CRICKET'S SECOND GOLDEN AGE

1920

Cheltenham, 18 August
W. R. Hammond   lbw b R. Tyldesley   0

1949

Adelaide, 5 March
Sir D. G. Bradman   b Johnston   30

CRICKET'S
SECOND
GOLDEN AGE

Gerald Howat

Hodder & Stoughton
LONDON SYDNEY AUCKLAND TORONTO

British Library Cataloguing in Publication Data

Howat, Gerald
  Cricket's second golden age: the Hammond–Bradman
  years.
  1. Cricket
  I. Title
  796.35'8'0904

ISBN 0-340-42345-5

First published in Great Britain 1989

Published by Hodder and Stoughton,
a division of Hodder and Stoughton Ltd,
Mill Road, Dunton Green, Sevenoaks, Kent TN13 2YA
Editorial Office: 47 Bedford Square, London WC1B 3DP

Photoset by Rowland Phototypesetting Ltd,
Bury St Edmunds, Suffolk

Printed in Great Britain by St Edmundsbury Press Ltd,
Bury St Edmunds, Suffolk

For
HUGH PICKLES

CONTENTS

ILLUSTRATIONS

ACKNOWLEDGMENTS

Hulton Picture Library, 1; *M.C.C.*, 2a, 2b, 3a, 3b, 3c, 5b, 6b, 7b, 7c, 8a, 9a, 9b, 10b, 11a, 11b, 16b; *Roger Mann*, 4a, 4b, 5a, 6a, 10a, 11c, 13a, 13b, 13c, 14a, 14b, 15c; *Ken Kelly*, 5c; *Sydney Morning Herald*, 7a; *Central Press*, 12; *Gloucestershire C.C.C.*, 15a; Sport & General, 16a.

AUTHOR'S ACKNOWLEDGMENTS

A book such as this draws extensively on the vast literature upon cricket, whether expressed in *Wisden Cricketers' Almanack*, in newspapers and journals or in any of the 8000 or so items listed in E. W. Padwick's *A Bibliography of Cricket*. The game is also well served by its archival sources and I turned again, as one must, to the Library of the Marylebone Cricket Club at Lord's and its curator, Stephen Green, for whom nothing ever seems too much trouble. Among first-class counties with particularly well-organised collections of material are Yorkshire and Warwickshire and I was glad to be able to use these. The staff of the P.P.E. room in the Bodleian Library, Oxford, and in the newspaper section of the British Museum were particularly helpful in meeting my requests.

I have, in the course of writing on cricket, talked to several of the players who belong to the years this book covers, the senior of whom were E. J. Smith, Canon J. H. Parsons and H. L. Hendry. All lived to be nonagenarians. The chapters on South Africa and New Zealand were read by Hayward Kitson and Walter Hadlee respectively and I am grateful for their guidance, and for that of Dr Ali Bacher, Professor Gavin Maasdorp, and Martin Donnelly in these areas. I am also indebted to the late R. L. Arrowsmith for his advice on Chapters 1 and 6.

I must single out in particular the research work undertaken in the field of cricket history by Dr Richard Cashman, Chris Harte and Ric Sissons who have published work of primary research relating to cricket in Australia, England and India. I acknowledge, with grateful thanks, my obligations to them. Their books should be mentioned: Richard Cashman, *Patrons, Players and the Crowd*, 1980; *'Ave a Go, Yer Mug*, 1984, and

11

Australian Cricket Crowds: the Attendance Cycle, 1984; Chris Harte, *The History of the Sheffield Shield*, 1987, and Ric Sissons, *The Players: A Social History of the Professional Cricketer*, 1988. Dr Martin Sharp of the Historical Research Section, Department of Foreign Affairs, Canberra, Australia, kindly allowed me to draw upon his (unpublished) thesis, 'Professionalism and Commercialism in Australian Cricket during the 1930s' (University of New South Wales, 1981).

My secretary, Nora Harragin, and my editor, John Bright-Holmes, have both brought a business-like approach combined with much courtesy in seeing this book through its various stages. Yet again, my wife, Dr Anne Howat, has compiled an index for me: as ever, I am in her debt. My dedication is to my cricketing friend and colleague of many years, Canon Hugh Pickles. *Crockford's Clerical Directory* reveals that he was born when 'Cricket's Second Golden Age' began and, not many months ago, he performed the hat-trick. To the *cognoscenti*, the legends of Hugh Pickles abound – weddings and funerals in juxtaposition with matches to be played or watched. He is, perhaps, to be compared to that Regency cleric, the Reverend John Mitford, who wrote, 'I lose all method, industry, fidelity and other virtues so long as summer lasts' – which brought the response from the essayist and poet, Charles Lamb, 'Mitford is crazy about cricket.' Canon Pickles' 'craziness' has been expressed in his skilled coaching of generations of young players.

North Moreton,   GERALD HOWAT
Oxfordshire
1989.

Author's Note: Both the first world war and the second world war find frequent mention in this book as chronological landmarks. To avoid needless repetition I have used phrases such as 'after the war' and 'in the years before the war' where the meaning is quite clear.

CRICKET'S SECOND GOLDEN AGE

PREFACE

> For if such holy song enwrap our fancy long,
> Time will run back and fetch the age of gold,

wrote John Milton in the seventeenth century. Every generation will look back to its predecessors and imagine a world in which stern reality gives way to romantic imagination. 'The good old days' do not need to present a balance sheet of loss and profit and the camera records only their sunny hours.

Cricket has certainly not escaped the pursuit of a golden past, set in that period before 1914 – the great watershed in modern history – when the inheritors of the Grace tradition shared in his Indian summers in the 1890s and offered their own Olympian cricket to a late Victorian and Edwardian public. It was a 'golden age' of great names – Fry, MacLaren, Ranjitsinhji, Trumper, Hill, Barnes; of lordly authority – Hawke welding his professionals into a formidable Yorkshire side; of style and elegance – the classical off-drive; and of experiment – Bosanquet and the googly. Then came war and W. G. Grace's appeal to sportsmen to meet the call to arms. Plum Warner went straight from Middlesex's match at Lord's to report to his commanding officer and, with stunning abruptness, the Golden Age had ended.

Yet no age can claim a monopoly of good things and the cricket which blossomed after 1919 has strong claims to be seen as enjoying a second 'golden age' even if, as in the first Golden Age, it is the names of batsmen rather than bowlers which we more readily pencil in. Two of them dominate the period – Walter Hammond and Don Bradman. The senior man, Hammond, made his first-class debut in August 1920; Bradman, his junior by five years, played his last first-class match in 1949. This book is an attempt to look at that Second Golden Age of cricket which their careers embraced. All that glisters is not gold and the burnished hue is tarnished by the events of 1932–33 and the struggle of many an English county to find the silver and coppers to survive. But throughout the years there was always the batting of Hammond or Bradman to watch; the elderly Hobbs centre up-stage; Headley making his entrances; Hutton playing the juvenile lead. There were bowlers such as Mailey, Grimmett, Larwood, Tate and Constantine and wicket-keepers like Oldfield, Cameron and Ames.

Australia and England (an alphabetical order denies prejudice or preference) set the standard; South Africa took an undisturbed third place; the West Indies, New Zealand and India put down markers for the future and the corps of English county cricketers and a smaller cadre of Australian State ones gave strength and breadth to the first-class game.

There were problems in how to arrange the material in this book. Chronology and Theme never make a perfect marriage. In the end I decided that a division might be made between the 1920s and the 1930s in discussing the English counties and the Anglo-Australian Tests. The other Test-playing countries make their appearance in the decade in which they first performed at that level. I hope the reader will be reasonably satisfied with a reasonable solution. Wheresoever they are mentioned, many of those cricketers who played in this period have their niche in this book. They are the cricketers of 'Cricket's Second Golden Age' – now either past the psalmist's span or recorded in the obituary notices of *Wisden*. Yet, as the aged Hambledon player William Beldham told the chronicler James Pycroft, 'We were all new once'. Never were cricketers more bursting with newness and talent than when England played Australia at Lord's in 1930.

ENGLAND v. AUSTRALIA: LORD'S, 1930

King George V, by meeting the players and interrupting the course of play, had taken the 'monarch's wicket' and Bill Ponsford was walking back to the pavilion, caught in the slips by Walter Hammond immediately after the royal presentation. Thirty thousand English supporters were not sorry to see him go, a man with two quadruple centuries behind him in Australian first-class cricket; but he was being replaced by another whose 452 not out had been made only six months before.

Don Bradman came out to bat at Lord's at 3.40 on Saturday 28 June 1930 on an afternoon of blazing sunshine. If there be a point when he set his sights on double and triple centuries in Test matches, on figures that dwarfed conformity, on the ruthless exploitation of the greatest bowlers in the game, it was in the two and a half hours of play that remained that afternoon.

By close of play he had scored 155 not out in exactly 155 minutes. Old campaigners like Maurice Tate and Jack White, newcomers to Test cricket like Gubby Allen and Walter Robins, were flayed without mercy. Hard as Percy Chapman, the captain, strove to set his field, every gap presented to Bradman seemed an inviting chasm. A maiden over from Tate earned a mighty cheer from the crowd, appreciative of his endeavours. Not a ball was put in the air by Bradman and only the remotest of chances was given when he nearly played on. Percy Fender watching in the press box thought that only two balls beat the bat all day. It was an innings of ruthless efficiency. Neville Cardus, in calling it a massacre and searching for some new and expressive word, wrote: 'Never before this hour has a batsman equalled Bradman's cool deliberate murder or spifflication of all bowling'.

On Friday and Saturday each side had scored 400 runs apiece – figures tauntingly similar until linked to the loss of only two Australian wickets. Before the match England had been rated the slightly better side: tenants of the Ashes and victors at Nottingham. The England innings had been opened by Jack Hobbs and Frank Woolley both close (Hobbs very close) to the end of their Test careers. Woolley had scored 41 in the first half-hour of the match, then had come Hammond, only by his own high standards playing a little below his best. The hallmark of England's innings had been the 173 by Duleepsinhji who, on his debut against Australia, made the highest score then by an England player against that country at Lord's. As for the Australians, their innings had been structured on the twin rocks of Bill Woodfull and Ponsford.

The Sunday papers praised Bradman and deplored Britain's 'black day' at Wimbledon where only Fred Perry remained as a representative. Sections of the press took the selectors to task for picking the Australian-born Allen and the Indian-born Duleepsinhji, something very properly defended by Plum Warner. Had not he and Lord Harris, both former England captains, been born in the West Indies? Nor did the Sydney *Referee* have any truck with such nonsense, reminding its readers that Archie Jackson of the current Australian party had been born in Scotland.

Bradman returned to business on Monday morning. Somehow the England bowlers kept the scoring rate below 60 an hour before lunch. Bowlers in this match on both sides needed commiseration and not condemnation. There was nothing for them in a benign, over-prepared wicket and England lacked the injured Harold Larwood (as indeed they did the batting of Herbert Sutcliffe). There were 140 runs before lunch and another 185 before a tea-time declaration. Bradman added a further 99 and his 254 became the highest score in an Anglo-Australian Test match in England. The rest of the Australians, Alan Kippax, Stan McCabe, Victor Richardson, Bill Oldfield and Alan Fairfax helped Australia to a declaration at 729 for 6 and to the highest score in the history of Test cricket. No proper seven could be found for one of the scoreboards.

To stave off defeat by an innings England needed just over 300 runs. Cardus, a little pessimistically for England supporters, thought that Australia ended the day on the verge of victory. Hobbs and Woolley had both fallen to the leg-breaks of Clarrie Grimmett. At the close Hammond and Duleepsinhji were still there. Hammond, with over 900 runs in the 1928–29 series against Australia, was due for a large score. The 25,000 who found a reason for not going to work on a Tuesday turned up at Lord's – not expecting victory, hopeful of a good fight, doubting that England would lose and perhaps aware of sharing in an occasion of classic proportions.

Within an hour Grimmett had got the measure of Hammond. He had dismissed him twice at Nottingham in the first Test and he did so now for a second time at Lord's. Eighty-two runs in four innings was a long way from vintage Hammond. 'Patsy' Hendren also fell victim to his flight, spin and varying height while the slow left-arm bowler, Percy Hornibrook, disposed of Duleepsinhji. At 147 for 5 before mid-day England's fortunes looked low and people who lived in Deal or Weymouth started consulting timetables for an early train home. Chapman put a ball from Grimmett in the air and farce intruded on the drama. Three Australians stood and watched and left the catch to each other. Chapman – dashing, stylish, debonair – rode his luck and made 100 in the cavalier and carefree manner which was the nature of the man. To a left-hander, Grimmett was bowling off-breaks and Chapman hit him for three mighty sixes, making mincemeat of his analysis. His partner was Allen, who usually worked for his living on Tuesday mornings at Debenham's, though Test match selection was not counted by them against his annual leave. He had a point to prove with those members of the press who had chided him for being an 'Aussie', not to mention being an amateur cricketer who was 'not quite good enough'. Always at his best when niggled – he once won a match for the MCC against the Gunners virtually single-handed after hearing the opposition pour scorn on the side he had brought – Allen made a half-century. The partnership of 126 between him and Chapman gave England a fighting chance of a draw, somewhat squandered by the tail-end batsmen. The total of 375 brought an England match tally of 800 exactly: not the sort of aggregate with which to lose matches but then it was not usual for the opposition to be already 729 on the way.

In the final three hours of the game the Australians embarked on their pursuit of 72. Scarcely had Ponsford gone at 16 when Bradman left to a catch by Chapman in the gully which led Sir James Barrie to turn to Cardus with the remark, 'What evidence is there that the ball which Chapman threw up into the air is the same ball that left Bradman's bat?' Catches like that were not taken by those who played for Barrie's 'Allahakbarries', a team of writers whose greatest performer was Conan Doyle, who had died a few days earlier. Just as Conan Doyle is remembered for creating Sherlock Holmes rather than for having bowled W. G. Grace, so Barrie is remembered for creating Peter Pan rather than for his cricket fanaticism. But fanatic he was and he had just written a letter to *The Times* inviting an imaginary brigadier to dine with him, 'Though I am not a brigadier, I too led my men into the tented field'. Barrie asked himself what they would talk about: 'Mr Hornibrook, their only slow left-hand bowler, I am a slow left-hand bowler. Mr McCabe, Mr Jackson and Mr Bradman; such a talk we shall have, if you will dine with me'. So Barrie and Cardus, old acquaintances, watched together in the Long Room. Nearby sat the essayist E. V. Lucas and Edmund Blunden whose *Cricket Country* would be a cheerful beacon written during the darkest days of the second world war. It was as if the men of letters had conspired to be together on an occasion which would imprint itself in the literature of cricket. Lord Harris who had captained England exactly fifty years earlier in the first Test played in England talked to Plum Warner who had led the first MCC side to Australia in 1903–04. A few yards away a very young journalist named E. W. Swanton was reporting his first Test match and boldly declaring that in Bradman 'a star of the first magnitude had arisen'.

Kippax went immediately after Bradman and the Australian total was 22 for 3. Improbable hopes of victory were entertained and Warner later wrote in *The Cricketer* which he edited, 'For a moment it had looked as if there might be a hard finish'. But the Australians had come determined to wrench back the Ashes, relinquished to Chapman at The Oval in 1926, and Woodfull and McCabe saw them home by seven wickets.

To the romantic, no-one was the loser as both teams trooped off the field. But how far did contemporaries see it as a great occasion – symbolic of the best of cricket since the end of the war? That one generation was giving rendezvous to another they recognised. Warner, always perceptive of young talent, wrote that 'Bradman stands on the threshold of a career which will equal and probably surpass that of any other batsman'. *The Times* wrote that King George V had been 'able to see an innings which would be destined to be famous as long as the game exists' and its correspondent, R. B. Vincent, compared the batting of Bradman to the acting of Marie Tempest, 'Both so exquisitely right in design and of execution'. He also adjudged, with perhaps more guesswork than informed knowledge, that Chapman's fielding had 'probably never been equalled in a Test match'. It was a time when the two great cricketing countries were evenly balanced. Hammond might be set against Bradman, Tate against Grimmett, man for man the two sides could be matched. That many of the greatest cricketers of the day had come together was generally agreed. Contemporary reports noted the record-breaking crowds, the glorious weather and the splendour of the occasion.

There is another sense in which this match may be seen in the context of its setting – England in the year 1930. The worst scars of the first world war were healing. Men and women flocked to see a play called *Journey's End* by R. C. Sherriff, which portrayed the inevitability of death for men in the trenches, and they could also find relaxation in the same playwright's portrayal of cricket in an English village. On *Badger's Green* people lay under the trees and heard the chock of ball against bat whilst old Hobson's mare watched over the gate. The sun shone in fiction as it had done in fact during those June days at Lord's.

The infant sons of the men who fell in Flanders were old

enough now to be watching, sent off for the day with their sandwiches by middle-aged mothers who had learnt to cope as single-parents. During the Test match the last French troops had left the Rhineland, and German pride, as an equal nation, was restored – though there still remained the matter of the Saar coalfield. No-one in June 1930 was paying much attention to the internal politics of Germany. The House of Commons, conscious of the value of those twenty-two miles which separated England from France, on the Tuesday threw out a bill by seven votes for a Channel tunnel. Both Ramsay MacDonald, the Prime Minister, and Stanley Baldwin had found time to get to Lord's. In India Pandit Nehru was sent to prison on the Monday for his membership of an unlawful association and, in the ensuing riots, the MCC felt it safer to cancel the proposed tour of India for 1930–31. In the United States Wall Street had collapsed but the crisis had yet to make a fervent mark on those who went to Lord's – or Badger's Green – though a poignant advertisement in *The Times* on the Saturday was a reminder of one kind of poverty which had been around since 1919: 'Ex-Officer, aged 39, willing to work at anything'. There was a world outside.

For those more fortunate and whose world was cricket a house might have been rented in St John's Wood with four bedrooms, three reception rooms and a good garden for £100 a year: convenient for Lord's and for that 1930 Test which conveyed so much of all that was best in the cricket of the period. The Test, wrote Bradman in his memoirs, was 'one of the golden chapters in cricket which connoisseurs revel in discussing by the fireside'. 'This was also a golden age,' conceded Cardus, 'the match of every cricketer's desire.'

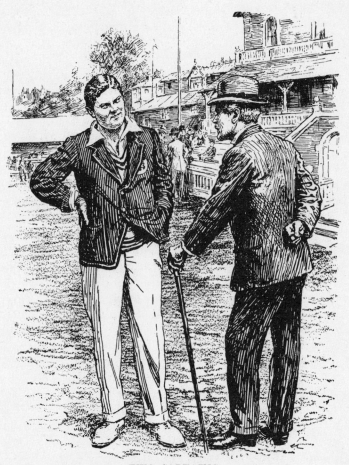

TWO CAPTAINS.

THE PREMIER. "GOOD LUCK! YOU'VE GOT A FINE TEAM."
MR. CHAPMAN. "YES, ALL KEEN; EVERY MAN ON HIS TOES."
THE PREMIER. "AH! I ENVY YOU. *MY* TEAM'S MOSTLY ON *MINE*."

1

THE ENGLISH COUNTY SCENE: THE 1920s

The man bowling had been too young for the war which had claimed his brother at Amiens three weeks before the end. The man batting was old only in experience for he had been so grievously wounded that it was a miracle he could play at all. In May 1919 Patrick Rucker of Oxford University bowled the first ball in first-class cricket after the Kaiser's War to Dick Twining of the Gentlemen of England at the Parks. Rucker was spared one war to fall in the next at Amiens just as his brother had done. Twining lived until his ninetieth year and became president of the MCC: such is life's lottery. The best cricketer on the field was Donald Knight, an undergraduate who would open the batting for Surrey with Jack Hobbs later in the summer.

In rather less exalted circles Walter Hammond had won his place in the Cirencester Grammar School first XI and made 15 against the local Church Lads' Brigade while two other schoolboys, Douglas Jardine and Raymond Robertson-Glasgow were dismissing each other in the match between Winchester and Charterhouse. Harold Larwood, a lad of fifteen, bowled for the Nuneaton Second XI in his sandshoes after his night-shift down the mine.

So the fabric of cricket was gradually being re-woven after Armageddon. It had been held to be unpatriotic to play during the war and W. G. Grace had said so. Only towards the end had opinion gradually changed and a few charity matches taken place. In the summer of 1919 a starved cricketing public flocked in their thousands to the game at first-class level, making what they could of the experiment of two-day cricket championship matches which went on until 7.30pm. Hobbs did not like the late finish: 'By the time one had dressed and dined it was too late to go anywhere'; Plum Warner declared himself 'a dead-dog' and the editor of *Wisden* remarked that by evening 'the craving for food was greater than the passion for cricket'.

In 1920 the county championship returned to its original three days and in 1921 Glamorgan joined the competition. In the seventy years which have followed the same seventeen counties have competed in what is still seen as the major groundstone of English Test cricket. Within the years this book covers it was the only competition, the lodestar of the domestic scene in England, nowhere more demonstrated than in the solid core of support in terms of membership and allegiance to be found in the two counties of Yorkshire and Lancashire.

Yorkshire and Lancashire

After a doubt or two about their bowling – Major Booth had fallen on the Somme and George Hirst was a player of past glories rather than future triumphs – Yorkshire created an attack in the 1920s that could meet all situations and produce so effective a batting side that the championship was won five times between 1919 and 1929 and Yorkshire were never lower than fourth. In 1925 – when seven of the side made centuries, not a match was lost and the championship was won for the fourth successive year – Yorkshire were at their peak. Ten professionals and the captain appeared almost without change and the Second XI provided a back-up of young men such as Cyril Turner and Arthur Mitchell who would take their place in due course. Arthur Lupton was the statutory amateur captain, appointed at the age of forty-six. He was usually near the bottom of the batting averages and not a bowler at that level but he satisfied the social conventions, commanded respect, left the big decisions to Wilfred Rhodes and held together a team whose toughness sometimes upset opponents, notably Middlesex in 1924. Rhodes was then the doyen of Yorkshire (though Hirst made occasional appearances throughout the decade). He headed the national bowling averages in 1919, a left-arm master of spin and flight, thinking through the aim and purpose of every ball, setting a field with mathematical precision, colluding with the ball in a batsman's downfall. 'For God's sake, Wilfred, give me a minute's rest,' Victor Trumper had exclaimed as far back as 1903. He would still be taking England wickets in the 1930s, to say nothing of his batting for Yorkshire, which H. S. Altham called pedestrian compared with the artistry of his bowling. Pedestrian or not, he had a range of strokes and a dourness in defence to the tune of just under 40,000 runs. Foremost after Rhodes was Emmott Robinson bowling his out-swingers, to whom the new ball was sacred, to be borne on a chalice at the end of each over. He and Rhodes would plot the opposition's downfall. Time not spent in dismissing them was time squandered. A wet Sunday morning in London was followed by dazzling sun – 'a lovely afternoon', commented Neville Cardus to the two of them whom he met filling in the day in Hyde Park. 'Aye, and a sticky wicket wasting at Lord's,' replied Robinson.

These were men, Robinson especially, to whom the business of playing cricket was all their being – a successful lbw appeal as vital to a day's work as striking oil to a driller; the memory of a missed catch or a rash stroke not to be eradicated in a lifetime. Their horizons may have been narrow but they were compelling; a faith simple but consuming.

Yorkshire batting opened with Percy Holmes and Herbert Sutcliffe: little to pick between them technically but Sutcliffe having the edge by his sheer imperturbability. Nothing ruffled either his concentration or his hair. Robertson-Glasgow – the schoolboy turned writer – saw them as the alderman laying the foundation stone and the punter off to the races. When they put on 253 against Lancashire in 1919 they established themselves as the post-war opening pair.

After them came Edgar Oldroyd and Morris Leyland, the one a solid county batsman scoring his 1000 runs or so, the other making a fistful of centuries for Yorkshire and playing a key role at the end of the decade for England in Australia – a batsman of strength rather than elegance. Such were the men who between 1922 and 1927 played 186 matches and only lost nine. Across the Pennines, in a rivalry as classic as Greek v. Trojan, were their Lancashire opponents.

Lancashire, who had strongly advocated the two-day

matches in 1919 were hoist by their own petard, half their matches being left drawn. By 1920 they were into their stride, a side of highly talented professionals in a county neither over-awed nor haunted by pre-1914 reputations and controversies.

Harry Makepeace gave the first half of the twentieth century to Lancashire cricket and a few years at the start of it to Everton Football Club and England. He won an FA Cup Medal at the Crystal Palace in 1906, the same year as he made his first runs for Lancashire. He was there again in 1919 with a dozen years to give as a batsman and a further twenty thereafter as the county coach. His selection against Australia in 1920–21 meant that he joined the ranks of double internationals. For Lancashire he and Charlie Hallows put on 270 for the first wicket against Worcestershire in 1922. Hallows was the newcomer in 1919, whom England used even less than Makepeace. Lancashire did not complain and the two were the foundation of many a county innings; the older man watchful, dour and defensive, the younger stylish and aggressive – foils to each other and sabres to the opposition. In May 1928 Hallows became the third man, after Grace and Hammond, to score 1000 runs in May.

Then came the Tyldesley brothers. From 1895 to 1936 one or other, John or Ernest, would be in the side. John (J.T.) was there to usher in the 1920s with 272 against Derbyshire before post-war cricket was a month old and to bow out two or three years later when approaching the age of fifty. Ernest remained to score many of his runs with a hook shot that took the ball from his eyebrows. In a period when England often needed great batting against the Australians, he could never command a regular place so he remained the county man, his periodic departures to play for England almost an intrusion.

Lancashire bowling was in the hands of Lawrence Cook and Cecil Parkin. They were among the many Lancashire players of those days whom Cardus got to know so well. In harness, he saw Cook as the craftsman, intent on duty, and Parkin as the artist playing cricket for self-expression. Cardus' subjects sometimes wondered what he meant. His literary allusions, flattering as they were, might be lost on them while any critical comments would make the bowlers want to have a go at him themselves. Cook toiled and strove, as a medium-pace bowler, while Parkin was always seeking to do something different – varying his pace, producing an awkward off-break, making it difficult for captains to set a field and batsmen to bat. Fact and fancy, Cardus called them. Both men had their differences with officialdom. Cook left the club in 1923 and Parkin in 1926. Parkin had also incurred the wrath of the influential Plum Warner who had in the 1920s a fear of Bolshevism. 'Can you imagine a cricketer being a Leninist?' he had written in *The Cricketer* in 1921. Three years later he could and wrote that the cricket world would regard Parkin 'as the first cricketing Bolshevist' if he did not apologise to the Board of Control for allegedly refusing to play for England. A journalist had rushed into print but Parkin was never picked for England again and he refused to disclose to his own Lancashire committee the name of the writer. Soon after, in 1926, he left the club for League cricket.

Meanwhile Lancashire had acquired the bowler who would make them champions. They offered the former Australian Test player, Ted McDonald, £500 a year, a benefit after five seasons and a house at low rent. In return he took 500 wickets for them with bowling of great pace and lift which carried Lancashire to the top in 1926, 1927 and 1928. Even on the mild Old Trafford wicket – which gave bowlers little help and encouraged batsmen to book accommodation for the day – he was devastatingly effective. Lancashire's policy clearly paid dividends but it was very advanced thinking for the time, made McDonald the best paid professional cricketer in the country and, in giving one player 'star' treatment, established a pattern for the long-term future. Yorkshire, always committed to local-born players, were disdainful.

No such financial generosity was extended to Richard Tyldesley, one of four brothers all of whom appeared for Lancashire and not related to J.T. and Ernest. He was a man of great bulk, a slow bowler who, from 1922 to 1931, flighted the ball tantalisingly and was an admirable foil to McDonald, regularly taking his 100 wickets. When, in 1930, he sought a further contract with a guaranteed wage of £400, he was unsuccessful and within a year returned to the Leagues.

The name George Duckworth seems to go with wicket-keeping. The first George, the half-brother of Virginia Woolf, had a substantial part to play in Eton's victory over Harrow at Lord's in 1886, making tail-end runs when Eton needed them and getting vital wickets behind the stumps. He got a trial at Cambridge but in competition with his famous contemporary Gregor McGregor he stood little chance. His reward for a career as secretary of the Commission on Historical Monuments was a knighthood. In his leisure moments, he would occasionally watch his namesake. The second George was a Warrington man, born and bred, who kept wicket for Lancashire between the wars and for England before finding competition in Leslie Ames. He squatted low, took the pace of McDonald, roared out his appeals and made a tail-end half-century against Nottinghamshire in 1924 when Lancashire needed the points. His county captain, Leonard Green, called him a man 'of good humour and unbounded thrills day by day'. Duckworth took a less jaundiced view of his captain than did Leyland of his: 'Skipper's aw reet. He does his job and we do ours'. Both Green and Lupton, Lancashire and Yorkshire captains for most of the 1920s, were war-time soldiers and peace-time territorials who were styled by their rank of 'Major'. Green was the better player of the two but both exercised the authority and displayed the enthusiasm which their committees felt essential.

Both Yorkshire and Lancashire gained in many ways from the existence of the Leagues which encouraged enthusiasm for the game and was good for crowd support at all levels. Young cricketers found their way to the county sides through League cricket and played there when not needed for the Second XI. In the best of relationships either party – county and League – helped each other. Nevertheless, the Leagues remained something of a threat as well. Players looking for the best financial return were tempted to play in a much less demanding situation than day-to-day county cricket. No-one minded a county player at the end of his days going to the Leagues where his contribution was invaluable – Oldroyd of Yorkshire, opening the batting for Pudsey St Lawrence with the very young Len Hutton and teaching him, is a case in point. The loss was more noticeable when a younger man cricketer scarcely needs saying. Nottinghamshire with the prestige of Trent Bridge and the comparative prosperity of the new light industries of the city of Nottingham, began the decade financially secure though the authorities never felt their professionals could be guaranteed more than £250 a year. Men who came from the mines would be helped in kind, with the purchase of kit, by the colliery owners. In 1920 eleven men were retained on the regular staff while, in Arthur Carr, the captain, there was an amateur of ability and a future England captain. The name of Tom Richmond, an extremely successful leg-break bowler, is no longer remembered but those of the Gunn brothers and the elder Hardstaff linger in cricketing memories. John Gunn, nephew of William Gunn, with whose career he just overlapped, was in the side from 1896 to 1925. His best years as an all-rounder had been before 1914 but at Trent Bridge in 1921 he secured three lbw decisions in his favour in four balls against Lancashire with his slow left-arm bowling. Both he and his brother George were among those great county cricketers on whose services the England selectors drew infrequently. At the end of the decade, in June 1929, George marked his fiftieth birthday by scoring 164 not out against Worcestershire, as he had promised Cardus he would do. It was the year in which Nottinghamshire won the title after a run of seven years in which they had always held their place in the first six.

Joe Hardstaff (senior), apart from his batting contribution to Nottinghamshire cricket (largely before 1914), afterwards became a well-respected umpire. He had worked in the Annesley mine alongside Robert Larwood and one day in 1923 he persuaded his friend to find the £9 to kit out his son Harold for a trial in the Nottinghamshire nets. The lad, pale from working underground with pit-ponies, thin, and only 5ft 4in. tall presented himself at the county ground. Three years later Surrey came to Trent Bridge and Larwood clean bowled Hobbs twice for a low score – a match in which there were plenty of runs about, George Gunn making 191 and Hobbs' partner, Andy Sandham, 144. At that time Hobbs had been co-opted to the selection committee for the series against Australia and Larwood believed that it was his influence which contributed to his own selection for the second

left the county side. Yorkshire was less affected than Lancashire. The Bradford League kept its payments within bounds. In Lancashire cotton manufacturers were ready to subsidise clubs who sought to attract highly paid professionals. McDonald first went to Nelson for £500 while qualifying for the county and, in 1929, the West Indian Learie Constantine went to the same club on a three-year contract of £500 a year with various side-benefits. John Kay, the historian of Lancashire League cricket, has argued that such men were stars rather than club servants. They were treated with much more respect by committees than were their county equivalents. Constantine, for example, moved in the circles of Nelson professional and business men, as well he might. He was earning an equivalent salary and five times that of a Lancashire cotton worker. In his first season in England he was foolish enough to give his views to the *Northern Echo* on 'Roses' matches: 'Cricket, as played between Lancashire and Yorkshire, where they take seven hours for 200 runs is a wash-out'. When there was a move for him to join the county in 1932, his remark was remembered by some Lancashire committee members.

Every year Yorkshire and Lancashire met twice, on the Whitsun and August bank holidays. As often as not, the result was a draw; the weather could be bleak, especially for the earlier game, and rain would hover over Old Trafford with its copper-domed pavilion of Lancashire dark brick. At Bramall Lane, Sheffield, a pall of smoke from countless factory chimneys would trim the light to puritan proportions. For the cricket would be puritan in its severity, tough, sometimes unenterprising and 'now't was given for now't'. Twenty thousand people would come each day, precious holiday hours snatched from a working week in the mill.

In a sense it matters not upon which match we intrude. The formula would be the same: the citadel had to be defended and conquest was a luxury. The match at Old Trafford in 1922, for example, was a perfect example of what the writer A. A. Thomson called 'two sides so tightly locked in a wrestler's grip that neither could move and often did not seem to try'. Lancashire made 118 and 135, Yorkshire 122 and 129 for nine. With five overs to go Yorkshire needed six runs to win yet scored only three of them, Rhodes playing out the last over for a maiden and defending the citadel. Two years later, at Headingley, in another low-scoring match, Yorkshire needed 57 to win and this time their citadel was stormed, Parkin and Richard Tyldesley dismissing them for 33.

In 1926, in the Whitsun match, Yorkshire, the reigning champions in their fifth year of success, beat Lancashire by an innings. At Old Trafford in the August game Lancashire won the toss and by Saturday night had scored 297 for 2, Makepeace having made a hundred. On the Monday morning, the bank holiday, 38,000 packed into the ground and Lancashire went on accumulating. At lunch they were 451 for 4 (Ernest Tyldesley 139). Rhodes got four wickets as Lancashire came to 499, then the captain, Green, scrambled a run to bring up 500 against Yorkshire for the first time and Lancashire declared. By close of play Yorkshire were 183 for none, Holmes and Sutcliffe bent on emulating Makepeace and Tyldesley. On the Tuesday morning Sutcliffe went for 89, the partnership worth 199. By the end of the match Yorkshire had reached 352 all out and Lancashire took three points for a first innings lead. Honour was satisfied and it was a match which halfway through the twenties was the symbol of change, the white rose yielding supremacy to the red for Lancashire crept ahead in the last ten days of the series, took the title from Yorkshire, and clung on to it for three years.

Yorkshire and Lancashire dominated the championship in the 1920s and both clubs were assured of the ability to balance their books and to be able to vote a proportion of their annual profits to maintenance and development. Membership, at £2 a year, brought in a guaranteed £10,000 and the total receipts for 1921, for example, were over £20,000 in each case. Both their committees were composed largely of businessmen who ensured that prudence reigned and resources were husbanded. Profit depended on success and success on players. The amateur, as we have seen, played little more than the role of captain and the core of Yorkshire and Lancashire cricketers were professionals who were paid about £10 for a home match and £11 for an away one, with a win bonus of £1 and a winter weekly wage of £2. 'Capped' players had greater security

than uncapped ones while for every establi
was the prospect of an *ex-gratia* benefit afte
benefits were tax-free (after a House of
in 1927) and much depended on the weat
occasion.

The temptation to leave county cricket for
ing world of the Leagues was understand
Professional cricketers were at the mercy
economic climate of the post-war years. Th
comparable with those of a skilled artisan,
from which many of them came. Yet char
way and a severe social division between the
professionals and amateurs could not for eve
Professionals with a grammar school backgrou
held commissions in the war, had they pursi
occupation, might be seen as white-collared
Sutcliffe, brought up by his aunts and himse
officer, may be seen as the professional cricket
touch his forelock to his amateur masters. The
lems which all counties to a lesser or greater
contemplate. The wiser ones harnessed the ex
acumen of their professionals, whatever their
and saw that some of them eventually found
committees. Nevertheless, any understanding o
cricket scene of those days cannot ignore the feu
expressed in so many ways – separate dressing-ro
ent hotels and two classes of railway compartme

Yorkshire and Lancashire, with Surrey, Nottir
Kent and Middlesex, were seen as the 'big six' m
do well and least likely to have financial proble
chapter (and in Chapter 5) it seems best to group th
counties geographically. None matched the res
professional strength of the two northern ones, th
of the Midlands ones offered some comparisons.

Notts, Derbyshire, Warwickshire

Nottinghamshire and Derbyshire both had strong
of drawing players from the mines. The contrast be
conditions and pay, sixty years ago and more, and

Test at Lord's. In the same year, 1926, another lad from the same colliery had a trial at Trent Bridge. Bill Voce was a left-arm bowler, though what sort remained a matter of doubt – he could spin the ball and he could bowl fast. It was as a spinner that he took seven wickets against Hampshire in 1928, as a fast bowler that he would make his name.

Not far from Derbyshire's beautiful ground at Chesterfield with its church with the crooked spire, Victorian bandstand and luxuriant trees are the Chesterfield coal-mines. There sprang the colliery sides from which came fast bowlers such as Bill Bestwick. There was never the money to pay a large professional staff and over the years a series of very ordinary amateurs turned out. Of the 38 players in the 1920 batting averages, only one exceeded 16. Yet, the County Report hoped that Derbyshire 'would be strengthened by more amateurs' (they cost only their expenses) but it would be on the professionals towards the end of the decade that their cricket would ultimately depend – men such as Stan Worthington, Harry Storer, Tommy Mitchell and Bill Copson. Under them Derbyshire began to lay foundations for the future. By 1929 they were a side with the aspirations which would eventually take them, if briefly, to the top.

As the elder George Gunn was to Nottinghamshire, so William Quaife was to Warwickshire. He joined the county in the 1890s when it was still second-class and, like Gunn, was still playing in the late 1920s when over the age of fifty. His photograph appears in *Wisden* of 1902, one of those sepia cameos taken by Mr E. Hawkins of Brighton of which cabinet-size copies might be bought for 1s. 6d. (7½p).

R. V. Ryder, on the administrative side, served the club for even longer, becoming assistant secretary in 1895, later secretary, and retiring in 1944. In a revealing article in *Wisden* in 1936 he called it 'something of a mystery' that Birmingham, in his day a city of commercial substance and municipal wealth, had never identified itself with Warwickshire cricket. Consequently, much of his time was spent wrestling with finance, recruiting members and praying for dry weather on bank holiday matches – the deciding factor in whether or not there would be an overdraft at the end of the season. A combination of his very strong personality and his longevity in office meant that Ryder, more than most county secretaries, was someone to be reckoned with, a man of whose authority the players were very well aware. Yet even Ryder appreciated that the support of his committee mattered and the need to keep them happy led to a match against Hampshire at Edgbaston in 1922 taking a most unusual turn. Warwickshire had made 223 in their first innings and Hampshire on an easy paced wicket were bowled out for 15, Harry Howell taking six wickets for 7 in 29 balls and Freddie Calthorpe, the captain, four for 4 in 24 balls. Hampshire followed on and lost three more wickets before play ended – on what was still the first day of the match. By lunchtime on the second, six wickets were down and they still required 30 runs to avoid an innings defeat. What happened next makes the game memorable. Hampshire reached a total of 521, with 172 coming from George Brown and 110 from Walter Livsey batting at no. 10. Set 313 to get, Warwickshire could only muster 158 and lost the match. Yet all was not quite what it seemed, as E. J. 'Tiger' Smith, the Warwickshire wicket-keeper, recalled a few weeks before he died in 1979. Calthorpe was asked by Ryder to let Hampshire get some runs after lunch. Several committee members were present for a meeting later in the day, wanted to see some cricket and thought that an extra 100 runs or so would make no difference to the result. Quaife bowled nearly 50 overs and the match slipped away from Warwickshire. It took a stronger man than Calthorpe to stand up to Ryder or his Committee.

Warwickshire was not without its strong men among both professionals and amateurs. Quaife was one of them, successful enough in his sports business to take an independent attitude. So, indeed, was 'Tiger' Smith, who had first kept wicket for England in 1911, without the security Quaife enjoyed. He was a player who belonged very much to the pre-first world war scene though his association with Warwickshire would last until many years after the second world war. Yet as a player he was less happy in the 1920s: he regretted the departure of the amateurs of independent means and real ability and his personal relations with Ryder were often difficult. 'The pros were still being treated as serfs in 1930' is a revealing judgment by a man who gave up playing left the county side. Yorkshire was less affected than Lancashire. The Bradford League kept its payments within bounds. In Lancashire cotton manufacturers were ready to subsidise clubs who sought to attract highly paid professionals. McDonald first went to Nelson for £500 while qualifying for the county and, in 1929, the West Indian Learie Constantine went to the same club on a three-year contract of £500 a year with various side-benefits. John Kay, the historian of Lancashire League cricket, has argued that such men were stars rather than club servants. They were treated with much more respect by committees than were their county equivalents. Constantine, for example, moved in the circles of Nelson professional and business men, as well he might. He was earning an equivalent salary and five times that of a Lancashire cotton worker. In his first season in England he was foolish enough to give his views to the *Northern Echo* on 'Roses' matches: 'Cricket, as played between Lancashire and Yorkshire, where they take seven hours for 200 runs is a wash-out'. When there was a move for him to join the county in 1932, his remark was remembered by some Lancashire committee members.

Every year Yorkshire and Lancashire met twice, on the Whitsun and August bank holidays. As often as not, the result was a draw; the weather could be bleak, especially for the earlier game, and rain would hover over Old Trafford with its copper-domed pavilion of Lancashire dark brick. At Bramall Lane, Sheffield, a pall of smoke from countless factory chimneys would trim the light to puritan proportions. For the cricket would be puritan in its severity, tough, sometimes unenterprising and 'now't was given for now't'. Twenty thousand people would come each day, precious holiday hours snatched from a working week in the mill.

In a sense it matters not upon which match we intrude. The formula would be the same: the citadel had to be defended and conquest was a luxury. The match at Old Trafford in 1922, for example, was a perfect example of what the writer A. A. Thomson called 'two sides so tightly locked in a wrestler's grip that neither could move and often did not seem to try'. Lancashire made 118 and 135, Yorkshire 122 and 129 for nine. With five overs to go Yorkshire needed six runs to win yet scored only three of them, Rhodes playing out the last over for a maiden and defending the citadel. Two years later, at Headingley, in another low-scoring match, Yorkshire needed 57 to win and this time their citadel was stormed, Parkin and Richard Tyldesley dismissing them for 33.

In 1926, in the Whitsun match, Yorkshire, the reigning champions in their fifth year of success, beat Lancashire by an innings. At Old Trafford in the August game Lancashire won the toss and by Saturday night had scored 297 for 2, Makepeace having made a hundred. On the Monday morning, the bank holiday, 38,000 packed into the ground and Lancashire went on accumulating. At lunch they were 451 for 4 (Ernest Tyldesley 139). Rhodes got four wickets as Lancashire came to 499, then the captain, Green, scrambled a run to bring up 500 against Yorkshire for the first time and Lancashire declared. By close of play Yorkshire were 183 for none, Holmes and Sutcliffe bent on emulating Makepeace and Tyldesley. On the Tuesday morning Sutcliffe went for 89, the partnership worth 199. By the end of the match Yorkshire had reached 352 all out and Lancashire took three points for a first innings lead. Honour was satisfied and it was a match which halfway through the twenties was the symbol of change, the white rose yielding supremacy to the red for Lancashire crept ahead in the last ten days of the series, took the title from Yorkshire, and clung on to it for three years.

Yorkshire and Lancashire dominated the championship in the 1920s and both clubs were assured of the ability to balance their books and to be able to vote a proportion of their annual profits to maintenance and development. Membership, at £2 a year, brought in a guaranteed £10,000 and the total receipts for 1921, for example, were over £20,000 in each case. Both their committees were composed largely of businessmen who ensured that prudence reigned and resources were husbanded. Profit depended on success and success on players. The amateur, as we have seen, played little more than the role of captain and the core of Yorkshire and Lancashire cricketers were professionals who were paid about £10 for a home match and £11 for an away one, with a win bonus of £1 and a winter weekly wage of £2. 'Capped' players had greater security than uncapped ones while for every established player there was the prospect of an *ex-gratia* benefit after ten years. Such benefits were tax-free (after a House of Lords' Judgment in 1927) and much depended on the weather on the great occasion.

The temptation to leave county cricket for the less demanding world of the Leagues was understandable, however. Professional cricketers were at the mercy of the uncertain economic climate of the post-war years. Their wages were comparable with those of a skilled artisan, the social class from which many of them came. Yet change was on the way and a severe social division between the background of professionals and amateurs could not for ever be sustained. Professionals with a grammar school background or who had held commissions in the war, had they pursued a different occupation, might be seen as white-collared salary earners. Sutcliffe, brought up by his aunts and himself a war-time officer, may be seen as the professional cricketer reluctant to touch his forelock to his amateur masters. These were problems which all counties to a lesser or greater degree had to contemplate. The wiser ones harnessed the experience and acumen of their professionals, whatever their background, and saw that some of them eventually found a place on committees. Nevertheless, any understanding of the county cricket scene of those days cannot ignore the feudal approach expressed in so many ways – separate dressing-rooms, different hotels and two classes of railway compartment.

Yorkshire and Lancashire, with Surrey, Nottinghamshire, Kent and Middlesex, were seen as the 'big six' most likely to do well and least likely to have financial problems. In this chapter (and in Chapter 5) it seems best to group the seventeen counties geographically. None matched the resources and professional strength of the two northern ones, though some of the Midlands ones offered some comparisons.

Notts, Derbyshire, Warwickshire

Nottinghamshire and Derbyshire both had strong traditions of drawing players from the mines. The contrast between pit conditions and pay, sixty years ago and more, and the life of a cricketer scarcely needs saying. Nottinghamshire with the prestige of Trent Bridge and the comparative prosperity of the new light industries of the city of Nottingham, began the decade financially secure though the authorities never felt their professionals could be guaranteed more than £250 a year. Men who came from the mines would be helped in kind, with the purchase of kit, by the colliery owners. In 1920 eleven men were retained on the regular staff while, in Arthur Carr, the captain, there was an amateur of ability and a future England captain. The name of Tom Richmond, an extremely successful leg-break bowler, is no longer remembered but those of the Gunn brothers and the elder Hardstaff linger in cricketing memories. John Gunn, nephew of William Gunn, with whose career he just overlapped, was in the side from 1896 to 1925. His best years as an all-rounder had been before 1914 but at Trent Bridge in 1921 he secured three lbw decisions in his favour in four balls against Lancashire with his slow left-arm bowling. Both he and his brother George were among those great county cricketers on whose services the England selectors drew infrequently. At the end of the decade, in June 1929, George marked his fiftieth birthday by scoring 164 not out against Worcestershire, as he had promised Cardus he would do. It was the year in which Nottinghamshire won the title after a run of seven years in which they had always held their place in the first six.

Joe Hardstaff (senior), apart from his batting contribution to Nottinghamshire cricket (largely before 1914), afterwards became a well-respected umpire. He had worked in the Annesley mine alongside Robert Larwood and one day in 1923 he persuaded his friend to find the £9 to kit out his son Harold for a trial in the Nottinghamshire nets. The lad, pale from working underground with pit-ponies, thin, and only 5ft 4in. tall presented himself at the county ground. Three years later Surrey came to Trent Bridge and Larwood clean bowled Hobbs twice for a low score – a match in which there were plenty of runs about, George Gunn making 191 and Hobbs' partner, Andy Sandham, 144. At that time Hobbs had been co-opted to the selection committee for the series against Australia and Larwood believed that it was his influence which contributed to his own selection for the second

Test at Lord's. In the same year, 1926, another lad from the same colliery had a trial at Trent Bridge. Bill Voce was a left-arm bowler, though what sort remained a matter of doubt – he could spin the ball and he could bowl fast. It was as a spinner that he took seven wickets against Hampshire in 1928, as a fast bowler that he would make his name.

Not far from Derbyshire's beautiful ground at Chesterfield with its church with the crooked spire, Victorian bandstand and luxuriant trees are the Chesterfield coal-mines. There sprang the colliery sides from which came fast bowlers such as Bill Bestwick. There was never the money to pay a large professional staff and over the years a series of very ordinary amateurs turned out. Of the 38 players in the 1920 batting averages, only one exceeded 16. Yet, the County Report hoped that Derbyshire 'would be strengthened by more amateurs' (they cost only their expenses) but it would be on the professionals towards the end of the decade that their cricket would ultimately depend – men such as Stan Worthington, Harry Storer, Tommy Mitchell and Bill Copson. Under them Derbyshire began to lay foundations for the future. By 1929 they were a side with the aspirations which would eventually take them, if briefly, to the top.

As the elder George Gunn was to Nottinghamshire, so William Quaife was to Warwickshire. He joined the county in the 1890s when it was still second-class and, like Gunn, was still playing in the late 1920s when over the age of fifty. His photograph appears in *Wisden* of 1902, one of those sepia cameos taken by Mr E. Hawkins of Brighton of which cabinet-size copies might be bought for 1s. 6d. (7½p).

R. V. Ryder, on the administrative side, served the club for even longer, becoming assistant secretary in 1895, later secretary, and retiring in 1944. In a revealing article in *Wisden* in 1936 he called it 'something of a mystery' that Birmingham, in his day a city of commercial substance and municipal wealth, had never identified itself with Warwickshire cricket. Consequently, much of his time was spent wrestling with finance, recruiting members and praying for dry weather on bank holiday matches – the deciding factor in whether or not there would be an overdraft at the end of the season. A combination of his very strong personality and his longevity

in office meant that Ryder, more than most county secretaries, was someone to be reckoned with, a man of whose authority the players were very well aware. Yet even Ryder appreciated that the support of his committee mattered and the need to keep them happy led to a match against Hampshire at Edgbaston in 1922 taking a most unusual turn. Warwickshire had made 223 in their first innings and Hampshire on an easy paced wicket were bowled out for 15, Harry Howell taking six wickets for 7 in 29 balls and Freddie Calthorpe, the captain, four for 4 in 24 balls. Hampshire followed on and lost three more wickets before play ended – on what was still the first day of the match. By lunchtime on the second, six wickets were down and they still required 30 runs to avoid an innings defeat. What happened next makes the game memorable. Hampshire reached a total of 521, with 172 coming from George Brown and 110 from Walter Livsey batting at no. 10. Set 313 to get, Warwickshire could only muster 158 and lost the match. Yet all was not quite what it seemed, as E. J. 'Tiger' Smith, the Warwickshire wicket-keeper, recalled a few weeks before he died in 1979. Calthorpe was asked by Ryder to let Hampshire get some runs after lunch. Several committee members were present for a meeting later in the day, wanted to see some cricket and thought that an extra 100 runs or so would make no difference to the result. Quaife bowled nearly 50 overs and the match slipped away from Warwickshire. It took a stronger man than Calthorpe to stand up to Ryder or his Committee.

Warwickshire was not without its strong men among both professionals and amateurs. Quaife was one of them, success-ful enough in his sports business to take an independent attitude. So, indeed, was 'Tiger' Smith, who had first kept wicket for England in 1911, without the security Quaife enjoyed. He was a player who belonged very much to the pre-first world war scene though his association with War-wickshire would last until many years after the second world war. Yet as a player he was less happy in the 1920s: he regretted the departure of the amateurs of independent means and real ability and his personal relations with Ryder were often difficult. 'The pros were still being treated as serfs in 1930' is a revealing judgment by a man who gave up playing

in that year because he was regarded as a trouble-maker. Later, the secretary and he were reconciled and Smith's contribution to Warwickshire as a coach until 1968 led another secretary, Alan Smith, to write that he was as much a symbol of Edgbaston as the Warwickshire Bear, 'the more endearing characteristics of which uncompromising animal he possessed to a considerable degree'.

A third player who also became something of a spokesman for the professionals was one of the most unusual characters playing in first-class cricket in the 1920s. Jack Parsons had been in the Warwickshire championship side of 1911 and was picked for the Players in 1914. He served in the war, transferring to the Indian Army in 1918, played a few games for Warwickshire, as an amateur, while on leave in 1919 and topped the averages. The price of his leaving the Army, he told the Committee, was a guaranteed income of £300 for six seasons with a benefit in 1924 which the county would underwrite for £900. Negotiations failed – no Warwickshire benefit had ever reached £900 – and Captain Parsons returned to his duties with 7 Hariana Lancers. In July 1923 he left the Indian Army, cabled the Warwickshire committee that he was on board ship and wanted a game. He landed at Southampton, boarded a train for Edgbaston and promptly scored 131. He was, said the *Birmingham Post*, 'the lion of the day': the man Warwickshire needed. Terms were agreed which meant effectively an annual income of about £400 a year and a guaranteed benefit of £750. He also had a clause inserted excluding him from ground-duties as a bowler, the bug-bear of many a professional's life. His role was that of an attacking batsman; what the county needed, as the chairman observed at the 1924 AGM when concern was expressed at the fall in gate-money. He was also the professional cricketer who had been an officer. A Yorkshire player was informed by an attendant that he was occupying Captain Parsons' chair: 'Tell him Private Oldroyd proposes to go on sitting in it'. Life had changed for someone who had enjoyed for many years the comfort and service of an officers' mess in India, with his horses and his batman. Parsons was the amateur who became a professional and, in 1929, as the Reverend J. H. Parsons, an amateur again.

Another player quite capable of speaking his mind was 'Bob' Wyatt, an amateur who might well have become a professional. He had little patience with the distinctions, resented a letter from Ryder to his father complaining of his friendship with Quaife – the two played hockey on the same side in the winter – and found the economics of amateur cricket difficult. The device of making him assistant secretary with permission to play all season was one way round the dilemma. Wyatt made his county debut in 1923. He was a tough, fearless cricketer in the Yorkshire mould – he liked nothing better than playing against Yorkshire. At first Warwickshire, with an attack depending too much on Howell, used him primarily as a bowler. But he forced the county to see him as a batsman and, by 1930, the year he became captain of Warwickshire and of England, he was in the front rank of batsmen at county and Test level. Ryder and the committee would not find him so easy to handle: the professionals respected his sense of command.

Despite these various players of talent, Warwickshire in the 1920s never quite got the balance right in terms of players. Between 25 and 30 would appear in most seasons, far too many of them undistinguished amateurs. Only when players such as Arthur Croom, Len Bates and Norman Kilner came on the professional scene would future prospects seem better.

Worcestershire, Leicestershire and Northamptonshire

The three counties of Leicestershire, Worcestershire and Northamptonshire surround all but the southern borders of Warwickshire. All three had a cricket tradition well established before 1914 and their fortunes in the 1920s were similar: all struggled to achieve much in the county championship, Worcestershire faring the worst. One may conjecture what Frank Chester might have done for Worcestershire had he not lost an arm in the first world war. *Wisden* considered that 'probably no cricketer of 1918 had shown such promise since the days of W. G. Grace'. Instead, Fred Root did his best to keep the county side alive, bowling his fast-medium in-swingers. In 1928 he dismissed Hammond for a 'pair'. He was also one of the pioneers of leg-theory. When he took seven for 42 for the North of England against the Australians in 1926, *Wisden* wrote 'to such purpose was Root exploiting his leg-theory that the Australians stood in actual danger of having to follow-on'. Root portrayed in his book, *A Cricket Professional's Lot*, the struggles of a professional playing for a county with limited resources. He was also a man with vision, suggesting as early as 1927 a Knock-out Cup competition in regional divisions with the first-class counties joined by a few other sides.

Worcestershire, the club with a cathedral at its gates and the Lytteltons and Fosters as its heritage, had known better days and would do so again.

What Root did for Worcestershire, George Geary and Ewart Astill did for Leicestershire. Altham, writing before the second world war, called them 'by reputation and statistic the greatest of Leicestershire's cricketers'. As bowlers, they complemented each other, Geary's pace matched by Astill's flight and spin. By the end of the 1920s – and aided by Astill's batting and the leadership and batting talent of the amateurs Aubrey Sharp and Edward Dawson – they had taken the county to halfway up the table. Both men represented the best kind of professional, men of humour and good temper and ready to help inexperienced amateurs. Yet their greatest contribution to the game might be considered from quite a different angle. In their later years they became the coaches at Charterhouse and Tonbridge respectively. Peter May has recorded that it was Geary who fired his enthusiasm at Charterhouse, while Colin Cowdrey was nurtured at Tonbridge by Astill who had the faith and courage to put him in the First XI at the age of thirteen and was rewarded by his making 75 in the match at Lord's against Clifton.

Leicestershire, often in deep financial trouble, owed a great deal to the generosity of Sir Julien Cahn, that furniture manufacturer, book collector and benefactor who did so much for Midlands cricket between the wars, and to a gift of £1000 from Leicester Football Club in 1924 at a time when the county was in desperate straits.

Leicestershire's neighbours, Northamptonshire, fared less well. They had finished as high as second in 1912 but were badly affected by the war and, immediately after it, by internal troubles. A stormy meeting led to the arrival of Vallence Jupp, who had been a pre-war Sussex professional, as an all-rounder and secretary. The county survived in the 1920s through his leadership and through the help of the millionaire, Stephen Schillizzi. The historian of Northamptonshire cricket, J. D. Coldham, has commented that 'he uncomplainingly "carried the baby" financially; entirely without help from the hunting and other well-to-do folk'.

By the middle of the decade A. H. 'Fred' Bakewell and John Timms had joined the professional staff, while Timms' cousin, Wilfrid, had played as an amateur since 1921. W. W. Timms had been given leave of absence in the middle of the summer term, while still a schoolboy, to play against Essex. Northamptonshire had fielded out over 600 runs and were striving to avoid an innings defeat when Timms made an undefeated 154, to be carried off the field in triumph by his schoolfellows – who had taken 'French' leave on the Tuesday. French and Spanish were Timms' subjects at Cambridge and he would become, in 1932, the first 'Master in charge' of cricket at Charterhouse. It was he who had brought Leicestershire's Geary to the school as professional and, like Geary, may take some credit for the moulding of Peter May. In the 1970s, across a breakfast table in a Cambridge college I heard a voice say, 'I wrote to David Steele about facing fast bowling: I once managed to get a fifty off Larwood before lunch'. Mystified as to who it was, I got into conversation with Timms, by now a chief examiner in Spanish and apologising profusely for what he thought was a lack of modesty on his part. *Wisden* confirmed the accuracy of his remarks: against Nottinghamshire in 1928.

Yet what he and others had promised as batsmen was never quite fulfilled. With debts of nearly £2000 in 1929 and membership of just over a thousand, the committee was forced to consider whether the county really wanted first-class cricket.

Less sombrely, we may reflect on how the umpires acted when the players ran for shelter in a sudden downpour when Northamptonshire were playing Worcestershire in 1924. The Worcestershire player, Humphrey Gilbert, had played a stroke and the ball remained in the field untouched. On resuming, the umpires decided that the stroke was worth two runs and everyone agreed. Gilbert, a barrister by profession, was no doubt satisfied at the equity judgment. Cricket in those days had its touches of innocence.

Gloucestershire, Glamorgan, Hampshire, Somerset

Cricket in the West Country in the 1920s remained a game associated with amateurs in multi-coloured blazers who could find the time to play three-day matches, and with professionals loyal enough to show their devotion to an occupation which would never make them rich and whose security was always dependent on their health and form.

Gloucestershire cricket was seen by *Wisden* in 1920 'to be a very modest and humble thing'. 'Whatever the present race of players may do, they cannot hope to equal the ancient glories. There will never be another W. G. Grace.' Perhaps not, but in 1920 the seventeen-year-old Walter Hammond made his debut and he appeared in the following year in the county side against the Australians. The Bristol crowds rolled up in their thousands and even the Prince of Wales happened to be in town and, perhaps because he had once met 'W.G.', came along. The Australians rattled up 500. Hammond went out to open the innings and moments later was bowled by Hunter Hendry. Yet the experience had not been entirely in vain, for he had studied the batting of Charles Macartney at close quarters. Two months later, the Australians came back to Bristol. Hammond was again picked and his schoolfriends came from Cirencester Grammar School to watch him. He scored 0 and 1 but the *Bristol Times and Mirror* loyally believed he had a great future. Hammond may have been despondent but the secretary, W. G. Tunnicliffe, son of the Yorkshire cricketer, was not. The revenues from the two Australian matches helped Gloucestershire to put £4000 on deposit. It was a bonus they would value in 1924 when they lost over £1000 in a wet summer.

Hammond's career began in earnest in 1922 when he scored 32 against Middlesex at Lord's. The consequences were unfortunate, for Sir Home Gordon saw him batting and eagerly told Lord Harris of what he had seen. Harris was a powerful figure in cricket circles – past England captain and past president of the MCC. The upshot was that the MCC disqualified Hammond from playing for Gloucestershire because he had been born in Kent and had no Gloucestershire qualification. If Harris hoped to recruit him for Kent, he was disappointed and the press was critical of obstacles being put in the way of a cricketer of ability. One nobleman is alleged to have greeted Harris in the pavilion at Lord's with the observation: 'May I congratulate you, my Lord, on having b-d the career of another young cricketer?' In the event, of course, Hammond flourished. Lord Harris' influence in 1922 was much more permanently effective in helping to bring down the Lloyd George coalition later in the year.

When, in 1923, Hammond started yet again, and made 110 and 92 against Surrey, Warner (not always the best of friends with Lord Harris) praised him in the *Morning Post*. Two years later, he made 250 against Lancashire at Old Trafford and Cardus was there to rhapsodise:

> To be present at the rise of a star in the sky and to know it is going to be glorious – here is a moment thrilling indeed to men who live their lives imaginatively. It was as plain as the nose on Bardolph's face that Hammond is an England batsman of tomorrow. In years to come we will remember August 19 1925 at Old Trafford for when in good time Hammond carves history out of Australian bowlers here and across the seas, we shall be proud to say that we understood well enough he was born for the company of master batsmen.

Hammond's arrival in the Gloucestershire team must have seemed like manna from heaven to the county authorities. Hardly any of the amateurs – some twenty of them turned out each season in the 1920s – was a cricketer of any great ability and certainly none had any pretensions as bowlers. The attack was in the hands of Charlie Parker, Percy Mills and George Dennett. Parker had been recommended to the county by Grace himself. His best years were the 1920s when, on four occasions, he took over 200 wickets, second only to Rhodes as a left-arm spin bowler. Among his many feats

were to take all 10 wickets against Somerset in 1921 and
hitting the stumps five times in five balls (one was a no-ball)
in his benefit match in 1922. None was more interesting than
a match against Middlesex at Bristol in 1924. Gloucestershire
were all out for 31, in just over an hour. Parker then took seven
for 30 in 10 overs to dismiss Middlesex for 74. Hammond took
command with 174 not out. It only remained for Parker
to take a further seven wickets to give Gloucestershire a
comfortable victory. Mills, changing from seam to spin,
bowled his way through the 1920s before departing to coach
at Radley College, while Dennett played an unheralded part
in grooming Hammond as an all-rounder.

As for the batting, the sheet-anchor was Fred Dipper. Year
after year he held the Gloucestershire innings together with
a solid defence. Only the emergence of Hammond gradually
let him feel free to play in more attacking style. Like Parker,
he only played once for England – both men were picked in
the 1921 series against Australia – and like Parker he represented the solid, dependable player around whom the real
strength of a county side was built. Yet both of them, on their
county record and, indeed, on their single Test appearances,
deserved better of the selectors. Parker certainly thought so
and his omission from the England side at Headingley in 1926
was something which he held very much against Warner,
chairman of the selectors, and the two of them nearly came
to blows a few years later in a lift in a Bristol hotel; only the
intervention of Reg Sinfield prevented Parker from doing
Warner serious injury. They were different, these two men:
Parker, voluble and irascible; Dipper, quiet and shy. Different
in temperament but typical, as the historian of Gloucestershire
cricket, Grahame Parker, has remarked, 'of the old guard
of professionals who had started their careers before the war
and who were expected to shoulder the burden and the
blame'.

Hammond and Parker had many a great match together.
'Someone' caught Hammond bowled Parker became standard
entry on any score-card, never more so than against Surrey
in the Cheltenham Festival in 1928 when Hammond secured
ten catches in the match, a record for a non-wicket-keeper.
In the Festival week as a whole he made 360 runs, took 16

wickets and secured 11 catches. No one else in the Gloucestershire side could compete with such figures. Hammond, in
1928, was on the threshold of greatness. He would return
from Australia having crossed it.

By then, his presence had enabled Gloucestershire to make
something of a bid for the county championship and, in 1929,
in finishing fourth, they came as high as ever they had done
since 1898. In a new captain, Beverley Lyon, they had an
exciting leader, in the vanguard of those who saw that county
cricket, as it stood in the 1920s, had no passport to eternity
and might die from dullness and neglect if heed were not
taken. By then, the Gloucestershire side wore a different face.
It was a solid bunch of professionals – men like Sinfield,
Billy Neale, Charlie Barnett and Tom Goddard who, with
Hammond, were to give Lyon the sort of side he wanted –
never better demonstrated than at Bristol in June 1929 when
a thoroughly professional Lancashire, led by their solitary
amateur, Peter Eckersley, were beaten by an innings and 31
runs.

Lyon's success allowed him to take some liberties and he
was backed by his committee. 'Freak' declarations (when rain
had lost many hours) or challenging ones were all part of his
philosophy. His professionals were not allowed in the Long
Room at Lord's so he joined his men by the gate so that they
might all walk out together. He was a captain in advance of
his time. Robertson-Glasgow wrote that 'he made people talk
about Gloucestershire and come to see them play. He clothed
a profession and a routine in the finery of rollicking adven-
ture'. He would have revelled in the limited-over game and
fitted into the scene in which everyone was a professional.
Hammond, the prime ace in Lyon's pack, as Grahame Parker
called him, sought to model himself on his skipper – a man
with a Rugby and Oxford background – with, in the end,
significant personal and social repercussions.

Glamorgan entered the list of first-class counties on 20 May
1921 and began their career by beating Sussex by 21 runs.
Their only other win that year was against Worcestershire at
Swansea but at least the two home victories assured the
authorities of some support in those major Welsh centres. An
immediate post-war boom in the South Wales Docks had

encouraged the decision to become a first-class county but soon the economic recession made its impact and Glamorgan struggled from a deficit of £97 in 1921 to one of £2951 in 1929.

Throughout the 1920s, as Wilfred Wooller recognised, Glamorgan 'was served by a wide range of indifferent amateurs' the exceptions being John Clay and Maurice Turnbull who, on his debut in 1924 at the age of eighteen, played a major part in the defeat of Lancashire. Clay would bowl for Glamorgan until as late as 1949 and share in their first championship title.

In 1927, without a win all season, they defeated Nottinghamshire, the leaders, by an innings in the last game of the season and so deprived Lancashire of the title. In this way Glamorgan from time to time did something unusual in what were, at base, desperately disappointing years until, in 1930, Turnbull became captain.

From 1923 onwards, the county played the visiting tourists on August bank holiday weekend and the victory against the West Indians in 1923 at Cardiff had something of the atmosphere of a victory at the Arms Park in a rugby international. What became a sort of mini-international, 'Wales' against the tourists caught the public imagination, brought in the crowds and helped to finance the county's small professional staff. So enthusiastic was the crowd at Swansea in 1926 against the Australians that Monty Noble, reporting the tour, visualised one day a Test match being played in Wales.

In the view of John Woodcock, Cricket Correspondent of *The Times* in the post-1945 years – native sentiment perhaps triumphing over objectivity – Hampshire resumed after the first world war with, 'the makings of one of the best sides in the championship'. Their performances proved otherwise and, in the 1920s, sixth was their highest place and thirteenth their lowest. Yet the county of Hambledon and Broad Halfpenny Down offered more entertaining cricket than many and no side could be reckoned of little account which in 1920 could score 456 for 2 against Yorkshire and 616 for 7 against Warwickshire.

Over thirty men were called upon in most years. Situated in Army country and with Portsmouth also in the county,

45

there was always a smattering of servicemen, among the best being Captain Edward Barrett. Other players included Altham, a master at Winchester, cricket historian and a future president of the MCC; Ronald Aird, future secretary of the MCC; and the old England and Sussex captain, Charles Fry. It was an impressive list on paper though *anno domini* and infrequency of appearance diminished its talent. The day-to-day burden was borne by the captain, Lionel Tennyson, and the professionals.

No man made more runs for a county or probably ever will than Philip Mead. He came to stay, occupying the pitch with the permanency of a Roman legionary on Hadrian's Wall. All bowlers of his day regarded him as the hardest man to get out. 'What other batsman,' uttered Robertson-Glasgow, 'whose broad back a bowler has so rejoiced to see receding?' Hampshire's other left-hand batsman was George Brown, a colourful cricketer, who could defend stubbornly, hit mightily (the first ball of a match against the Australians for six), bowl and keep wicket – reputed to have done so sometimes in his motor-cycling gauntlets. Both men could have their dour moments: all nine hours of them, and 'wearisome to a degree' as *Wisden* noted when they put on 344 for the third wicket against Yorkshire on the United Services Ground at Portsmouth.

These two professional batsmen were supported year in and year out by Alec Kennedy – the Scotsman who looked like the comedian George Robey – and John Newman, of whom John Arlott might have said: 'And what is happening at Southampton today? Why, Kennedy and Newman are bowling in-swingers and off-breaks'. These were contented men even if their benefits in the 1920s were half of what a Yorkshireman received: perhaps because they were Hampshire men or perhaps because they had in Tennyson a leader who treated them like gentlemen and who batted like the Ulysses of whom his grandfather wrote: 'to strive, to seek, to find, and not to yield'.

Tennyson came of a family of parsons and poets – Alfred, the poet-laureate, had no monopoly of verse-making. After Eton, the Guards and the Rifle Brigade, he came to lead Hampshire through most of the inter-war years. Cricket he combined with working in the wine trade, commanding a Scotland Yard Special Constables Flying Squad, a colonelcy in the Territorials, big-game hunting, journalism and gambling. Gentleman he always was, nobleman he became, but the Establishment never quite accepted this outspoken cavalier who batted fearlessly whether facing the 1921 Australians virtually with one hand or taking a double century off the West Indian fast bowlers in 1928. A half-century at Bradford against Yorkshire in 1922, when the total runs in the whole match scarcely exceeded 300, was another typical performance.

Everything about Hampshire in those days was a little unusual. The secretary was Colonel John Greig who had played for the county whenever he was on leave from India, scoring 249 not out against Lancashire in 1901. Under him Hampshire had some 1200 members and money was found for development and for a 'nursery' – more and more a need as successive Annual Reports noted the dependency on Mead, Kennedy and Newman. Later, Greig was ordained and became a Canon of the Roman Catholic Diocese of Portsmouth. The two future Canons, John Greig and Jack Parsons of Warwickshire, never played against each other in county cricket but as Indian Army officers, the one a colonel and the other a captain, they put on 170 for the Europeans against the Parsees at Bombay in 1920. Greig retired from the secretaryship in 1930 and in the same year Mead, Brown, Kennedy and Newman played together for the last time. Tennyson would remain to see what the much talked of 'nursery' would bring forth.

Schoolmasters and farmers rather than soldiers and sailors were to be found in the Somerset side and the county approached cricket after 1919 with scarcely a professional in sight, save for Len Braund, a survivor from W. G. Grace's London Counties side at the turn of the century. Year by year some twenty-five amateurs would turn out and only one or two professionals were retained. Later, as Somerset languished near the bottom of the table, professionals such as the Lee brothers, Frank and Jack, and Arthur Wellard were recruited.

Yet Somerset were lucky in some of their amateurs, a

colourful bunch, none more so than John Daniell, the captain
through most of the 1920s. He had captained England at
rugby, tea-planted in Ceylon, led Somerset and retired from
first-class cricket all before 1914. The committee recalled him
and he would become an England selector – an appointment
which he also held in the rugby world from 1913 to 1939. A
career of combative leadership, pejorative comments, and
effective performances, was crowned when, in 1925, he
scored 174 not out and 108 at Taunton against Essex. A few
weeks later on the same ground Hobbs was the centre of
attention when Surrey played Somerset in circumstances
which caught the public attention. Hobbs needed one more
century to equal Grace's record of 126 centuries. For a month
the press followed him around and placards bore the heading
'Hobbs fails again' (when he had made a mere 54). This
time, on Saturday 15 August, the journalists and film-crews
thought the moment had come, and so did charabanc-loads
of Surrey supporters. Somerset won the toss and not till late
afternoon did Hobbs bat, reaching 91 at the close.

On the Monday the spectators were duly rewarded. Among
the amateurs who virtually did all the Somerset bowling in
the match were White and Robertson-Glasgow, universally
known as 'Farmer' and 'Crusoe' respectively. Jack White, one
of the best slow left-arm bowlers in England, had taken
sixteen wickets in a day against Worcester at Bath in 1919
and in 1929 he would captain England in four Tests, one in
Australia, three in England. Robertson-Glasgow was the
epitome of the amateur cricketer in the first-class game in the
1920s. A surprising number of them knew each other, met
on the county circuit, stayed in each other's homes, had been
to the same schools and to either Oxford or Cambridge. Men
like Warwickshire's Wyatt and Northamptonshire's Jupp
were only on the fringe of that world. 'Crusoe' first saw
what batting could be like captaining the Under-Sixteens at
Charterhouse when Knight made 90 for Malvern. He was in
the First XI with Rucker whom we met at the start of this
chapter. Up at Oxford, he took 5 for 20 to give the University
a victory against Somerset and Daniell invited him to play
for the county. As a Scot, he had no English qualifications
for any other county but his cousin was the MP for Bath. It

was enough and someone who would have been less at home in the ranks of, say, Lancashire or Derbyshire, settled happily enough into the atmosphere of Somerset. Luckily for Somerset, Lord Harris and Kent made no claims. Daniell stood no nonsense and banned 'Crusoe's' straw-hat, while contriving to field in his own Homburg.

The chemistry of 'Crusoe' and Somerset worked. Somerset, like every dog, had its day especially at Lord's in 1924 when he took 9 for 38 against Middlesex, twelve wickets in the match; and Somerset won a low-scoring game by 37 runs. Fast bowler, raconteur, humorist, journalist, prep-schoolmaster – he was all of these and in his autobiography *46 Not Out* he described how Hobbs equalled Grace's record at Taunton in August 1925:

Hobbs was 94 when I took up the attack. How I longed to unloose something supremely and eternally unplayable, an inswinger, say, pitching on the leg stump and sending the middle flying. Never the time and the place and the 'snifter' all together! I bowled four running that were very straight and proper. He played back to each one, and I chose to believe that he was nearly late to the fourth. Then, Lord bless me, I bowled a no-ball. Whack went she, to the square-leg boundary. From the sixth and last ball he scored a single: 99. Then, with a single to leg off Bridges, he was there.

On the Tuesday, Hobbs scored a second hundred before a tiny crowd and Grace's record was beaten. Even the *New York Times* caught the flavour of the occasion:

Any American in London or elsewhere in England yesterday and today realised that something had turned the country topsy-turvy. Barbers, bus conductors, stenographers, financiers – all had a topic in common which made them kin for the moment. Jokes have been hastily interpolated into the reigning London theatrical successes about Jack Hobbs.

Among the spectators at Taunton was a ten-year-old school-boy called Harold Gimblett. It was the school holidays and he had made his way from the family farm at Bicknoller where he played cricket with his brothers, caught rabbits and already possessed a gun-licence. The player who would be Somerset's greatest attraction for a generation had crossed the Quantocks and entered the county ground.

Surrey, Middlesex, Kent, Sussex, Essex

Cricket supporters in the south and south-east of England have always been spoilt for choice with five first-class counties playing and a choice of Test cricket at Lord's and The Oval. This chapter began with our noticing the batting of Knight as an undergraduate in the first post-war season. Once the Oxford term was over, he opened for Surrey with Hobbs and their partnerships were a major factor in bringing large crowds to The Oval in 1919 including the twelve-year-old E. W. Swanton, one of whose early memories was of Knight scoring a century in each innings off Yorkshire. Knight had the temerity to finish above Hobbs in the averages but he had a living to earn and, after two appearances for England in 1921, he became a schoolmaster at Westminster. Above both him and Hobbs in the Surrey averages was another amateur, Jack Crawford, who had first played for Surrey as a schoolboy in 1904. Few matches in 1919 equalled the excitement of that be-tween Surrey and Kent at The Oval when he and Hobbs went in at 6.45 on a murky August evening to pursue 95 runs to win. Both men scored almost 50 and the runs came in 29 minutes.

Surrey, by comparison with other counties, were fortunate in their playing strength. Their amateurs were cricketers of talent – Knight, Crawford, Fender and Jardine – while their professionals were impressive. Yet, highly placed though they were throughout the 1920s, Surrey never took the title and the explanation must lie in the failure of their bowlers to dismiss the opposition twice on The Oval wickets. Batting, rather than bowling, was both the county's strong point and its public attraction.

Pride of place must, of course, go to Hobbs. In 1919 he would still have a further hundred centuries in front of him but he was already 'The Master'; the acceptable face of English professional cricket; a man of charm and modesty; and, above all, the batsman whom the public came to see for the variety of his strokes, for his poise and authority of manner, for his craftsmanship on treacherous wickets and for the consummate ease with which he batted. Perhaps he was not a leader nor wanted to be: in the occasional absence of the captain others would take the task over though there was a famous exception at The Oval in a Test match in 1926. Two biographies of him, by Ronald Mason and John Arlott, have demonstrated that contemporaries were in no doubt that it was he, above all others, who was at the pinnacle of the English cricketing scene from the day he made 88 in 1905 for Surrey against an XI captained by Grace until his final century in Duckworth's Benefit Match at Old Trafford in 1934.

Andy Sandham, his regular opening partner rather than Knight, also made a hundred centuries in his career. Like Holmes of Yorkshire, he had to play second fiddle and his England opportunities were few. Andrew Ducat, who resumed his career in 1919 with a triple century, combined batting for Surrey with playing football – leading Aston Villa to an FA Cup victory in 1920. He played both sports for England and later managed Fulham FC.

Players such as these, together with Herbert Strudwick, the wicket-keeper, and John Hitch, a fast bowler of immense energy, who would in many other counties have been reckoned an all-rounder, were treated responsibly by the Surrey authorities, paid a guaranteed wage in excess of £300 and received substantial benefits from their generous South London supporters. Hobbs, in financial terms, was in a class apart. He had his own successful sports business and the County guaranteed him over £440 a year. With bonus money, Test matches and advertising revenue he earned, as John Arlott has recorded, 'a most handsome' living.

Throughout the 1920s, Surrey were led by Fender who quickly established a reputation after making a century in 35 minutes against Northamptonshire in 1920. Two years later against Hampshire he scored a devastating 185 in just over two hours. As a bowler, against Middlesex at Lord's in 1927 he took six wickets in 11 balls. Year after year he accomplished the 'double'. Nothing was predictable about Fender – neither his batting, his bowling nor his captaincy. If orthodox tactics failed, he tried the unorthodox; if a gamble might bring victory, then a gamble there would be; if he himself could turn the tables on the opposition, he would bat or bowl accordingly. Fender never captained England – too outspoken for some, too outrageous for others, though he became a favourite with the journalists ('He is always up to something,' wrote H. J. Henley in the *Daily Mail*); but he did less than nothing to ingratiate himself with men like Lord Harris. As his biographer, Richard Streeton, put it, 'Incidents attached themselves to Fender like barnacles to a ship'. When he gave way in 1931 to Jardine (of whom more in later chapters), the *Daily Express* wrote, 'Life at The Oval without Fender in charge will be much duller'.

One of Fender's earliest exercises in captaincy was in the match against Middlesex at Lord's at the end of the 1920 season, an occasion which caught the public imagination for a variety of reasons. Middlesex had to win to become champions, a draw was insufficient. It was a grand London 'derby' and, above all, it was Plum Warner's last match.

The match has been well documented, notably by Ronald Mason in his *Plum's Last Season*. Richard Streeton and myself in our biographies of Fender and of Warner each looked at the match from the angle of the respective captains. It was an occasion for which 30,000 Londoners turned out to watch on the August bank holiday weekend. Middlesex on the Saturday scored 253 for 8 after a somewhat perilous start. Early on the Monday they were all out for 268, Warner making 79 and Fender taking 4 for 76. So far, both skippers had led from the front. Sandham held the Surrey innings together with 167 not out and, with a comfortable lead of 70 or so, Fender declared, leaving Middlesex a nasty 40 minutes in dull, grey conditions. Overnight came the news that Lancashire had virtually beaten Worcestershire already – their passport to the title: a Middlesex victory therefore remained essential. On the Tuesday, with the odds stacked against them, Middlesex set about giving themselves enough runs to bowl Surrey out. By four o'clock in the afternoon they had scored 316 for 5, and Surrey were set a target of 244 to win in three hours. Ten minutes before the end of play they were bowled out and Warner had the climax to his career which his schoolboy nature craved; but Fender certainly did not present Middlesex with the game for Warner's sake, as one journalist, who was present, suggested to me in his old age. He set out for victory, though possibly contributing to defeat by signalling to *one* of his batsmen to accelerate: both took the instruction and wickets fell. It is a curiosity of the occasion – perhaps a reminder of the innocence of years when prize-money played no part – that both Hendren and Jack Durston, a bowler, left the field early on the Monday (while Surrey were batting) to go and play for Brentford in a Third Division South match against Millwall.

Middlesex duly won their title and they would do so again in 1921 in another crucial match at Lord's. Surrey were in the driving-seat and had to win to be champions. All Middlesex needed was to draw but they rubbed salt in the wound by winning comfortably. Durston and Jack Hearne were the principal figures in Middlesex's 1921 success – typical of a score of professionals in a county which could always command a large number of amateurs: rather too many of each for the coherence of the team.

Middlesex in the 1920s never quite recovered the glamour of those two championship titles. They had plenty of talented cricketers but many were amateurs unable to spare the time from work. A close analysis of the side which beat Surrey in 1920 showed that even for such an important occasion Warner was struggling to fill the eleventh place. Victory in that game had owed a great deal to Greville Stevens, a schoolboy only a year earlier, whose googly bowling was an effective weapon as, indeed, was his batting for some seasons. More important to Middlesex, if only because they wanted another fast bowler, was Gubby Allen. After leaving Cambridge in 1923 he worked in the City of London from which precious days of leave were wrung from his employers for cricket matches. He made his mark early, taking 6 for 31 against Nottinghamshire in 1924 in a match in which Middlesex, forced to follow-on, won the game. Talented as he was, there was little to suggest in those days that he would one day captain

53

England, be the president of the MCC, hold the prestigious post of MCC treasurer and become the doyen at Lord's – in the lineage of Harris and Warner.

'Patsy' Hendren and Jack Hearne represented the hard core of Middlesex batting. Hendren was a short, stocky man of great strength who had played for Middlesex since 1907 but his best years were the 1920s and he appeared for England 51 times. Ian Peebles, who played with him latterly and was his biographer, called him 'the complete craftsman' who only 'lacked the ultimate spark of genius'. He was a man of great humour and a mimic, at one with the crowds wherever he played and one of the outstanding personalities of his day in cricket. Secure in his position, not anxious for the morrow, creating happiness wherever he went, he represented the professional cricketer of the period at his best, serving but not servile. Even Warner, a conservative in approach if ever there were one, invited Hendren to come with the amateurs to stay at his home at Caring in Kent and take part in pre-season nets. It made the business of going back to Lord's (or wherever) and occupying different dressing-rooms even more absurd. Hendren and Hearne were to Middlesex in the 1920s what Compton and Edrich were in the 1940s. Their 375 partnership against Hampshire in 1923 for the third wicket being beaten by the later pair against Somerset in 1948. Compton had the edge on Edrich as a batsman but Edrich made a greater bowling contribution, and the same was true of Hendren and Hearne. Middlesex cricket in the 1920s was for those who liked watching determined batting. Hendren was lucky in his skills, temperament and health. A Middlesex player of much less talent, Harry Lee, saw the other side of the coin and wrote: 'A cricketer who was sick or out of form had nothing to fall back upon except charity'. Hendren, with a century and a fifty did his best for Lee in his Benefit Match in 1928.

It was to Kent that the cricket follower of the 1920s turned for a side studded with elegance and style. It was a county of great amateur talent – the three Bryans, Charles Knott and, above all, Chapman – but, as often as not, the amateurs would play at Canterbury in August rather than at Headingley in May. When they were not available a professional staff, insufficient in depth, bore the heat of the day.

Chapman joined Kent from Berkshire in 1926 – he had already played for England while a minor county cricketer. Twelve months later, he faced Lancashire, the reigning champions at the Mote Park, Maidstone. At 70 for 5, Kent were in trouble until he and Geoffrey Legge took 284 runs in two-and-a-half hours off the Lancashire attack. Chapman scored a hundred in 100 minutes, a second hundred in a further 70, and his last 50 runs in 15 minutes, eventually reaching 260. Yet wonderful performances such as this were too often marked by sudden Kent collapses, especially against fast bowling. Kent, for these sort of reasons, would be fifth or thereabouts in the championship rather than at the top.

Among the professionals, 'the long and short of it' as the press were never tired of saying, were Frank Woolley and 'Tich' Freeman – the professional axis on which Kent cricket pivoted day in and day out. Woolley had much in common with Chapman – height, personality, public appeal and the ease of movement which left-handers seem to make peculiarly their own. Woolley was already a folk-hero long before 1919 and the 1920s simply added stature. One does not look for the massive score to make the point (he had already made a triple century before 1914) but simply record what contemporaries remembered – a superb sense of timing, drives off the back foot, a majestic command. Robertson-Glasgow who bowled to him so often observed, 'there weren't enough words' to describe him.

Freeman was a gnome of 5ft 2in., with a balding head and a habit of hitching up his trousers. The gnome became a wizard when he bowled. His skills lay in his ability to bowl a leg-break which the batsman had to play, a well-disguised googly and a top-spinner with exactly the right amount of spin to clip the edge of the bat, so adjudged Leslie Ames to whom 'c. Ames b. Freeman' occurred on exactly 100 occasions, besides affording a further 259 'st. Ames b. Freeman'. 1928 was a hot summer when batsmen up and down the land prospered and five players made over 3000 runs, yet Freeman enjoyed what his biographer, David Lemmon, called 'a season of continuous triumph', justly rewarded by a first appearance at Lord's in a Test match. Although he was regarded as one of the worst bats in the game he had already made 50 not out on his Test debut in Australia. Some years earlier, Kent were playing Sussex at Hove in 1922 in the last match of the season. After seventy minutes' play, punctuated by rain, Sussex (Ted Bowley, George Cox, Maurice Tate, the Gilligan brothers) were back in the pavilion for 47, and Freeman had taken nine wickets for 11 runs. Kent declared at 196 and Freeman took a further eight wickets at a cost of 56 runs. It was the last week of the season and his total haul in the last two matches was twenty-nine wickets.

The keynote of Sussex cricket was its cheerfulness and the side was seen at its best in fielding. Both qualities stemmed from the leadership of Arthur Gilligan and it was he who persuaded Tate to become a fast bowler: for a year or two they were a formidable pair, bowling out South Africa in a Test match for 30, and dismissing Surrey for 53 and Middlesex for 41, all within a fortnight in 1924. Tate was a Sussex man through and through – Cardus called him 'the last of the rustic cricketers'. Ill fared the batsman who faced him at Hove on a green wicket with a sea-breeze harnessed to his aid. He would be there to bowl for Sussex – and bat – until, with a dismissive sum of £250 for twenty-five years' contribution, the Sussex committee parted with him less than graciously in 1937, though later he was made a life member of the club.

Sussex cricket was very much a family affair. Tate's father was Fred, forever associated with England's defeat at Old Trafford by 3 runs in 1902. Arthur Gilligan's brother, Harold, was county captain in 1930 and towards the end of the decade the Langridge brothers were establishing themselves. In 1895 another family association began which would last ninety years when George Cox made his debut. As late as 1926, when well over fifty, he took seventeen for 106 against Warwickshire on the pretty Horsham ground which E. V. Lucas called 'preposterous, like the haunt of some cricketing pierrots'. Three years after Cox's retirement in 1928, his son George made his debut. By then yet another family pair had begun to play their part, the Parks brothers. In the wider sense, Sussex cricketers were seen as 'a happy family' by Sir

Home Gordon, the 12th baronet who travelled with them to almost every match, got himself awarded a county 'cap' for his role as a supporter, and talked and wrote rather garrulously on the game. Arthur Gilligan's leadership coupled with the debut of Duleepsinhji, gave just the hint that the greatness associated with Duleep's uncle, Ranjitsinhji, might be found in Sussex cricket in the 1930s.

The historians of Essex cricket, David Lemmon and Mike Marshall, have called the immediate post-war period until 1929 'The JWHT Years'. Essex cricket *was* 'Johnny Won't Hit Today' Douglas, never better demonstrated than in a match against Worcestershire in 1921. Essex were dismissed for 90 and Worcestershire replied with 245, Douglas taking 7 for 91. Essex then made 560 for 5 declared, to which he contributed 123 not out. Worcestershire were bowled out for 273, Douglas taking a further seven wickets for 65 runs. A century had also come from A. C. (Jack) Russell, both men (Douglas as captain) just back from the MCC tour of Australia.

Russell had first played for Essex in 1908 and his father had been the county wicket-keeper in the 1890s. He was the first man to score two hundreds in a Test match for England and his last three innings in his Test career were 96, 140 and 111. Yet it is as an Essex player that he is remembered, not exciting to watch but a sound interpreter of what the circumstances of a match demanded. When he retired in 1930 he had scored over 17,000 runs.

Apart from these two, there was little continuity in the Essex side. As many as 38 players would turn out in most years and when Essex finished sixteenth in 1928 the committee felt that the time had come for change. Douglas was asked to resign and he never played for Essex again. It was an unfortunate end to the career of a man who had done the double on four occasions and, like Russell, scored over 17,000 runs — besides taking over 1400 wickets.

At the root of Essex's problems was money to pay professionals (Russell had a very poor benefit), and a lack of sufficient members. Leyton, the old county ground, was proving a liability and the county experimented in playing at various centres for a week, such as the Garrison Ground,

Colchester, and Southend. In 1924 the first match was played at Chelmsford. It was at Leyton, nevertheless, that a little bit of cricket history was made when Canon Frank Gillingham, himself an Essex player for twenty-five years, gave the first commentary on the BBC of a cricket match when the county played New Zealand, an event on which both *Wisden* and *The Cricketer* were curiously reticent. Then, and for a long time afterwards, the press was suspicious of the new medium of broadcasting. When Warner began broadcasting the same year, the editor of the *Morning Post* insisted that his newspaper be mentioned at the start of each broadcast.

Better times lay ahead for Essex. Maurice Nichols and Jack O'Connor were players for the future and a tall youth who played for Gidea Park impetuously walked out on his job in a Baker Street bank one morning in 1930 and boarded a tube to watch the Australians play Essex at Leyton. His name was Kenneth Farnes.

Throughout the decade county cricket had had its share of criticism. A correspondent in *The Cricketer* in 1922 declared he would rather know 'the destinations of the Public School cracks than the results of the county championship'. Such destinations – Oxford, Cambridge, Woolwich or Sandhurst – were regularly published in *Wisden* but, one might ask, to what cricketing effect if there had been no championship for 'the cracks' to participate in? The era of country-house cricket had never really survived after 1914 and patrons and hosts such as Sir Julien Cahn and H. M. Martineau were typical of an earlier generation rather than their own. Serious weekend club cricket was the form and Sunday cricket was becoming prevalent, even being advocated at first-class level. To Warner, in 1926, the 'interest in cricket was intense' and he saw no reason for reforming the championship as it stood though he viewed events that year through metropolitan-tinted spectacles – Middlesex were able to give Hampshire £500 and Surrey had a profit of nearly £3000. In later years he was not the arch opponent of change some of his critics might think. Where criticism in general was more specifically directed was in the mastery of bat over ball. Cardus challenged anyone to find bowlers to match their pre-1914 predecessors.

In the 1930s the simple but unequal equation of bat over ball would be refashioned by events in Australia and by a change in the lbw law. Yet it would remain true right up to 1939 that batsmen rather than bowlers were fashionable, and high-scoring was the stock-in-trade of the game.

2

THE FIGHT FOR THE ASHES: THE 1920s

'Last year in the great cricket match of England against Australia, the former accepted the victory of the latter with chivalrous acknowledgment of her opponent,' wrote Kaiser Wilhelm II to his uncle, Edward VII. Australia had, indeed, won the 1899 series and 'W.G.' had played his last Test.

The Kaiser, German Emperor of that most uncricketing of countries, had sought some aphorism or *Gedenkensplitten* which the cricket-loving Edward VII would understand. The time had come, he thought, for Britain to accept with equanimity the claims of the Boers in South Africa. Edward VII replied that there was a great deal of difference between a Test match and a war. Was there such a difference, the Kaiser might have wondered, had he read the speech of Warner, the England captain, on returning from Australia five years later in 1904? 'I tried to convert that strip of twenty-two yards into a battlefield on which no quarter was given. I have led great men into battle and we have come out of the fray victorious.' Nevertheless, the Kaiser had touched a chord and Anglo-Australian encounters in the brief twenty years since the first one in 1877 had become, within the British Empire, a symbol of the Mother Country challenged by a colonial fledgling. By 1914, the two countries had played each other on 94 occasions, of which England had won 40 and Australia 35.

If the Australian officials and the British public had had their way, there would have been a series in 1919 (rather like the Victory Tests of 1945). Instead, the crowds had to make do with the tour of the Australian Imperial Forces before returning home from the war. In a summer of two-day cricket, this was almost the only chance to see the three-day game. What was remarkable – again, as in 1945 – was that a side gathered from the Armed Forces should have done so well.

The Australians were led for most of the summer by Herbert Collins and the party included Bert Oldfield and Jack Gregory – all of them would make their mark when Test cricket was resumed. The editor of *Wisden* thought them a better fielding side than many a Test team and, until August, they had only lost two matches. It would be sixteen months before England met the full might of the Australians again but Gregory's fast bowling alone had given a hint of what might be in store.

The MCC sent out a side to Australia in 1920–21 in pursuit of 'The Ashes', a label firmly accepted in the public mind after nearly forty years. How wrong were the journalists in 1904 who called it 'a slang term of very temporary significance' and 'a rather undignified borrowing from the Yellow Press'! The Ashes had come to stay, the hallmark of Anglo-Australian context, a prize of mythical substance and elusive value forever kept at Lord's. If the crowds at St Pancras Station on 18 September 1920 were anything to go by, the MCC departed for Australia loaded with goodwill and a considerable amount of optimism. Every engine passed on the short journey to Tilbury proclaimed its support with a shrill whistle and ships in the Thames Estuary hooted their good wishes as the SS *Osterley* began the six-week voyage to Australia, punctuated with various stops where cricketers might taste French food, discover Naples and get some practice at Colombo. On reaching Australia they spent a week in a Quarantine Station near Fremantle because there had been a typhus death on the voyage. It was a healthy week with sea-bathing, no alcohol, and even dancing lessons for those who had shown least skill on the voyage.

The captain of the MCC party was Douglas, who had led the 1911–12 side after Warner took ill – though Warner's role from his sick-bed was not inconsequential and the Australian press had given him, rather than Douglas, the credit for England's success. The principal batsmen were Hobbs, Woolley, Hearne and Hendren. In support were Russell and Makepeace (preferred to Holmes). The all-rounders were Douglas himself, Fender and Rhodes, who shared the bowling with Howell and Parkin. Strudwick was the first-choice wicket-keeper. Critics thought that runs would be made but doubted whether the Australians would be bowled out on their own superbly hard wickets. The more discerning wondered about rather elderly gentlemen and players chasing balls in the outfield under hot Australian skies and were distinctly less optimistic than the crowds at St Pancras. The 'unknowns' in the Australian Imperial Forces side in 1919 had done well and there was a feeling, not entirely justified by the facts, that English cricket had suffered more by the war than Australian. The Australians, despite losing to Douglas' side in 1911–12, were eager to play as soon as an MCC side could be got out there. The parallels with 1946–47 and 1948 are close in so many ways. After both wars the Australians would outgun England in captaincy, batting depth, fast bowling and fielding.

At this distance of time the two series of 1920–21 and 1921 may be seen collectively as a period in which England and Australia played ten Test matches, Australia winning the first eight handsomely and England recovering some vestige of pride in the last two. The two sides got to know each other extremely well, even travelling back on the same ship at 'half-time' and individual friendships were formed, as for example that between Fender and Arthur Mailey, one a fit subject for the other's cartoons. When the MCC reached Adelaide, they heard the first of many speeches about 'brotherhood' and the forging of Anglo-Australian relations through the recent war. The strains on this relationship would not be tested even by the superiority of one team over another.

Warwick Armstrong, the Australian captain, symbolised Australian supremacy right at the start by scoring 158 in the first Test. He had been a thorn in the side of English cricket for twenty years; 'no apology is needed,' wrote *Wisden* in 1903, 'for giving his portrait, so successful has he been as an all-rounder'. In 1920 it needed a different portrait to reveal a man of some twenty-two stone who by appearance, experience and authority conveyed the power of the post-war Australians. It is difficult to find a real chink in his armour – a thoroughbred in performance, an uncompromising leader of men, an outstanding tactician. Only some lack of tact, demonstrated in England in 1921, blots the scutcheon while, in 1932, he was to use the emotive word 'unsportsmanlike' in a newspaper cable, from which verbal acorn sprang the oaks of controversy about bodyline bowling.

His vice-captain, Collins, also made a century in the first Test and confirmed the reliance of the man who had captained the AIF team in England and who would succeed Armstrong. Collins in private life was a 'bookie' but he took no gambles as a batsman, playing with a stubborn determination and winning the nickname 'Horseshoe' for his luck with the toss. As a captain he proved as shrewd as Armstrong but without his sharpness and acerbity. Collins and his fellow opening partner, Warren Bardsley, would open the Australian innings and one or other would usually make a half-century. There was a permanency about Bardsley which one might compare to the bats on which he had endorsed his name. My own club in Oxfordshire expended £1.10s in 1926 on such a bat. It was still being used in practice in 1971, retaining all the durability and strength of its patron.

Once the opening batsmen had gone, there came Macartney, the 'Governor-General', as much a predator of bowlers at no. 3 as Don Bradman would be in the 1930s. Solid foundations, undressed masonry, had come with Collins and Bardsley. The public looked for some architectural style in Macartney, as displayed at Sydney in the fifth Test or at Lord's the following summer. Only once in ten Tests did these four men all 'fail' and make only 73 runs between them, but rain – at Old Trafford – forbade England taking the advantage.

Strong as the Australian batting was, the real difference between the two sides was in bowling. Gregory (with a batting average of 73.66 in the 1920–21 series) and McDonald were a pair of fast bowlers as psychologically terrifying as any comparable pair in cricketing history; the orthodoxy of their pace and technique as theologically sound as a divine. Gregory was a farmer who bounded and leapt to the wicket as if rounding up his cattle. McDonald was more languid in approach, yet rigorous in accuracy. England had no-one comparable and again we are reminded of the post-1946 parallel: Lindwall and Miller and the search for speed bowlers in England.

Armstrong himself was also a bowler, though less so in Test cricket after the war, and the main attack was completed by Mailey whom one might think of as the Australian Freeman, a short man dispensing googlies and leg-breaks and statistically highly successful. In the 1920–21 series he took a record 36 wickets. Mailey's artistry went beyond cricket and earned him a living as a cartoonist, painter in oils, humorist and journalist. John Arlott called his book *Ten for 66 and All That* (1958) among the finest 'in the entire literature of cricket'. His later years were in distinct contrast with his earlier ones, spent as an employee of the Sydney Water Board delving in drains and pipes.

In Henson Carter and Oldfield, Australia had two wicket-keepers who, in their contrasting appearance and even apparel, seemed to span the generation from the turn of the century until modern times. Carter was the last man to wear open-slatted pads in a Test and the first one to adopt the squatting position behind the stumps. He was an undertaker by trade and, if business was pressing, would arrive at a cricket match in his hearse. When he played at Headingley in the 1921 Test he was the only Yorkshireman on the field. Oldfield brought a new professionalism to wicket-keeping: he never read a book or went to the cinema during his career for fear of straining his eyes and kept in constant practice in his Sydney sports shop by requiring his assistants to throw goods at him.

Among those picked to go to England in 1921 who had not played in the 1920–21 series was Hendry. He was an all-rounder whose chances to shine in this exalted company were few but who made a major contribution in the slips. Bill O'Reilly called him one of the most gifted all-rounders in Test cricket and his comparative obscurity in the Australian sides of the 1920s simply highlights how strong they were.

Australia established an ascendancy on the third day of the first Test at Sydney which remained unchallenged eight weeks later, by which time the Ashes had been regained and all five Tests won. Four times they led England on the first innings; twice they scored over 580 in the second innings; never (in a completed innings) did they score less than 250. England, by contrast, only once scored over 400 and twice scored under 200. Even when a game was evenly balanced, or briefly in England's favour, the Australians successfully turned the tables. At Sydney, in the first Test, the margin of difference on the first innings was a mere 77 when Australia proceeded to make 581, and so set England 659 to win. At Melbourne, in the second, England had seven Australian wickets down for 282 when Gregory, batting no. 9, made a century and the final total was 499. At Adelaide – almost a carbon copy of Sydney – the margin in the first innings was less than 100 and in England's favour. Australia then made 582 and left England to chase 490 – that they got as many as 370 of them (a new record for a fourth innings) was greatly to their credit. While Hobbs was in, victory was always a possibility. Nevertheless, after three games the Ashes were lost. *The Times*, in its leading article, remarked:

> It must always remain a great feat when one of the Dominions defeats the Mother Country. But if we did not know it before, the war showed us how it is they do it. They are a magnificent fighting stock these brothers of ours beyond the seas, and they play, as they fought in France and at Gallipoli, to win – but to win like gentlemen.

There is a distinct danger in assuming that the England players accomplished nothing of any note simply because they were so outclassed. They had the more experienced side, in terms of Test cricket, but the men were older. Among the batsmen, Hobbs sustained his great reputation with an average of 50 and two centuries. Russell, with 135 not out and 59, did a great deal towards reducing the margin of defeat in the second Test and Makepeace, with 117 and 54, bore the burden of the England batting in the third. The best bowling sustained over the series, came from Parkin who took 5 for 60 in the third Test, yet overall, like all the others, he was very expensive.

Much of this has to be seen as clutching at straws by a side regularly outplayed in all areas of the game. The Australians were a better fielding side, held their catches and Armstrong was the more imaginative captain. It is, of course, easier to command a winning combination and Armstrong had few problems – only one England partnership exceeded 140. Nevertheless, Douglas showed some lack of initiative in field-setting and was strongly influenced by the recollection of how effective the fast bowling attack of Barnes, Foster and himself had been in 1911–12. Neither he, a few years older, nor Howell could be compared either with 1911–12 or the current Australian attack. Hobbs believed the difference lay in the pace and lift of Gregory which assaulted the England batting at the outset, leaving Mailey to clean up the innings.

The tour was reported by two of the MCC players, Rockley Wilson and Fender, amateurs seeking to eke out their expenses. Fender often took a tram to a match rather than hail a taxi. Neither got into really serious trouble for what they said, though Wilson's reports, and especially his criticism of the umpiring, in the *Daily Express*, led very soon to the MCC banning such writing by players on tour.

Fender produced the only book on the tour, written on the voyage home and seen by the newly-launched magazine *The Cricketer*, in Warner's review, as 'a censored letter from the front'. It is narrative though much less so than much of Warner's own writing in, say, *The Fight for the Ashes in 1926*. It hints at errors of judgment on Douglas' part. With wife and parents accompanying him, he was as much the absentee captain off the field as Hammond, for different reasons, would be in 1946–47. There was less consultation between Douglas and his senior professionals than Rhodes, for example, wanted. Fender himself, once he was selected after the second Test, ultimately topped the bowling averages and the lack of variety in Douglas' use of the attack was something he discussed with his biographer, Richard Streeton, sixty years later. Yet, in the search for 'what went wrong', one is brought back to the simple fact that one side outplayed the other and would continue to do so in England in the following summer.

It says much for the equanimity of the MCC side that they seem to have travelled back to England happily enough on board ship with the Australians – they danced better (all those lessons in the Quarantine Station) but lost at deck quoits. Nor was the returning team consigned to the dustbin in public

esteem. The crowds who had sent them on their way from
St Pancras greeted them with equal enthusiasm at Victoria:
'What would have happened had we won?' Fender pondered.
The enthusiasm displayed towards a well-beaten side would
find few echoes in our own day. The last ball bowled by the
MCC had been on 15 March. Six weeks later, on 30 April,
Gregory bowled the first ball of the Australian tour, Carter
took the catch and the Australian road-show was in business
again.

On a cold May day in Norfolk the Australians played an
XI raised by Lionel Robinson – a prosperous fellow-colonial
who had made his money on the Turf – and captained by
Archie MacLaren, Grace's successor as England captain in
1899. The elder statesman scored a dignified 25 not out and
a Cambridge undergraduate, Clement Gibson, took 4 for 34.
The country-house XI at Old Beckenham Hall had far the
best of the match and MacLaren devoted the summer to
claiming that the Australians could be beaten. Little heed was
paid to what he said as the Australians came to the first Test
with several victories by an innings and still less when the
Test at Trent Bridge was barely minutes old. Douglas won
the toss and within a few overs Gregory with, as *Wisden*
reported, 'very fast and rather intimidating bowling' had
dismissed Knight, Ernest Tyldesley and Hendren in four
balls. As Ronald Mason in his book on the tour wrote: 'In a
single over, Gregory destroyed the morale of England cricket
for the best part of a season'. From England's dismissal for
112 there was no remission and a match which began with
some expectancy and huge public support on Saturday was
all over by Monday afternoon. Even such lines from *The
Times* on England's second innings as 'Mr Gregory bowled
very fast and Mr Knight played him delightfully' did not
conceal the dismay at yet another defeat. It had been the 100th
Test match between the two countries and, curiously, each
side had won forty times before it began. Australia had
made a formidable beginning to the second century of
matches.

Order, counter-order, disorder seemed to attend the
England selectors' efforts to redeem things at Lord's. Fourteen
men were summoned up, including Fry, who had first played

for England in 1899. In *Wisden*'s words he 'begged off on the ground' because he was not in form. Hobbs, transparently unwell, as was Hearne (though he made a century for his county) also withdrew. Alfred Evans, a Kent amateur, on the basis of 69 not out for the MCC against the Australians, made his solitary Test appearance as did the solid Dipper of Gloucestershire who had taken a long look at the Australians while batting at Bristol but who seemed to take even longer to get to the ball when fielding.

From a match in which Gregory, McDonald and Mailey plucked 19 victims and Australia won by eight wickets, some small English prestige was salvaged. For the second Test running, no Australian was allowed to make a century and three Englishmen batted in ways worthy of the first Test match played at Lord's since 1912. Dipper played courageously off the front foot for 40 runs, strong and fearless – 'a morale influence' wrote the aspiring young Cardus. The crowd gave him an ovation as he made his way back to the pavilion. Woolley made 95 and 93 – no pair of 90s is better remembered in the history of Test cricket. Among those watching was A. A. Thomson who, in the proverbial phrase, 'saw every ball received by Woolley'. Not for thirty years would he become a cricket writer, a whole range of plays and novels would come first, but he was storing up the memories for the books which gave him, for a few years, a following second only to Cardus. 'I cannot think of any innings I have seen that was finer in essence than those two of Frank Woolley's. While partners came and went he progressed serenely towards the hundreds he never reached. Tennyson's effort was a different cup of tea and a very strong one.' He got 74 not out in the second innings, runs that foreshadowed gaiety and courage in the next Test.

For the third Test at Headingley only the England selectors had to be jugglers; the Australians had merely to decide whom to omit from a highly talented squad. It was a simple decision – no-one! There had to be a change of England captaincy in that Douglas was so tainted with defeat. *The Times* declared that 'Colonel Douglas was not a lucky captain'. He kept his place, made 75 runs and took three wickets while Tennyson assumed responsibility. More names were chosen: Ducat by a solitary appearance becoming a double international and Brown of Hampshire coming in as wicket-keeper to strengthen the batting. Hobbs declared himself to be fit or at least ready to make a brave show for England's sake. He fielded on the Friday, rested on the Saturday, felt better on the Sunday and was relieved of his appendix on the Monday, possibly in the nick of time.

These matches, one is reminded, were all of three-day duration. The counties, in the 1920s, did not like further inroads into the championship matches. Armstrong set England a target of 422 in four-and-a-half hours and comfortably won the rubber by 219 with an hour to spare. Tennyson's batting for 63 (in an hour) and 36 virtually with one sound hand was, said *The Times*, 'one of the greatest exhibitions of determination ever seen in a Test match'. For the Australians, Macartney made a century and the two undertakers by occupation, Tommy Andrews (92) and Carter (47) hammered appropriate nails into the coffin of English fortunes. Every Australian except Hendry made at least 30 runs or got four wickets.

Then came a Scottish interlude. In Glasgow, Armstrong met a businessman which led to his securing a profitable Australian agency for the rest of his life and Hendry looked up his second cousins. In Edinburgh, John Kerr, for Scotland, made one of the few centuries against the Australians all summer. Hobbs ranked him as one of the best batsmen in the world.

The eighteenth-century diarist, Horace Walpole, tells us of cricketing parsons fetched 'by express from different parts of England to play at Richmond Green'. So did the England selectors summon fifteen men from the shires to Old Trafford for the fourth Test to sit in the rain all Saturday. The match was thus reduced to two days and was (arguably) governed by the law applying to two-day matches. Tennyson declared less than 100 minutes before the close of play on Monday and Armstrong objected. After flurries of discussion, his objection was sustained and Fender, by now in his bath, had to dress and bat again. Years later, Armstrong confessed to Fender that it had been a 'try-on' suggested by his wicket-keeper. The laws were broken even further when no-one noticed

Armstrong bowl successive overs either side of the dispute.

England, on the Tuesday evening, could have enforced the follow-on but with half an hour remaining chose not to. It was all something of a storm in a tea-cup yet this England side had allowed no Australian to make 40 and led them by 200 runs. The occasion allowed Parker of Gloucestershire to join the '1921 Club': those that year who made a solitary appearance in their careers for England.

Declaring and then gaining a first innings lead almost became a habit when Tennyson repeated it at The Oval but again rain reduced the match to absurdity in the closing session, compounded by Armstrong reading his paper in the deep field – a personal protest at travelling 13,000 miles to play three-day Tests and a sad, if not entirely uncharacteristic end to his career as Australian captain. Cricketers since Armstrong have offended more and been pilloried less but his nonchalance hurt English pride after ten unsuccessful Tests. Mead's 182 not out was the highest score by an England player in a Test match in England. He had been lucky (or unlucky: there are two ways of looking at it) not to go to Australia the previous autumn.

By way of innings victories against Somerset and Gloucestershire (Hammond's second encounter with them), the Australians came to Eastbourne to meet 'An England XI'. MacLaren, the captain, still believed that the Australians could be beaten and everyone who has read Cardus knows all about the result. The young Cambridge men whom MacLaren had gathered around him were dismissed for 43 and the Australians got 174. Cardus, defying his sports editor to be there in the first place rather than watching a key county match, enjoyed Sunday by the sea and – he tells us – lingered on Monday morning before going to the station. It matters not now whether he booked out of his hotel or not, or what he did with his suitcase. He could always tell a tale and let literary licence quell the awkward fact. What does matter is that he was assuredly there among the retired colonels and saw the Australians vanquished by 28 runs and MacLaren (his boyhood hero) come off the field a 'conqueror in the last great match of his career in England'.

Public euphoria at the victory and Cardus' piece in the

Manchester Guardian were typical displays of English cheerfulness in the face of adversity. Aubrey Faulkner (who made 153 in the second innings) was a South African, MacLaren was a survivor from the Victorian era and Gibson (who took 6 for 64) would spend his life in the Argentine: in none of them lay candidates for later England success against the Australians.

Next day the Australians played further along the coast at Brighton, were badly behind on the first innings but won the match thanks to Mailey's 5 for 13. The nine-year-old Ronald Mason watched his first match and he would come to write rather like Cardus but with more respect for the facts. You must eat a man's bread with him if you would write a book on him, declared Samuel Johnson. So Mason, munching his sandwiches on the benches, established his claim to write a fine book on Warwick Armstrong's Australians.

By now the summer was over. The Australians lost again at Scarborough to a more orthodox England XI and, no doubt desperately tired and perhaps a little homesick, set sail for Australia via three Test matches in South Africa. They reached their own shores in mid-December. The odyssey of the 1920–21 Australians was over, but in the case of seven of them, their long-suffering families did not even have them for Christmas. Victoria played New South Wales over the holiday.

When the fight for the Ashes was resumed in 1924–25 English hopes were cautiously optimistic, the Editor of *The Cricketer* observed, though he prophesied that Tate would be the only effective bowler. Noble, a former Australian captain, thought that 'man for man, team for team, the Lion would twist the Kangaroo's tail'. This time there was no dallying around in Quarantine Stations and the MCC played three games in Western Australia, whose captain, Fred Taafe, did sufficiently well against them to be asked to play for a Combined XI at Brisbane against the MCC: with 96 undefeated runs and the unusual record of being at the wicket on every day of the match his round trip of 6000 miles by train was not in vain. Distances in Australia remained immense and travel by air was still a novelty.

Lack of air communications in the 1920s meant that Australian sporting links with the outside world were few and far between. A Test match against England aroused massive interest throughout the continent. Those in distant sheep stations or wheat farms who might never visit one of the great urban centres followed the progress of a game on the newly developing radio links. A county court judge in Melbourne arranged for reports of the Sydney Test to be supplied throughout his sitting and he passed on the scores to counsel and defendants! In Sydney itself, from English place-names such as Liverpool, King's Cross or Paddington, huge crowds flocked to the Sydney Cricket Ground intent on spending every day except Christmas Day itself watching the First Test. What wives and families made of it we cannot know but there they all were, this predominantly male crowd, in trilbies or caps, dark suits and stiff collars, willing victims of the heat in the stands or on the Hill; 165,000 of them over seven days, casting their cheers and sallies, survivors of Gallipoli, boys who had queued in 1915 to see Trumper's funeral cortège, three veterans who had played in the first-ever Test in 1877 – men in work and men out of it, a microcosm of humanity intent on what twenty-two of mankind might achieve on twenty-two yards of earth.

Making his debut in the Australian side was Bill Ponsford, outstanding among the new generation of post-war Australian batsmen. He had made a century on his debut in Sheffield Shield cricket and he did so again in this Test. His 429 for Victoria against Tasmania in 1922–23 had been ruled to be first-class only a week or two before the Test and so became the highest score in first-class cricket till he himself, and then Bradman, both eclipsed it later in the 1920s. Ponsford would play Test cricket for ten years. Sixty years after this initial Test match he was still playing bowls beside the Melbourne ground while inside they played a 'day-night' match, 1980s style. Instant cricket was not his forte. As in life, he was a man for a long innings.

The captain, Collins, also made a century and Australia reached 450. England's reply demonstrated the new opening partnership of Hobbs and Sutcliffe, forged the previous summer against South Africa. They put on a century and, when

Australia made a further 452 in their second innings, they repeated their performance. But runs from them, and a century from Woolley, were never quite enough and England failed gallantly in pursuing 605 for victory. 411 was the highest score in the fourth innings of a Test. Noble in the press box, ever critical of his own side and desperately hoping for parity between England and Australia after 1920–21, believed that the Australian bowling did not really trouble England and he was unimpressed by Australian fielding. As for the England bowling, Tate had worried the Australians most and his 11 for 228 won generous recognition from the Australian critics. His bowling, and Sutcliffe's century on debut against Australia – Noble called him a 'wonderful colt with a great future' – seemed to leave the series wide open. England, he wrote, 'must keep a stiff upper-lip and a stout heart'.

In many ways the second Test at Melbourne was similar to that at Sydney. Ponsford, Hobbs and Sutcliffe made centuries, Sutcliffe making another in the second innings; Gregory, Mailey and Tate got most of the wickets; England lagged behind a huge Australian score (600) in the first innings and failed, by 81 runs, to reach a stiff fourth innings target. Notwithstanding Australian loyalties, the feature of the match was seen to be the partnership of 283 by Hobbs and Sutcliffe who batted undefeated for a whole day. 'English cricket at its best,' said the Melbourne *Age*.

Adelaide and the third Test demonstrated how the Australians, after losing 6 wickets for 119, could recover. A double century by Jack Ryder helped them to reach 489 though injuries to all the main England bowlers diminished the achievement somewhat. Ryder was a major figure in Australian cricket for over fifty years, as player and selector, and he would survive to be the oldest Test cricketer present at the Centenary Test in 1977.

Yet again, England had chased a fourth innings total of substantial proportions and in reaching 363 fell only 11 runs short. They had been the better fielding side and Hobbs had made another century, yet once again they had lost. Despite it all, *The Cricketer* could comment: 'English cricket is at its high water-mark again. Even Italian waiters indulged in bets as to what would happen'.

It is time to mention the England captain. Arthur Gilligan, scarcely able to bowl in the match through injury, and out of his class as a Test batsman, had stayed in at the end for nearly two hours in getting 31 runs and taking England close to victory. He was an immensely popular leader, seen by the Australian public as the pipe-smoking, dignified and charming Englishman but without any airs and graces and they liked the way he accepted defeat. Within minutes of losing at Adelaide he was allowing himself to be surrounded by youngsters with autograph albums cheerfully signing his name over and over again. And Australians remembered that he had refused to slow down the over rate and waste time when Victoria successfully snatched victory against the MCC on the stroke of time. Warner, in *The Cricketer*, was rather less impressed and felt that his light-hearted manner was not attuned to the atmosphere of Test cricket.

The thorough admiration for the England cricketers as a whole brought genuine Australian pleasure when Gilligan won the toss in the fourth Test and England (instead of Australia) made over 500 runs – with yet another Sutcliffe century. England won by an innings and 29 runs, the first victory against Australia since The Oval in 1912, but all else on the tour was something of an anti-climax. The side met Clarrie Grimmett at Sydney in the fifth Test for the first time and his was a sumptuous debut with 11 for 82. England lost by 307 runs: salvaged from the wreckage was Sutcliffe's record 734 runs in a series, Tate's record 38 wickets and the four century-partnerships of Hobbs and Sutcliffe.

Even more than Hobbs, the England batsman of the tour had been Sutcliffe. His career had started late because of the war but in half a dozen seasons he had established a personal authority which demonstrated itself in a total confidence in his abilities: bowlers came close to apologising for the indignity of taking his wicket. In technical terms, his hooking of fast bowling was the distinguishing feature of his batting. He had style in everything – cricket, dress and manner – and Len Hutton would be his most apt pupil.

Noble, in his book *Gilligan's Men*, believed that no MCC side had done so much to cement goodwill between England and Australia and he admired England's ability 'to take a licking with a smile'. It is, of course, easier to be generous to a chivalrous but beaten foe than one who has come and conquered. Would Hobbs and Sutcliffe still have been presented with their silver coffee and tea sets by the Melbourne public had the series gone the other way?

A lot of importance was rightly attached to the winning of the toss: on the only occasion on which Gilligan won it, his team won, and with an innings to spare. The wicket at Sydney, composed of Bulli soil, would begin to wear after the fourth day, causing a fine dust to accumulate. This helped bowlers such as Mailey and Grimmett immeasurably and it is a further tribute to the England batting in the first Test that over 400 runs were scored in the fourth innings. By contrast Freeman, who only played in the first and third Tests when England batted last, had no opportunity to bowl in such circumstances. At Melbourne, where each side won a Test, conditions were equable for the first three innings of the match. The black Merri Merri soil, looking like polished ebony, gave a perfect surface for the first four days before cracking and becoming rough, something which the bowlers of each country used to their advantage in the second and fourth Tests. Similar conditions prevailed at Adelaide and England's batsmen, chasing nearly 400 runs, had little with which to reproach themselves. All this made, as we have seen, for a sequence of high scores. Over the five Tests 5847 runs were scored in the first three innings of each match, an average of 365 runs per innings. In the fourth innings, which came England's way in all four Tests which ran to a fourth innings, the average was 302. Australia never made less than 250, nor did England until their double collapse in the fifth Test. Australia made over 600 runs in three Tests and over 800 runs twice: England made over 600 runs in three Tests and over 700 runs thrice. Ten of the Australian batsmen averaged over 24 while eight of the English ones did so. Over the four Tests the differential was not great but sufficient in a series in which batting dominated and decided the winners. Yet, in the end, bowlers win matches since twenty wickets must fall. Tate carried the heaviest burden, bowling a hundred more overs than anyone else on either side. Discounting the performance of Grimmett in the fifth Test, all bowlers had to work hard for their wickets and Tate did so to best advantage. Had he had a partner of his calibre at the other end, the series might have turned out differently. There are comparisons to be made between his role and that of Alec Bedser in 1950–51. Both men, on the losing side in each case, took more wickets than any other bowler in either team.

Cricket made a lot of money out of the tour. All the England professionals got £400 plus £30 a Test match, and every Australian got £30 a match, expenses and a bonus. The MCC took home a £20,000 share of the profits from which the game as a whole in England gained. Many a struggling county was grateful for its share of Australian largesse. With every justification, the editor of *Wisden* could write 'the actual difference between the two sides was small and the dark days are coming to an end'. *Wisden*'s editor wrote as an Englishman. For Australia there had been nothing but golden days on which the sun was just beginning to set for a spell.

With his *The Fight for the Ashes in 1926* Warner wrote the first of many books, by different authors, which would use the same style of title. An alternative version, never widely adopted, was to name an Anglo-Australian series after the visiting captain: thus, *Gilligan's Men* (1924–25) by Noble and *Collins' Men* (1926) by Gilligan, now a selector instead of a captain. Noble, in his *Those Ashes* was the third author of a book on the 1926 series. All three brought to a head the debate on three-day Test matches in England against Australia where a definite result was hazarded both by weather and by high scores. As Armstrong had graphically demonstrated by reading his paper in 1921, 13,000 miles was a long way to come for a draw. So it proved in 1926 with no result coming from the first four Tests though just a hint that the Australians were striving not to lose rather than to win. Subsequently, some Test matches in England would be lengthened with the 'timeless' option retained if a rubber was at stake. The English domestic programme imposed a realistic limit since counties wanted their men back. Abroad, time was only a factor in the sense that amateurs had jobs to return to. No-one questioned the absurdity of removing the time dimension, an essential tactical part of the game, until after the matches at the end of the 1930s.

The Australians were led by Collins, and Noble was not entirely convinced that he had the vigilance of Armstrong as a captain. Their team was largely picked months before it sailed, rather than on Sheffield Shield form in the immediate preceding weeks. In the event, Gregory was manifestly unfit and had none of the fire of the earlier years. The overall weakness in fast bowling became apparent very quickly, in the matches preceding the first Test.

'What cricket we saw was good,' wrote the ever-enthusiastic Warner of the first Test, but there were only fifty minutes of it before rain ended the entire proceedings. The second Test at Lord's illustrated the other hazard of three-day Tests. To an Australian score of 383, with Bardsley taking out his bat for 193 – a grand finale to his four tours of England – England replied with centuries or half-centuries by every principal batsman, Hobbs, Sutcliffe, Woolley, Hendren and Chapman, and a total of 475 for 3. Since Macartney then made 133, it was batting rather than a result which gave any currency to the Test. Hobbs came to the match fresh (or perhaps not so fresh) from making 261 against Oxford University the day before. It was said the University had been offended that Surrey had, in the past, been reluctant to put their best men out against them! Hobbs went to the Parks to recompense.

Controversy surrounded the third Test at Headingley for Arthur Carr, the England captain, put the Australians in and by 5.30 they had made 366 for 3. There had been a thunderstorm the night before and doubt existed on how the wicket would play. Cricket is littered with captains whose brave decisions have made them heroes or villains. Carr compounded his 'villainy' by dropping Macartney in the first over when Australia had already lost Bardsley. The crowd settled down to enjoy Macartney's batting in what Warner later called the greatest innings he had ever seen: 'every sort of stroke came in rapid succession and it mattered not what length the bowler bowled'. He was less magnanimous at the time and Carr recalled him during lunch 'with a face like nothing on earth', which brings us back to the nature of the controversy. How far was Carr 'his own man' in putting the Australians in or was he, as sections of the press asked, acting under the directions of Warner, the chairman of selectors? And what of the omission of the left-armer, Parker, of all slow bowlers in England the one most likely to exploit the wet conditions at Headingley? 'Carr had exactly the side he wanted' and made his own decisions, Warner would later argue. Carr would not be picked as captain in the fifth Test and whether or not he voluntarily stood down was another 'grey' area.★

Australia made 494, Woodfull making his first century against England. He and Ponsford would come to play as effective a role as Hobbs and Sutcliffe without the style and artistry. Both would be formidable accumulators; Woodfull intensive, solid, a fortress of defence. England had to follow-on and Hobbs and Sutcliffe remedied a minor fall from grace in the first innings by scoring almost a century each and saving the day.

Once again, rain rendered sterile the best efforts of men at Old Trafford. As if putting on a show in a pre-television age for those in the North who had seen nothing that summer, the 'stars' all made centuries or half-centuries and Lancashire's own Ernest Tyldesley joined the parade. The match has its place in history as Carr took ill and Hobbs, at the selectors' request, became the first professional to lead England. If you were 'someone' in Lancashire you went to dine in the Midland Hotel in Manchester one evening during the Test and you heard that master-spokesman between the wars, Sir John Simon. After-dinner speeches are not really to be compared with the port which they accompany: they do not get better with age but, in our own troubled times, we may recall his message that cricket, of all games, was one in which the umpire's decision was accepted without delay and without comment.

The England selectors met on Sunday 8 August 1926 and Warner, the chairman, has recorded that the 'prestige of

---

★ This is all past history now but a discussion of it in my biography of *Plum Warner* gives the matter an airing and suggests a rather less than straightforward side to Warner.

English cricket seemed to depend on our decisions for England had only won one Test against Australia out of the last 19'. Those decisions included the appointment of Chapman as captain, to become the youngest holder of the office, and the recall of the forty-nine-year-old Rhodes who had played his first Test under Grace's captaincy in 1899. Nor would this be the end of Rhodes in Test cricket. There are England players alive today (1989) who played in the same Test side as Rhodes in 1930. No other Test cricketer can span the game from Grace and Fry to Wyatt and Ames in such a way.

England won the toss in what was to be a 'timeless' Test to get a result. Hobbs, they say, laughed when Mailey bowled him with a full toss; Mailey, they say, had dreamt that he would dismiss Hobbs in exactly that fashion. Mailey bowled well in this his last Test match and his 6 for 138 brought England's dismissal for a modest 280. By the end of the first day, Australia had lost four wickets for 60 though their final total of 302 assumed large proportions when a thunderstorm drenched the ground on the second night with England in their second innings barely 20 ahead. Grimmett and Mailey had itching fingers.

Four hours on the third day were decisive in establishing England's claim to victory. Hobbs and Sutcliffe, in circumstances made for the bowlers, put on 172 and each made a hundred. *Wisden* called Hobbs' innings 'one of the most masterly displays of his career'. He and Sutcliffe, on a wicket more venomous by the minute as the sun played havoc with the turf, countered everything which spin and speed could devise for their downfall. Hobbs' century – the only one he ever made against Australia before his own crowd at The Oval – has been seen by his biographer, Ronald Mason, as the finest hour of his cricketing life. Australia were set a target of 415 and it was the unholy alliance of Rhodes, the old warrior, and Larwood, the young lancer, who bowled them out for 125. The Ashes were won back at last and Warner went off to his club, had a whisky and soda, and wrote his piece for the *Morning Post*: 'Had we been beaten, despondency would have crept over the land'. Perhaps an over-statement, for there were other things to worry about in 1926 besides cricket and the nation had been paralysed by a General Strike.

THE GREAT RECOVERY.
JOHN BULL. "WELL, SO MUCH FOR THE ASHES; NOW FOR THE COAL."

But England's success merited leading articles in most of the papers, and even caught the attention of the New York press who found it odd that a man of forty-nine could win the match in a game that seemed 'more closely related to tiddly-winks than baseball'.

Noble did not find it so much odd as disturbing and

commented on the fact that older men had played a large part in the series as a whole. 'Where are the successors of Hobbs, Mailey and Macartney coming from?' he asked his Australian readers. A rhetorical question to which answers might be found in, say, Sutcliffe, Grimmett and Ponsford or, with some help from the crystal-ball, Bradman, O'Reilly and Hammond.

A dampener on England's success came in a letter to *The Times* which asked if there were not 'a respectable body of opinion in favour of the abolition of Tests altogether'. Devotees of county cricket deplored the inroads which extra days for Test cricket and the visits planned for four successive years from 1928 onwards of other Test countries would make. Had the correspondent known, there would be visitors every year henceforth. 1927 would have a unique quality: the last year of county cricket undisturbed.

This was not the only letter to *The Times*. John Trumble, who had played for Australia in 1886, deplored the fact that conditions unduly favoured the batsman. He called the situation in Australia 'farcical' and made a plea for English cricket to put less emphasis on binding soils and heavy rollers so that Test matches would cease to be a matter of 'patience and endurance'.

And so with a gentle win against Somerset and final matches as far apart as Folkestone and Forres, the 1926 Australians went their way; as did Warner, to captain a side including Allen and Lord Dunglass (Alec Douglas-Home, the future prime minister) against the Argentinians – led by Gibson, the bowler who had devoured the Australians at Eastbourne in 1921.

Collins' 1926 Australians could not be compared with those of Armstrong and, though they only lost one match, theirs, said *Wisden*, 'was a sorry record' – a somewhat harsh judgment on a side hampered by a dreadful summer, Gregory's unfitness and Hendry's scarlet fever. In the months of isolation that dread disease of those days imposed, Hendry recalled that no-one dared visit him. More positively, Oldfield had shown the English public how great a wicket-keeper he was and his captain declared he 'could not remember him making a solitary mistake during the entire tour'. The corporal dug out more dead than alive from a Flanders wood in 1918 became, in the view of two of his peers, 'Tiger' Smith and Herbert Strudwick, the greatest wicket-keeper of them all, moving to the ball with the precision and accuracy of a compass needle. He, but not Strudwick who had played for England since 1910, would be there when battle resumed in 1928–29.

Chapman, victor at The Oval, had no serious rival for the captaincy against Australia in 1928–29. Two of his predecessors, Douglas and Gilligan, were the selectors, while Fender, in the view of his biographer, Richard Streeton, was 'never a candidate in the eyes of those who had to make the decision'. Instead, Fender went to Australia as reporter for the London evening paper, the *Star*; was very close to the MCC team – breakfasting with Jardine, for example – and wrote another 'tour' book. In *The Turn of the Wheel*, he was critical of the lack of all-rounders in the party and mentioned the career-figures of one P. G. H. Fender. He invited Warner to write the Preface which proved to be a defence of the selectors. Fender then wrote a footnote to the Preface criticising what Warner had said – much washing of dirty linen in public, especially as England retained the Ashes and won the series 4–1! Chapman led a side so strong in batting that no place could be found for Woolley, and both Warner and Altham called it the strongest side to leave England in the twentieth century.

Australia gave the captaincy to Ryder and the appointment signified Board of Control policy: a reluctance to shed the players who had served Australia well in the early 1920s despite the passing of the years. Gradually, as the matches were played, an older man or two would disappear and a younger one emerge. Noble, who wrote the only other 'tour' book, was extremely critical of this and attacked the Australian Board for 'neglecting opportunities to encourage the young of the land'. There were 'men of proven ability never called who might be pirates or bushrangers for all the Board cared'. Two young players, he declared, had forced themselves into the Australian XI, 'not because of the selectors but in spite of them'.

The two were Archie Jackson and Don Bradman who

emerged first and second in the batting averages. Of Jackson, the critics were unanimous in their praise. He made 164 on his debut in the fourth Test, displaying, recorded Fender, 'a perfection of execution and the confidence to play forward which English youngsters did not possess'. He was seen, even more than Bradman, as the most promising discovery Australia had made. Sadly, this would be Jackson's only Test century and tuberculosis, the scourge of the times, would strike him down four years later. Bradman was picked for the first Test, as twelfth man for the second, and made a century in the third: thereafter a place was his automatically in the Australian side for twenty years. Fender had some reservations and, in the light of Bradman's career, they have some interest:

> He may well become a very great player; and if he does this, he will always be in the category of the brilliant, if unsound, ones. Promise there is in Bradman in plenty, though watching him does not inspire one with any confidence that he desires to take the only course which will lead him to a fulfilment of that promise. He makes a mistake, then makes it again and again; he does not correct it, or look as if he were trying to do so. He seems to live for the exuberance of the moment.

Noble had no such reservations: Bradman was 'resolved to rectify any deficiency there might be. His rise has been meteoric'.

Despite the five years' difference in their ages, Bradman and Hammond made their first appearances in an Anglo-Australian Test match at the same time. Illness had prevented Hammond's selection in 1926. If for nothing else, it makes the first Test ever played at Brisbane a memorable one. From now onwards, until Hammond's retirement in 1947, their respective performances went a long way to determine the outcome of each series between their two countries. When Bradman imposed, Australia won. If Hammond dictated, England were victorious.

Chapman's side came to the first Test at Brisbane with a reputation for making a lot of runs against the States but not being able to bowl them out twice. Nearly 900 runs in two innings (and 169 from Hendren, hooking and humorous in equal measure) occasioned no great surprise, though England profited from the breakdown of Australia's opening pair of bowlers, Gregory and Charles Kelleway, the last bowling relics of the AIF side of 1919. What devastated Australian public opinion was the home country's dismissal for 122 and 66, their batsmen in the second innings 'hitting out wildly immediately on going in', reported S. J. Southerton who accompanied the MCC for *Wisden*. Larwood made 70 and took 6 for 32 which proved his best analysis in the series. More remarkably, Somerset's White took 4 for 7, establishing an accuracy of length which he retained throughout the tour. Mailey, now a journalist, wrote that there was no Australian player whom he did not embarrass. Hobbs was run out for 49, an anonymous dismissal for which no bowler could claim credit. He had run two, looked for a third and – too late – saw extra-cover gather the ball and deliver it, like an unerring dart, to Oldfield. Bradman had arrived and no batsman in future would ignore him. Hobbs, great cover as he himself was, could appreciate the deed done.

The second Test at Sydney belonged to Hammond, though it is nice to record that Hendry made his only Test century and took 3 for 56. Hammond had given notice of runs from the start of the tour and especially with a double century against New South Wales, enshrined forever in Herbert Fishwick's famous photograph of him displaying his cover-drive and pocket-handkerchief. On the same ground he amassed 251 of England's 636. The *Sydney Morning Herald* doubted if a player in the world hit the ball harder, and the *Sydney Sun* organised a shilling collection for him. England won by eight wickets, owing something to Geary who made 66 and took 7 for 90. Fender's criticism of a lack of all-rounders was lacking in substance. This was also the match in which Don Blackie, enticed from gardening back to cricket, made his Test debut at forty-six as an off-break bowler.

After this eight-wicket victory, the MCC came to Melbourne for the third Test over the New Year. Bradman made his first Test century (brought back into the side, wrote Fender with some irony, 'to strengthen the fielding') and

Hammond another double-century, but the real drama lay in England's pursuit of 332 runs in conditions which were expected to yield them barely a hundred. Hobbs and Sutcliffe set about the task after lunch on the sixth day, with the ball popping like an ambitious champagne cork and Oldfield conceding numerous byes over his head. The tactics were to play the ball only if you had to and play back with a dead bat while silly point and short forward short leg awaited their dues. Hobbs and Sutcliffe had not demonstrated the united front of four years earlier but their partnership in this England's second innings more than compensated. Hobbs made 49, out to an lbw decision which some observers doubted, and Sutcliffe remained to get a century. Both men, in later years, would say that the other's performance was a greater one than that at The Oval in 1926. Jardine joined Sutcliffe, survived another lbw appeal and kept company with him for the remaining hour of the day. Fender doubted whether anyone else (Hammond included) would have batted so well. Jardine's matchless courage was never a quality in dispute. When Sutcliffe finally left on the morrow the Australian crowd greeted his departure in muted silence, for only a few runs away lay England's retention of the Ashes.

Jardine had contributed in every Test and in the fourth, at Adelaide, he made 98, sharing in a partnership of 262 with Hammond in the second innings. His introduction to Australia should not go unnoticed. Noble called him 'this self-possessed aristocrat of the cricket field' and the public endorsed this judgment less articulately but more vociferously. Courage they reluctantly admired: the patrician outlook won him only plebeian derision. Jardine stored up their taunts and his day would come.

Hammond made a century in each innings and England secured a win by 12 runs, revenge for the 11-run defeat at Adelaide four years earlier. It was in this game that Jackson made his debut with batting, wrote Ray Robinson, which made even Bradman look pedestrian. White bowled out the Australians in the second innings, taking 8 for 126 and earning the unexpected reward of captaining England in the final Test when Chapman felt unfit. England made 519 runs in the first innings and Hobbs made his last century against Australia but, in a match which lasted until the eighth day, Australia were successful by five wickets.

Fender wrote in *The Star* that the great difference between the two sides was in the field. England never dropped a catch until the series was won and the Australian ground fielding was far below Test standards. Chapman set England an example in catching and in close-fielding and his absence in the fifth Test allowed Australia to score more freely. Southerton wrote in *Wisden* that his leadership on and off the field 'created a favourable impression wherever the MCC went in the Commonwealth'.

There is always much one can say about cricket and the imperial relationship and the parodied thought is never far away but the analogy gains conviction from the knighthood conferred on the MCC manager of this and both the earlier tours in the 1920s. Gilligan called Sir Frederick Toone the greatest manager ever and declared that the knighthood – only the second for services to cricket – was a tribute to what he achieved for Anglo-Australian relations by 'tact, diplomacy, and kindness'. Toone – scarcely remembered now – was a man of stature in his day. He had played rugby football for Leicester and been secretary of the county's cricket club before his life's work as secretary of Yorkshire from 1903 to 1930. He was a master of detail, a magnificent organiser, a friend to the professionals and amateurs alike, and a person who combined authority, efficiency and courtesy in equal measure. He died soon after the tour, in 1930, and one can only speculate how he might have handled events in 1932–33. Another speculative thought: the Australian press wanted to see White as England captain for the next tour in 1932–33. Would Cricket history then have been deprived of one of its greatest dramas?

Captaincy and management apart, the central figure in England's success had been Hammond whose 903 runs established a new record. Noble, in calling him the sheet-anchor of a talented England side, asked if Australia had much grounds for viewing the future with confidence. Jackson and Bradman apart, he was pessimistic especially in terms of bowling. In contrast, English cricket, in the doldrums in the first half of the 1920s was breezy with success in the second half. Hammond received most acclaim from the huge crowds who mobbed the returning MCC at Victoria Station as if looking for a new hero as Hobbs began a gentle descent from the highest pinnacles of achievement and veneration. Even in Australia he had been acclaimed by a public not quite sure where its own next heroes were coming from, though it would not be many months before Bradman's ability to assume that role would be established beyond doubt.

The fight for the Ashes in the 1920s was concluding with the gladiatorial rivalry of Hammond and Bradman.

3

SOUTH AFRICA:
CRICKET FOR THE FEW

'The occasion is unique,' Charles Fortune, doyen of South African cricket writers, said, as I joined him in the commentary box at the new Wanderers Ground in Johannesburg. 'Never before has the Currie Cup been played in autumn.' With the sun pounding down from a deep blue sky and a temperature in the mid-seventies Fahrenheit, April had arrived, and we were watching Natal play Transvaal in the closing stages of the 1981–82 competition.

I had arrived that morning from London and my first sight of cricket in South Africa was the West Indian Alvin Kallicharran and the South African Graeme Pollock batting for Transvaal. Kallicharran had made 'a superb contribution to South African cricket', Jackie McGlew, the former national captain, remarked 'and he is immensely and deservedly popular as a performer and a coach'. Here was a West Indian playing for a South African provincial side in the same season in which a 'rebel' English XI had played three matches against South Africa, for which official Springbok caps had been awarded. South Africa had last played a Test match in March 1970, before being banned from the international cricket scene. During my visit I was to learn how much cricketers themselves were doing to make the game multiracial. 'What else can we do?' pleaded one. The 'else' had to be the total dismantling of apartheid by the politicians: without it, the efforts of cricketers were mere straws in the wind.

Test cricket had begun in South Africa at Port Elizabeth in March 1889 though no-one realised it at the time. The occasion would make the English actor, Sir C. Aubrey Smith (*The Prisoner of Zenda, The Lives of a Bengal Lancer*, et al.) an

88

England player on his only appearance. Ten years later, *Wisden* still did not recognise matches between England and South Africa as Test matches and Warner, in making 132 not out at Johannesburg only retrospectively claimed the distinction of making a century in his first Test. By 1914 South Africa was accepted as the third of the Test-playing countries, as the 1912 Triangular Tournament had demonstrated.

England's defeat by South Africa at Johannesburg in December 1922 was as galling to the losers as it was encouraging to the victors. For England, it continued the long run of Test matches without success since the war; for South Africa, it was the first which they had won in ten years. The margin of England's defeat was only 8 runs less than the 176 runs scored against them by Herbert Taylor who had led South Africa before the war and who would play his last Test in 1932. He was a product of Michaelhouse, Durban and of the coaching there of George Cox, the Sussex professional. Before 1914, he had been the only batsman in the world to score consistently off Sydney Barnes at his best. He became captain of South Africa at the age of twenty-four and won a Military Cross with the Royal Flying Corps. An untimely descent into the Bristol Channel might have ended disastrously and put paid to his resumption of the leadership when the 1920–21 Australians visited South Africa on their way back from their triumphant tour of England. In the days of matting wickets, he was South Africa's foremost exponent in the art of playing back to the bowler.

Immediately after the Johannesburg Test, both the MCC and the South Africans boarded a train at Johannesburg and travelled south to Cape Town where England, in a low-scoring Test, won by one wicket. Not many people were there at the end to see them do it. More gaps were exposed than spectators in the single row of seats in front of a marquee and the owners of three large cars watched comfortably from under the trees. The photograph which is the evidence of this shows the umpire hopelessly out of position as the fielder attempted a run-out from the winning hit. It was as well he was not called upon to make a decision. Cricket, of all sports, does not admit the 'measurement' of progress but many a photograph lends testimony to the view that in three areas of the game, fielding, the setting of fields, and umpiring, standards have risen immensely.

In both the third and fourth Tests, which were drawn, the two sides were evenly matched and they came to Durban for a six-day game to decide the rubber. The MCC, on the tour, had been at full strength save for an unfit Hobbs who had stayed in England. South Africa had no one to equal the batting of Taylor though 'Dave' (a nickname throughout his career) Nourse would come nearest. He had played first-class cricket in 1897, after coming out to South Africa from England as a bugler with the West Riding Regiment. He would appear for South Africa in 45 consecutive Test matches and still be playing at first-class level at fifty-eight. Although two of South Africa's pre-war bowlers, Sibley Snooke (the only man to be out 'stumped sub.' in a Test match) and James Blanckenberg, played in the 1922–23 series, neither belonged to the tradition of googly bowlers who, in a few seasons, had given South African cricket so much prominence before 1914.

England won the deciding Test comfortably thanks to a century in each innings by Russell. Taylor, with a century, alone offered any real challenge to the bowling of Gilligan, Kennedy and George Macaulay. It had been one of the least memorable of series: South African cricket, especially in bowling, lacked 'both the novelty and excellence of earlier years', reported *Wisden* and English cricket had not demonstrably reasserted itself.

The 1924 South Africans, under Taylor, ran into trouble right from the start of their tour. Several counties beat them and they came to the first Test with wins only against Scotland and Cambridge University. The batting was brittle and the bowling ineffective. In a desperate effort to improve the bowling, Taylor brought Sidney Pegler out of retirement. He had been the best bowler in the 1912 Triangular Tournament but war-wounds had led him to give up the game and he had come to England simply to watch the series. In the match against Oxford University, immediately preceding the Test, Taylor picked George Parker, a South African playing for Eccles Hill in the Birmingham League. All Wednesday and Thursday it rained at the Parks but in a few brief hours on the Friday afternoon Parker took four undistinguished

Oxford wickets and found himself on the evening train to Birmingham to open the bowling against Hobbs and Sutcliffe on Saturday morning. Sutcliffe, by a rather more conventional path, was also making his Test debut. England's two openers scored 136 before lunch against the attack of Taylor's two recruits. Parker kept his head, was not over-awed and yorked Sutcliffe immediately after the interval.

By late afternoon he had added Woolley, Hendren and Chapman to his haul before having to leave the field before the end of play, utterly exhausted. It was the first time he had ever played through a whole day's cricket and, since he was neither injured nor ill, South Africa could not ask for a substitute and had to make do with ten men.

England were finally dismissed on the second day for 438, Parker taking 6 for 152. His sensational first appearance was immediately eclipsed by what followed. In 75 minutes – scarcely time for the batsmen to go to and from the wickets – South Africa were dismissed for 30 runs in 75 balls. Gilligan, in his first match as England captain, took 6 for 7 and his county colleague Tate, 4 for 12. *Wisden* wrote that 'there was nothing in the wicket to excuse such a collapse'. The South Africans fought back in the second innings to reach 390, Robert Catterall making 120, but they lost the match by an innings and, in the public esteem, the damage had already been done.

Many had stayed away from the match anyway because of the high admission charge of 2s. 6d. (12½p) and only at Lord's, where 3s. (15p) was asked, did the South Africans command large crowds in the remainder of the summer – crowds which came, as much as anything, to see England batting and to relish success after the bitter taste of constant defeat against Australia.

Catterall scored another century in the second Test. He was a Rhodesian in origin with a cheerful approach to cricket and to life, very different in temperament from Aubrey Faulkner whom Taylor also persuaded to come out of retirement. Faulkner was one of the grandees of the pre-war googly bowlers who had made himself into a batsman able to average 73 in a tour of Australia. He stayed in England after the Triangular Tournament, won a DSO in the war, taught

Freddie Brown at a preparatory school, played for MacLaren's XI at Eastbourne in 1921 and founded the first indoor cricket school, pioneering an idea which is now commonplace. He worked long hours, spotted talent, charged 10s. a lesson, made very little money and, in a depression, took his own life in 1930.

In the Lord's Test match neither Faulkner nor Parker could be said to have 'failed' but both passed immediately from the first-class scene forever: the one still remembered in the cricket world, the other totally forgotten, one of the few Test cricketers not to command an obituary in *Wisden*. Parker took the only two wickets which South Africa secured in the match, Hobbs and Sutcliffe, in a partnership of 268, coming to within five runs of South Africa's first innings total. Hobbs made a double century, Sutcliffe and Woolley centuries and Hendren a half-century. England declared at 531 for two and bowled out South Africa to win by an innings. It was the first Test match in which Frank Chester umpired, a young man embarking on the first of his forty-eight Test matches and using the same six pebbles with which he would count throughout his career.

South Africa narrowly escaped another innings defeat in the third Test, while the fourth, at Old Trafford, was limited to three hours because of rain. Rain probably saved them from being at risk in the final Test though they would need to have batted as badly as at Edgbaston to have lost. Sometimes a touring side between the wars finished on a note of triumph at Scarborough. Not so the 1924 South Africans where a sort of England 'B' XI (in the usual guise of H. D. G. Leveson Gower's XI) overwhelmed them.

In summing up the tour, the editor of *Wisden* caustically observed that English cricketers had not been in the least apprehensive as to what was likely to happen. 'Even figures do not give a true idea of how little the South Africans were to be feared.' Part of the problem had been the captaincy. Taylor had always been a greater player than a leader and, in adversity, he had lacked the ability to instil a sense of purpose into a struggling side. He and Nourse scored nearly 2000 runs and Pegler and Blanckenberg took over 100 wickets, but few of those playing had any future. Three were veterans and

Blanckenberg accepted an offer to play in a League. The one lesson learnt was to invest in turf wickets at home, something which had been advocated at the start of the century and which now gained gradual support in official circles.

The MCC, in selecting the party for South Africa in 1927–28, rested players such as Hobbs, Larwood and Jardine who would be needed a year later in Australia. A side which included Sutcliffe, Holmes, Wyatt, Ernest Tyldesley and Hammond as batsmen and Geary and Freeman as bowlers was thought strong enough for the purpose. The captaincy went to a regular soldier, Ronald Stanyforth, a natural leader, fluent speaker and capable wicket-keeper, though not a county player. A place was also found for the young Scotsman, Ian Peebles, a pupil at Faulkner's School of Cricket, in the belief that on matting he might be effective, and he would certainly gain experience. The series began on Christmas Eve at Johannesburg. For the first time since 1909, England were without Woolley but Hammond was there instead. It was his 151st first-class match and he had waited nearly seven and a half years to appear in a Test match, in marked contrast to the debuts of Stanyforth and Peebles. Hammond celebrated with a half-century, Sutcliffe and Tyldesley made centuries and England reached 313, enough to bring a ten-wicket victory to which Hammond contributed with 5 for 36 in South Africa's second innings. At one point, South Africa had lost eight wickets for 38 and Hammond had taken three wickets for no runs.

On the last day of 1927 England were dismissed for 133 by mid-afternoon in the second Test at Cape Town, George Bissett, a fast bowler brought in from a lower League side in Cape Province, taking 5 for 37. Despite leading by over a hundred runs on the first innings, South Africa let the opportunity slip. The Yorkshire pair, Holmes and Sutcliffe, paved the way for a large England total and the home side failed, by 87 runs, to achieve a target of 312 in four hours.

South Africa's new captain, Herbert Deane, made a pair of 70s in the third Test at Durban. Batting late in each innings, he saved the side from potential defeat. If not in a winning position at the end, their second innings total of 464 earned

South Africa a creditable draw. Throughout the tour England had had a long and undistinguished 'tail', especially in evidence in the fourth and fifth Tests when the leading batsmen did not accomplish much. Bissett proved far too fast for the majority and in each case South Africa were able to seize their chance. At Johannesburg in the fourth Test they successfully chased 156, and at Durban in the fifth, they only needed 69. Twice Deane had won the toss, put England in and the gamble had come off. The squaring of the rubber meant much to South African cricket in a country where the game always played second fiddle to rugby, though the editor of *Wisden* in his 'Notes' chose to pass the event by completely in total absorption with England's forthcoming prospects in Australia.

Just before the visit of the MCC opinion had mounted in South Africa that there must be changes in policy. Taylor wrote publicly that too much emphasis was being placed on picking cricketers from Transvaal to the neglect of other provinces. He also attacked the custom of choosing selectors insufficiently experienced in the game at first-class level, and continued to urge a transfer from matting to grass. Until that happened, South Africa could not hope to compete on equal terms with England or Australia. Taylor believed that matting led to a weakness in off-side play: far too many batsmen were content to pull the ball on the leg-side – a weakness which can still be observed in the Dutch cricketer of today who plays on matting. Changes did not come immediately but events in 1927–28 had pointed the way. The 1930s may be seen therefore (despite some evidence to the contrary) as a period of advance in South African cricket. Gradually matting disappeared from South African grounds and the selection of the 1929 side to go to England (although the veteran Taylor was deservedly in it) marked the beginning of a new generation of young cricketers drawn from a wider band of players and of batsmen confident of moving forward to the pitch of the ball without fear of the pronounced spin caused by the mat.

The 1929 South Africans began their tour of England on the village green at Bearsted against P. F. Warner's XI. It was (and is) one of the historic grounds of England, surrounded by Tudor, Georgian and Victorian houses, set amidst oak trees (which survived the hurricane of 1987) and where Alfred Mynn, 'The Lion of Kent', Fuller Pilch and W. G. Grace had all played. For many years, Warner made Bearsted his village 'local', in cricketing terms, but the 1929 visit was the last occasion on which he brought a touring Australian or South African side to play there.

From Bearsted (Warner recalled a day of freezing cold and shivering in a tent as he waited to bat), the South Africans went to Worcester for the traditional start to the first-class programme. Deane's young side – only he and Taylor were over thirty – were a better batting combination than a bowling one, with players such as Bruce Mitchell and 'Tuppy' Owen-Smith. In the matter of fielding, English cricket had nothing to teach them. Day after day, wrote the editor of *Wisden*, they maintained a uniformly high standard and 'on many occasions became positively brilliant', none more so than Owen-Smith at cover and 'Jock' Cameron as wicket-keeper.

They came to the first Test having been beaten by three counties and troubled by a pattern of injuries, accidents and illnesses which would dog them throughout the tour. Players who might have been rested could not be spared and a dry summer gave no respite. As occasional cricketers, they felt the strain of day-to-day cricket. The press called the first Test at Edgbaston a very unsatisfactory match. Mitchell, on his Test debut, made 88 and 61 not out but he averaged 15 runs an hour and displayed the stubborn resistance which would be the hallmark of his batting on three visits to England. Set 304 runs to get in three hours the South Africans made no attempt to get the runs and when Catterall was out for 98, stumps and the match were drawn.

Every touring side seeks to impress at Lord's and South Africa began the second Test by taking three England wickets for 18. They maintained the upper hand until early on the third and last day but centuries from Leyland and Tate enabled England, as at Edgbaston, to set them a target of 300 or so in three hours. Walter Robins turned the ball on a worn wicket and the South African innings crumbled to 90 for 5 when Cameron was struck senseless by a ball from Larwood.

In the days before meters, everyone agreed the light was too bad and, as the players went off, 'not a murmur of dissent from the crowd was heard', recorded one reporter.

So beset were South Africa by injuries for the third Test at Headingley that a summons went to Johannes Duminy, a former Test player on business in Switzerland. Continental timetables were hastily consulted and he got to Leeds on time. When Duminy was dismissed in the second innings on the evening of the second day, South Africa led England by only 24 runs with four wickets left and the match was as good as over. Those who came on the following morning were rewarded by a spectacular display of batting from Owen-Smith who hit a century in under three hours and shared in a last wicket partnership of 103 with Sandy Bell. Owen-Smith's innings was marked by his ability to choose the right ball and by the cutting at which so many of his colleagues (brought up on the mat) excelled. If South Africa felt that a batsman for the future had been discovered, they were sorely disappointed. This was his only Test series. He returned to England as a Rhodes Medical Scholar at Oxford, played some cricket for Middlesex and captained England at rugby.

The England cricketers, eventually set 184, won by five wickets. There was a point – just – when England might have failed to get the runs. Those who had paid their 2s. for what might have been a couple of hours' cricket at the most had a day to remember, not least 95 not out from Woolley, the only pre-1914 Test player on the field: for a parallel, one looks to Compton and Washbrook playing against the 1956 Australians. Woolley again plagued South Africa in the fourth Test at Old Trafford, sharing in a partnership of 243 with Wyatt. Both made centuries, Wyatt's being the first by an English amateur since the war. Freeman overwhelmed the South Africans, taking 12 for 171, and they were beaten by an innings.

One problem which the South African selectors had not anticipated had been the constant failure of the opening batsmen. After century partnerships for the first wicket in each innings of the first Test, nothing seemed to go right and in the fourth and fifth Test matches the first three batsmen scored 30 runs between them in nine completed innings.

Nevertheless, in the fifth Test, the later order batted magnifi-
cently. Taylor, in his 32nd Test match (a remarkable figure
for those days) made his only Test century in England and
there were four half-centuries. Sutcliffe made a century in
each innings and England, needing 234 to avoid an innings
defeat, finished up 30 ahead with nine wickets left at the close.
Interest in the South Africans had been sustained by the
English public throughout the summer and 47,000 people
had come, over three days, to see the game at The Oval. *The
Cricketer* considered they would 'in the near future be a
difficult side to beat' and, in Deane they had a captain who
inspired them 'with the power to hit back'. By now, the West
Indies were also a Test side. They and South Africa would
have been well matched, but no encounters were ever contem-
plated.

The 1930s brought change in South African cricket in two
areas. The gradual transition from mat to turf meant that
three of the Test matches played by the visiting MCC side of
1930–31 were played on matting and two on grass. At Durban
one Test was on grass and one on matting, while Newlands,
in Cape Town, staged the first grass pitch Test in South
Africa. It was also a transitional period in the South African
captaincy. Deane had retired and was then recalled; the ever-
green Taylor was considered; the long-serving bowler Eiulf
Nupen, of Norwegian origin, was appointed for one match
and finally the captaincy was given to the wicket-keeper/
batsman, Cameron. The confusion surrounding the captaincy
extended to the selection of sides. In a domestic series the
selectors gave too much attention to the personality of players,
a quality rather more important when choosing a side to tour.

The MCC, under Chapman, were near enough as strong
as could be and they, too, had – in a different sense – a surfeit
of captains: Wyatt and White had already led England. In a
low-scoring first Test at Johannesburg, over Christmas,
South Africa won by 28 runs, owing their success to the
eleven wickets secured by their new captain, Nupen. He was
the last of the great bowlers on matting with an off-break
which came viciously off the surface. It was the only result
in the series and gave South Africa the rubber.

In the second Test at Cape Town, played on turf, South Africa made 513, after an opening partnership of 260 between Mitchell and Jack Siedle. England, in making 350, had to follow-on and narrowly avoided defeat. It was a match of records and curiosities: eight Test captains, past, present or future, played; never before had South Africa made 500 against England; Hammond was both England's opening batsman and bowler, and he took over as wicket-keeper when Duckworth was injured; Nupen, on turf, was as ineffectual as he had been effective on matting; Taylor proved to be the last of the pre-1914 Test cricketers in any country to make a Test century.

Taylor might well have made another century in the third Test at Durban and he alone, with 64 not out, stood between South Africa and defeat in a rain-ruined match. England lost only one wicket in the whole game, South Africa having inexplicably left out (on matting) Nupen. They brought him back at Johannesburg and again he was by far their most successful bowler. South Africa's third captain in the series, Cameron, played an aggressive innings which almost secured a South African victory before time was called. By the time the fifth Test was played, the turf was ready at Durban which was more than could be said for the bails. None could be found to fit the new, larger stumps (the law had just changed) and a pair had to be made after a fruitless search of Durban sports shops. The delay was compounded by rain and South Africa secured the draw which gave them the series.

From England's point of view, the series had been distinguished by the batting of Hammond and Hendren and the bowling of Voce, Tate and Peebles. Tom Goddard had been disappointing and the constant changes between matting and turf, in a time of transition, affected him most of all. Successful as the South Africans had been in the series, they had solved no bowling problems for the future, but Mitchell's consistency as a batsman was endorsed and Cameron had excelled in the formidable role of captain, wicket-keeper and batsman.

The South Africans had done the right thing in moving over to turf and, eventually, their players would be better equipped to cope with conditions abroad. But nothing, in their experience, could prepare them for a combination of Bradman and the Australian bowlers on 'glue-pot' pitches. The team that set off for Australia in 1931–32 under Cameron's leadership was photographed with everyone holding a 'Don Bradman 4-star bat'; a fine advertisement for the man who would make over 800 runs against them in the forthcoming Test matches.

South Africa lost all five Tests by substantial margins. It was a tale of almost unrelieved woe. Kenneth Viljoen made one century but only 41 runs in his seven other innings; Taylor and Mitchell, with scores over 70 in each innings of the fourth Test at Adelaide, helped to make something of a game; Cameron found the triple burden he carried too much and could average only 15. The fast left-arm bowler, Neville Quinn, in Bradman's view the best of the bowlers, was unlucky in having a lot of catches dropped off him. His very early death two years later was a tragedy for South African cricket.

Bradman's performance eclipsed everything he had so far done in Test cricket. He made a century in every Test in which he batted, two of them double centuries. At Adelaide he was left stranded on 299 not out when his last partner was run out. Those who watched believed that the South African bowlers developed an (understandable) inferiority complex when he batted and performed below their true worth.

The bowling of Grimmett was as much a jinx as was the batting of Bradman. Batsmen would jump out to him impatiently and be bowled or give Oldfield his opportunity behind the stumps. The fourth Test alone illustrates the mastery of the two men. By making 308 and 274 the South Africans were by no means disgraced but Bradman's 299 not out and Grimmett's 14 for 199 overwhelmed them. Yet Australia was not a two-man band: Woodfull averaged 70 in the series and Bert Ironmonger took 31 wickets. The crowning irony came in the fifth Test at Melbourne when Bradman (through injury) did not bat and Grimmett was not needed to bowl. On the Friday, and on a Melbourne wicket of teasing malevolence, South Africa were dismissed for 36 and Australia for 153. Not until Monday afternoon did the weather allow a resumption and in an hour and a half the game was all over. South Africa's dismissal for 45 meant that

20 wickets had fallen for an average of four runs apiece. Ironmonger took 11 for 24. Badly as South Africa had batted their bowlers deserved some credit for their own exploitation of the conditions. Ten days later (see Chapter 7), the South Africans got their own back by defeating New Zealand in a series as convincingly as they themselves had been defeated. On their way home their ship stopped at Fremantle and some self-respect was salvaged by their beating Western Australia. Throughout the Australian part of the tour, Cameron's personality and his sense of playfulness displayed in pranks and practical jokes, saved his young team from being utterly demoralised.

Not until the Cheltenham Festival in mid-August did the 1935 South Africans, after four months of almost daily cricket, suffer a defeat. The side under Herbert Wade caught the attention of the public by winning their first four matches in almost Australian style, drawing a rain-ruined first Test, comfortably defeating the unbeaten Yorkshire side and coming to the second Test at Lord's with every prospect of beating England for the first time in England.

Lord's presented the England selectors with an unusual problem. The wicket had been reduced to near-desert conditions by a plague of leather-jacket insects and, in one of the longest selection meetings ever held, the discussion centred on who would bowl best in the conditions. The selection of Tommy Mitchell rather than Robins turned out to be the wrong one. A curiosity of selection was the choice of Bill Farrimond, the Lancashire Second XI wicket-keeper, over his county colleague Duckworth (who would keep wicket in the fourth Test). Ames, who kept wicket in three others, was slightly injured and retained for his batting. The South Africans, less aware of the circumstances at Lord's, had a side which, on form, virtually picked itself. Balaskas had taken twelve wickets against Yorkshire four days earlier, and in him South Africa placed their greatest hopes. From the start, the wicket proved difficult and South Africa had lost four wickets for 98 before Cameron took charge. In half-an-hour he had made 58 out of 60 runs. During the innings Louis Duffus telephoned Johannesburg for the Saturday night papers reporting 'there is no need for alarm. Cameron is playing the innings of his life'. He would never make a century in Test cricket but his 90, made in attacking style and at some speed, enabled South Africa to reach an acceptable 228. On the second day Balaskas, with 5 for 49, secured South Africa a first innings lead of 30. 'There followed,' declared *Wisden*, 'the classic batting of the match': Mitchell, in scoring 164 not out, batted throughout the South African innings until Wade declared, leaving England nearly five hours in which to score 309. The decision was brave rather than generous and he staked everything on the bowling of Balaskas. Once Sutcliffe and Hammond had gone, the England innings crumbled and South Africa won by 157 runs, Balaskas and Arthur Langton securing the wickets.

Xenophon Constantine Balaskas, who had modelled himself on Grimmett, bowled with accuracy and imagination. From a short run-up he was unusually fast for a googly bowler. This would be his finest hour: an injury afterwards virtually ended his tour, though he would make four more appearances for South Africa. In the 1980s, he was still practising his profession as a pharmacist and still coaching in his garden in Johannesburg. He had gathered together some of his contemporaries to talk to me and we sat around, as if in a Socratic market-place, with the benevolent old Greek handing round honey-cakes and cream. He modestly attributed his success to the lbw(N) rule and deplored the decline of bowlers of his kind of art. Presently the small boys arrived to be coached – generations had come over the years and some had become Springboks. Bruce Mitchell picked up a bat and Balaskas bowled to him, the small boys impatiently awaiting their turn: the god whom they worshipped was a younger one called Pollock.

The 1935 series was the last in which South Africa had to accept three-day Test matches in England. With the win at Lord's behind them, they were determined not to concede the advantage. The remaining three Tests were drawn. When time prevented them winning, they ensured they would not lose. All were reasonably poised and, in the third and fourth, South Africa were set targets possibly within their reach if they had batted more adventurously. Wyatt, the England captain, did all he could to force a result. At Leeds he bowled full-tosses to entice the batsmen; at Old Trafford he made a very generous declaration; finally at The Oval he gambled on victory by putting the South Africans in on a perfect wicket. South Africa proceeded to bat for a day and a half to make 476 and achieve their objective. Mitchell took nearly five hours over a century, while their depth of batting was shown by a century from Eric Dalton and 73 from Langton at nos. 8 and 10. Yet Wyatt did not give up hope entirely. England scored very quickly and, after centuries by Leyland and Ames, he declared when England were 58 ahead. With two hours left, South Africa were only nine runs in front with seven wickets left, in some danger, and on a wearing pitch an (unselected) Hedley Verity would have been very useful. Instead he was spending the afternoon taking 5 for 20 in 12 overs against Middlesex at Leeds.

Wyatt was sacrificed on the altar of a lost series. Warner, as so often between the wars, was chairman of the selectors and he began the process which would eventually lead to Allen becoming captain and taking the England side to Australia in 1936–37. Wyatt had his defenders – notably Fry – and he believed that Tests of four-day duration would have brought victory to England rather than drawn games. As for Wade – 'a captain of unostentatious efficiency', wrote Altham – he returned home to be at once appointed captain against the visiting Australians. He would play ten Tests for South Africa, every one of them as captain.

His predecessor, Cameron, had had a tremendous summer as wicket-keeper/batsman, ending it with an innings of 160 in the Scarborough Festival. The journalist Gerald Pawle drove Cameron to the night train from York to London and recalled his delight at the reception the South Africans had received from large English crowds. Cameron boarded the ship for home, contracted typhoid fever after a stop at Madeira and was dead within seven weeks. *Wisden* made him one of the 'Five Cricketers of the Year', placing him second only to Oldfield as a wicket-keeper. Wyatt, taking his batting into account, would have put him into his World XI. Duffus saw him as 'the most scientific and calculating of all South Africa's big hitters' who stood out in a generation of defensive players.

The 1935 South Africans had been greeted on their arrival at Southampton with the hope expressed by the president of Hampshire, 'We should like you to win one Test'. They did! There had been a confidence and assurance about them which was displayed in all areas of the game. 'Of the batting one might write columns and then leave the subject unexhausted,' wrote the editor of *Wisden* exuberantly. Even in those days *Wisden* struggled for space and wisely he left the thought unfulfilled. Nevertheless, a side which could face England five times without defeat was assuredly well equipped with batsmen. The measure of their achievement was the profit of £8000 they took home.

Then came the rude awakening! For the first time, Australia sent a side direct to South Africa and they ran roughshod over the provinces and the international side. Not a game was lost and the great majority (and three Test matches) were won with an innings to spare. All that had been promised by the introduction of turf wickets and by success in England seemed to have come to nothing.

The Australians were without Bradman, which was probably just as well. Stan McCabe and Jack Fingleton were prolific scorers in the Tests, while Grimmett and O'Reilly achieved such mastery that batsmen often seemed demoralised before they even faced them. Only in one Test did South Africa put up any serious resistance. After being 93 behind in the second Test at Johannesburg, they scored 491, Dudley Nourse making 231, a new South African record. Duffus called his innings 'a monument to the rough wrought metal of his cricket'. Even then, only rain on the last day saved them from defeat, with McCabe 189 not out and some hundred runs wanted with eight wickets in hand. Earlier Wade – unusual in a fielding captain – had appealed unsuccessfully against the light, believing his men to be in actual danger from McCabe's hitting.

The Australians established a psychological mastery which they never relinquished, symptomatic of which was the close-fielding and catching of the captain, Victor Richardson. The better they fielded on the tour – and particularly in their Tests – the worse did South Africa become. In wicket-keeping there was no Cameron to equal Oldfield and his sad absence was felt by a team which had been so closely knit together a few months earlier. The claims of business and the mischances of injury further weakened the South Africans. In a country where cricket was totally an amateur enterprise, it was argued that there had been too much of it at first-class level within a twelve-month period. Be that as it may, it would be the best part of three years before another Test match was played. The final match of the Australians was against Western Province at Cape Town. The two veterans of pre-1914 cricket in South Africa, Dave Nourse and Herbert Taylor, both played and made runs, Nourse's 55 being three below his age. In this, the one exciting finish of the tour, the Australians successfully chased 63 runs in 38 minutes on the stroke of time.

Within weeks of England's historic encounter with Australia at The Oval in the timeless 'Test' of 1938, the MCC embarked for South Africa with a side thoroughly representative of the best in English cricket, save for the absence of Denis Compton – playing for Arsenal. The batting was immensely strong so that the 'failure' of Hutton to make a century in the forthcoming Test series proved of little significance. There were seven others who did. Hammond was the captain and, in those pre-war years, the burden of responsibility touched him lightly. He made over 1000 runs on the tour and averaged 87 in the Tests. Despite the presence of Hedley Verity and Farnes, the England bowling would lack penetration. South Africa were led by Alan Melville, who had played much of his cricket for Oxford University and Sussex and in Norman Gordon they had a bowler of striking potential. Their batting would depend on Mitchell and Dudley Nourse.

The first Test at Johannesburg, played over Christmas, was a distinctly high-scoring affair with both sides making scores around 400. Paul Gibb, on his debut, made 93 and 106 and, after a collapse, the South African pair Dalton and Langton batted as they had done at The Oval three years earlier, with another late partnership of over a hundred. Dalton – pianist, baritone, South African amateur golf champion, tennis player – was one of the finest all-round sportsmen of his generation of South Africans. Langton, as an all-rounder, was also one of the great assets of South African cricket just before the war which he would not survive. The Test was drawn, though not without a brief moment of excitement. Just before the close of play on Boxing Day, Goddard got Nourse caught and bowled. Ames promptly stumped the night-watchman and Billy Wade, on his debut, was bowled first ball. It was only the sixth hat-trick by an England player and it gave zest to the remarks of Swanton, making his own debut in a running commentary on a Test and in the first live broadcast of a cricket match sent back to England. Broadcasting of the Tests 'caught on' in South Africa and was increased as the series advanced. Journalists in the country gave the games plenty of coverage but only one Fleet Street paper sent out its own man.

Both sides boarded the train for Cape Town, travelling across the Great Karoo Desert in a temperature of 145° with frequent stops for water to meet the thirsty needs of the huge Garratt locomotive. Of all the grounds in the world, Newlands, Cape Town, was the one Hammond loved the best and he chose the occasion of the second Test to play one of his finest innings. It is a ground on which nature has bestowed all her favours. The spectator may choose to look at play with the massive backcloth of Table Mountain skirting an entire length, its colour predominantly grey but changing in shadow and shade as the sun reaches and passes its northern zenith. Creeping like some hesitant caterpillar along a bank is an occasional train, its murmur attracting the ear rather than the eye. If you are lucky, you will see a grey squirrel casting a critical eye on the game as he hurries to his next destination.

A change of seat gives a view of massive oaks which are old enough to have seen and heard it all: the veld and pond cleared to make a ground; tea under the old pine trees for crinolined ladies and their boatered escorts; sixes into Newlands station; excursion trains from Cape Town at 7d first class; Bradman drinking Newlands' health in the Long Room but never playing there; Arthur Mailey pacifying an irate crowd with blackboard cartoons. The scene is completed by the green-roofed white pavilion and stand on one side and the new Memorial scoreboard and the Nursery on the other.

Central to it all is the deep green turf on which play takes place. In the changing and turbulent scene which is the South Africa of the late twentieth century, the ground at Newlands remains a continuing home of urbane tranquillity.

The Test, like those at Johannesburg and Durban, produced large scores on over-prepared wickets. Groundsmen were preparing tracks which were plumb without pace, 'so far overstepping perfection as to be of little use to the bowler', as Robertson-Glasgow observed. Hammond, as captain, was acutely aware of the problem: 'Bowlers on both sides could break their hearts and exercise every guile in the calendar, and still stand very little chance of getting a normally careful batsman out.' The effect of all this was to produce some tedious cricket throughout the tour which was relieved only by the attractive batting of Hammond himself, Eddie Paynter and the South African captain, Melville. The first two were mainly responsible for England's huge score in the third Test at Durban which brought the only result in the series, an England win by an innings. Paynter (243) made the highest score in Test cricket in South Africa until Graeme Pollock's 274 against Australia in 1970.

The brief visit to Rhodesia after the third Test had its curiosities both at Bulawayo and Salisbury. Neither ground had yet gone over to turf, while that at Bulawayo had no grass at all. White sand was used to dry the outfield, giving the impression of snow. At Salisbury, the clay which formed the base of the matting wicket was dried by lighted petrol, amid sheets of flame and black smoke. Despite these hazards – or counter-attractions – two matches took place.

Rain reduced prospects of a finish in the fourth Test and the two sides came together at Durban in a match designed to be played to a finish. The pleasant Kingsmead ground at Durban, with its bank of trees planted by individuals who had distinguished themselves there, became the scene of a game which has gone down in history as the second 'timeless' Test. The Test at The Oval the previous September (see Chapter 6) had shown the consequences of giving batsmen unlimited time but the lesson was not learnt until after this Durban game. The players went on to the field one Friday morning. In not the following week but the one after, they came off it for rain on a Tuesday. The contest was unfinished but abandoned.

To South Africa's 530, England replied with 316. A further 481 from South Africa left England 696 to win. In poor light on the evening of the sixth day, Hutton and Gibb set about a task which the South African press regarded as hopeless. Hammond knew he had a strong batting side and encouraged the attempt. By the evening of the seventh day, England had made 253 for the loss of Hutton. On day eight it rained and then came a Sunday. On the ninth scheduled day, England advanced to 496 for 3. A mere 200 were needed as Hammond and Paynter made the final assault on the tenth day. Rain punctuated their efforts. Hammond's 140 had been an innings of powerful drives and hits to leg and brought England within 40 runs of an incredible victory when a thunderstorm ended play. There could, of course, be an eleventh day – and indeed a twelfth – but the charade had to end. The boat home beckoned and the *Athlone Castle* could not delay its departure. The MCC cabled to Hammond that they might consider bringing the party home by flying boat but after a conference between Hammond, his manager and the South African authorities, the decision was taken to end the match.

The Test had become a way of life to its participants. To Mitchell, 'it was like going to work every day. You seemed to be going for endless fielding sessions, watching countless runs being accumulated'. Melville recalled being woken up by the groundsman every morning at five o'clock for instructions. Even when the decision was Hammond's rather than Melville's, Melville had to take the call and relay it. 'Those five o'clock calls went on and on . . .' And the game went on and on for South Africa's wicket-keeper, Ronnie Grieveson, and he liked it that way. He had batted for the first time in a Test, got himself what proved to be a Test career average of 57, stumped Hammond twice and simply enjoyed it all. Gordon remembered with rather less enthusiasm bowling over 90 overs for a single wicket.

But the man of the match, long before such trophies were offered, was Edrich. This gifted young Middlesex cricketer had a string of Test failures behind him both against the Australians in 1938 and on this tour. Hammond believed, with his shrewd judgment of technique and temperament, that Edrich was a genuine Test player. What must have been his last chance came when Hammond selected him for the fifth Test and dispatched him to the wicket in the second innings as no. 3, charged with making a major contribution to the England target of 700. To a man who had compiled a mere 19 in all the Tests in the series, the prospect lay in the realms of fantasy. Had England needed 70, and he had been asked to get 20 of them, it would have been a realistic proposition. Hammond felt otherwise, encouraged the young man and told him when his first hundred came up at the end of the day to settle down and double it. That Edrich made 219 and became a peerless player in the post-war years owes much to Hammond's confidence and judgment. His captaincy on this tour Louis Duffus called 'exemplary'. His opposite number, Melville, also had a high regard for him, though others have suggested that Hammond learnt much from the smooth self-assurance of Melville. As a pair, their contribution to a happy Test series was significant. They had far more to say to each other than Bradman and Hammond. This is the part of Hammond's career as England captain best remembered: not the sad, even sullen leadership in Australia after the war.

The MCC caught the 8.05 pm train on 14 March 1939 from Durban to Cape Town. The night that they spent on the train, Hitler spent in the ancient royal palace at Prague: Czechoslovakia had fallen. The following morning, as they boarded the *Athlone Castle*, newspapers carried reports of the speech of the British prime minister, Neville Chamberlain. Boat drill on the ship was taken very seriously. It would be Christmas 1939 before another first-class match was played in South Africa: by then war had broken out and the Currie Cup suspended. The game itself, Border versus Natal, was in great contrast to the 'timeless' Test and produced less than 600 runs in four innings.

Like all Test-playing countries except England, the first-class game in South Africa made only intermittent demands on players who had to earn their living. From 1890 onwards, the provinces in South Africa have competed for a cup presented by Sir Donald Currie, chairman of the Union (and, later, Union Castle) Line, so important in the links between South Africa and other cricketing countries. Currie had originally given the cup to the captain of Major Warton's touring side to South Africa in 1888–89, C. Aubrey Smith, with instructions to present it to the side which did best against them. Kimberley were the recipients and they chose to offer it for competition thereafter among the provinces.

The competition, between the wars, did not happen regularly nor necessarily attract entries every year from all the provinces. When the MCC or the Australians visited, time and distance made it impossible for cricketers to meet both the demands of tourists and a domestic first-class programme. In the eleven competitions between 1919 and 1939, Transvaal were the winners on seven occasions. Western Province and Natal each being successful twice. Eastern Province, with their headquarters at Port Elizabeth, were unsuccessful and their claim to fame must rest in producing for a later generation the Pollock brothers, Peter and Graeme. At a time when Graeme Hick is staking his claim to be one of the greatest batsmen in the game, the participation of Zimbabwe, his country of origin as Rhodesia, in the Currie Cup should not be forgotten. From Rhodesia came eleven South African Test cricketers, not least that fielder of breathtaking brilliance, Colin Bland. The ban on his entry to England after 1965 was one of the early and sadder demonstrations of the interaction of cricket and politics.

Currie Cup cricket was well supported despite indifferent accommodation for spectators. In the 1920s some development took place though not without internal acrimony: the treasurer of Western Province resigned, for example, over differences of opinion about expenditure. Transvaal, dominant in talent, achievement and membership, had most money to spend and the old Wanderers ground at Johannesburg (eventually taken over for railway development) saw the provision of better facilities to meet a large membership and a growth in public response. The City of Durban Corporation contributed £10,000 towards improvements at Kingsmead.

Some of the matches have a particular interest. The Orange Free State played Western Province in (literally) 1925–26, beginning on 31 December at Bloemfontein. Orange Free State were 188 for 9 when the last pair, Len Tuckett and Lance Fuller, came together. Their partnership of 115 helped Orange Free State to a first innings lead of 44 over their opponents. Orange Free State, in their second attempt, were 121 for 9 – a mere 165 on – when, once again, the last pair put on over a century for the tenth wicket, though there was a different no. 11. Fuller's 84 had won him promotion in the order! Tuckett made 70 and Frank Caulfield 56 not out; Western Province, set a much harder task than they expected, lost a match in which the umpires gave thirteen lbw decisions in the bowler's favour.

One particular game at Christmas 1932 should not go unnoticed. Western Province played Natal and the Nourses faced each other. Dave, born as far back as 1878, made an undefeated double-century for Western Province and Dudley an undefeated half-century for Natal. Dave had never coached his son but they had a few years playing together and Nourse senior lived long enough to see Nourse junior become captain of South Africa.

There was a curious game between Eastern Province and Transvaal in the 1937–38 season at Port Elizabeth. Eastern Province were dismissed for 36 and Transvaal declared at 38 for 0. They then dismissed Eastern Province for 62, and proceeded, all in one day, to win the match by eight wickets. Throughout the years Transvaal dominated the competition. In 1923–24, for example, they won every match by an innings and, in the 1930s, the side was virtually indistinguishable from the South African side despite the pleas of Taylor, a few years earlier, that selectors should look further afield. Strong as provincial cricket often was, especially in batting in the 1930s, many players found it difficult to raise their game in Test matches. The strength of provincial cricket in South Africa was never the measure, which the Sheffield Shield sides in Australia provided, of the potential strength of the national side.

During the voyage up the coast to Durban to report the Test between South Africa and England in January 1939, E. W. Swanton had found himself in conversation with Lord

Nuffield in the ship's gymnasium. Nuffield asked Swanton if he could possibly get him a ticket for the Test and the car manufacturer and philanthropist was invited to sit on the players' balcony. On the Saturday evening, at the end of the first day's play, he went to a dinner-dance at the Country Club and made an impromptu offer of £10,000 for South African schools' cricket if a satisfactory scheme could be produced within two days, before he sailed. A committee was at once set up, met on the Sunday under the chairmanship of Hammond and proposed a scheme to encourage cricket among schoolboys. Lord Nuffield's representative on it had indicated that the money should be used 'for the benefit and extension of South African cricket from a national stand-point'. Lord Nuffield approved the scheme, gave an extra £500 and went on his way. In 1940 the Nuffield Trust launched the annual Schools Week bearing his name. In announcing it a member of the Board of Control declared: 'It is the greatest thing that has ever been done for South African cricket. It will make the boys of South Africa just one big family regardless of any considerations of race or birth.' These were fine words and many fine Springboks were first spotted at successive Schools Weeks but there proved to be no place for non-whites. Their role in the context of cricket as a whole in the years before the Nationalist Government was a very different one.

What the Nationalist Government did in 1948, in heralding the policy of apartheid, was to extend and to consolidate the segregation in sport which had been as inherent in South African society as all other segregation. Historically, white dominion has prevailed since the arrival of the European and those of colour – the term Black is officially used for those not genetically White – have had to see themselves in a social, economic and political role which is at once different and inferior. Cricket has not stood apart from this.

When Warner took the 1906–07 MCC side to South Africa on what was in part a goodwill mission (after the Anglo-Boer War) he was told by the *Cape Times* on his arrival that 'the world of cricket was a United South Africa'. Cricket, then and later, was much more the game for the Europeans of British extraction rather than the Afrikaners. Louis Duffus has written that even up to 1939 the game 'appealed little to them'. Broadcasts on cricket in Afrikaans in the post-war years brought much more enthusiasm at all levels. Unity in white society, as Warner had been told, and cricket played by those of British and Dutch extraction was one thing: cricket among the Blacks was quite another: distinct, different, and very much down-grade.

Promise which was not fulfilled lay in a match between 'Africander Boers and Hottentots' in the Cape as early as 1854. By the end of the nineteenth century cricket among Malays and Coloureds was played in the Cape while an England touring side under W. W. Read played the Malays at Cape Town in 1892. *Wisden* does not record the event in its report of the tour. Not for eighty years would a white side on tour again play one of black cricketers.

There was a Malay fast bowler, Krom Hendricks, who reached the final squad for the South African party to tour England in 1894 but he was not selected and the *Cricket Field*, in its issue of 31 March 1894, commented on South African concern about the colour rather than the talent of its players. However good any black cricketer might be, he would not find a selection for South Africa or any provincial side though he might, as did C. J. Nicholls, bowl in the nets to white South African players or, indeed, to Australian ones as did Taliep Salie in 1928–29.

Black cricket perforce went its own way, often played among miners in the Transvaal as well as in the Cape; Natal remained predominantly committed to football. By 1914 it was administered by the South African Coloured Cricket Board though the authority of that body suffered through various breakaway movements in the 1920s and 1930s and the Board itself was defunct from 1932 until 1944. Under whatever auspices, the inter-war years found black cricketers competing, for example, for the Barnato Trophy, presented by Sir David Harris, or the NRC Trophy given by the Chamber of Mines. Perhaps more significant than any of their endeavours was the cricket being played by a small boy born in the Malay quarter of Cape Town in 1931. Basil D'Oliveira learnt his game in the streets and tenements and eventually found his way to the Lancashire League. His name would become synonymous with the events that ended South Africa's participation in Test match cricket.

In my visits to South Africa on two occasions in this decade I saw a genuine endeavour by men of goodwill to whom the problem was one of competitive standards as much as of doctrinaire politics. The deprivation which black cricketers had endured in terms of participation, pitches, equipment and coaching could not be remedied overnight, though in all these areas much has been accomplished. Coaching by English cricketers has done a great deal towards raising standards. Yet, I have to record that one distinguished South African Test player of the 1930s and 1940s told me in unequivocal terms that he supported apartheid. For the foreseeable future – and endorsed by the decision of the International Cricket Conference at Lord's in 1989 – South Africa has played its last Test match, and 'Rebel' tours are no substitute. However hard white cricketers in the South Africa of the 1980s may have striven to create a climate of multi-racial cricket, they are powerless against the politics of apartheid.

4

WEST INDIES:
THE FORMATIVE YEARS

Learie Constantine had been among the crowds in Port of Spain who watched the return to Trinidad in 1919 of the survivors of the 1500 men who had served in the West India Regiment in the first world war. In 1939 he would be on the quayside watching his fellow-members of the West Indies Test side leaving Britain for home on the outbreak of the second world war. Within those twenty years West Indies cricket came of age and Constantine was an integral part of that process.

His father, Lebrun, visited England twice and either father or son was a member of every West Indies tour to England between 1900 and 1939. Lebrun Constantine, on 12 June 1900, lost his wicket to W. G. Grace at the Crystal Palace and exactly twenty-eight years later to the day his son gave a display which established the status of West Indies cricket. The 1928 tour of England was doing badly: the weather had been poor and attendances thin. Constantine was unfit but the manager begged him to play against Middlesex otherwise the fortunes of the tour and, indeed, the prospects for any future tours, might be jeopardised. As if in sympathy, the weather changed and on a baking hot day the West Indies went out to field. Middlesex ran up a total of 352 for 4, with a century from Hendren, but the West Indies were 79 for 5 when Constantine came in to avert the follow-on. In an hour he had scored 86, an innings of tremendous driving and pulling, and he then went on to take 7 for 57 in the Middlesex second innings. His team were set the task of getting 259 to win but with five wickets down for 121 their chances seemed slight. Then, on Tuesday 12 June, Constantine came to the wicket again and within an hour had scored the century which ensured a West Indies victory by three wickets. His personal contribution had been 189 and eight wickets, to say nothing of his brilliant fielding.

The members in the pavilion and the entire Lord's crowd stood to him as he walked off the field. Memorable as that reception was, the long-term implications of the match were important both for Constantine and for West Indian cricket. He received an invitation to turn professional for Nelson in the Lancashire League where he would remain until 1937, while also appearing for the West Indies and occasionally for Trinidad. Living in England eventually led to his becoming a barrister, a governor of the BBC and a member of the House of Lords while his own country briefly claimed his services as a High Commissioner and as a cabinet minister. As for West Indian cricket, the Australian Macartney had also watched the match against Middlesex and it was his influence which led to an invitation to the newly formed West Indies Board of Control to send a side to Australia in 1930–31.

Cricket in the West Indies at colony or representative level was controlled by the influential families in white society whose leadership in the affairs of the colonies went largely unchallenged before 1939. Among these Sir Harold Austin takes pride of place. He was a Barbadian, the son of a bishop and a member of a family with deep-rooted political and business associations. He eventually became Speaker of the House of Assembly. He had intended to lead the first West Indies side to England in 1900 but cricket gave way to the claims of Empire and he departed to fight against the Boers in South Africa. He led both the 1906 and 1923 sides to England and he was foremost in the advocacy of Constantine's claims. It was he who insisted Constantine should go to England in 1923 and for that decision, if for no other, he justifies the judgment of the West Indian cricket writer, C. L. R. James, that he 'more than any other made West Indies cricket what it is'.

George Challenor came of another Barbadian family (there were seven cricketing brothers) and his influence as a batsman, especially in 1923, did much towards gaining Test status for the West Indies. As a youngster playing in 1906 in the nets at

Lord's, his talent had been spotted by 'W.G.' He was a pioneer in the great tradition of Barbadian batsmen and, as a schoolmaster, bore the not insignificant responsibility of coaching Frank Worrell. He was a product of his times: the white West Indian, formally coached, classic in style, an off-driver primarily, who was the batsman. Black men bowled.

In Trinidad, the Grant and Stollmeyer families had a similar importance. The Grants had a large family business in Port of Spain: two of them, in the 1930s, Jackie and Rolph, were successive captains of the West Indies. The Stollmeyers were substantial plantation owners: Jeffrey and Victor both played for the West Indies, Jeffrey becoming captain.

Families such as these dominated the political, social and economic life of what were British crown colonies. As such, leadership in cricket was a natural role and sufficient cricketers of ability emerged to assume the captaincy of colonial or representative sides: for the white West Indian one reads the amateur in English terms. They were not necessarily the best cricketers but they were worth their place in the sides. Only as 1939 approached might one find the same innuendoes emerging as did in England. Hammond became an amateur and therefore acceptable as captain: black men could not change the colour of their skin and therefore contestants for leadership such as George Headley and Constantine received no consideration. The voice of political change was active in the colonies before 1939 but it would not make an effective impact until after 1945. The pre-war social structure remained unchanged and the fabric of society still had a colonial hue; not least in the West Indies Board of Control which had been set up in 1926, at the instigation of the MCC, when the West Indies were deemed ready for Test cricket. The Board of Control represented in policy and personnel the leading colonial families and its reflection of the white society at the helm remained unchallenged until the 1950s. Thus one finds family names such as Austin, Grant and Stollmeyer among the presidents of the Board.

Cricket was – and remains – the only expression of unity in the West Indies, especially after the collapse of the ill-fated Federation. Geographical distances and local loyalties have led the colonies (or independent nations) to mean more to

their peoples than the larger Caribbean concept. As late as
1953 the Jamaica *Gleaner*, for example, could speak of a
Trinidad newspaper as 'the foreign press'. Accordingly, the
Board of Control, however effective in arranging overseas
tours, had to accept local autonomy in matters of domestic
Test matches. Of all clubs in the West Indies, Queen's Park
Cricket Club in Trinidad exercised the greatest authority,
owned Queen's Park Oval in Port of Spain and held a role
analogous to that of the MCC in England. It was the club
officials who selected the Test teams, with a bias towards
local candidates.

By 1919 cricket in the West Indies had become well established. There had been visits from English sides, including
the return of Warner in 1897 to his native Trinidad, and
an inter-colonial tournament had existed since 1893. In the
immediate post-war years West Indies cricket began to set its
sights on achieving Test status and there began the tradition
of producing black fast bowlers. George John and George
Francis, together with Constantine, performed with such
effectiveness at the Scarborough Festival in 1923 that a strong
Leveson Gower's XI was reduced to 26 for 6. Thereafter,
though the spinners in the 1950s would have their moment
of glory, fast bowling would become the hall-mark of West
Indies' ascendancy and later dominance.

Although bowling was the virtual monopoly of black West
Indies cricketers between the wars, they brought their own
especial contribution to batting. The classical batting of the
well-coached white players contrasted with the romantic approach of the black ones. Formalism was matched by infor-
malism; orthodoxy by unorthodoxy and, above all, the black
cricketer displayed a swiftness in footwork and a suppleness
of wrist. His cricket had been learnt, not in the sanctuary of
nets and true wickets but in the courtyard of some plantation
or on the beach. What the ball did at the last moment came
not so much from the wit of the bowler as the whim of the
pitch. Ingenuity and improvisation were called for, characteristics which Constantine displayed as a batsman throughout
his career. His flexibility of muscle and his impulsiveness
evoked the response of romanticism. He offered the cricket
of lyric and freedom; the joy of those whose forefathers

had shed the bondage of slavery. Deep-rooted in the black cricketer was the yearning to express the liberalism which was more and more coming the way of his people. The full expression, in terms of technical achievement, of this philosophy would be found in the batting of George Headley.

Headley spent his early years in Panama where his father was helping to build the canal. His mother brought him to Jamaica when he was ten and he began to play cricket instead of baseball. In 1928, when he was eighteen, he planned to go to the United States to study dentistry but there were delays in getting him a Panama passport. Instead, he played for Jamaica against Lord Tennyson's side. In the first match he made 71, in the second 211 and in the third another 71. The passport was forgotten and cricket had won a batsman who would rival Bradman in talent, bring Jamaica into the orbit of West Indies cricket and carry on his shoulders the burden of West Indies batting in the 1930s: not for nothing did Warner call him 'Atlas'. The selectors left him behind when the West Indies went to England in 1928 but from 1929 onwards until the war he never failed in a single Test series. He was the first black West Indies batsman of outstanding quality. Not much coaching had come his way and, like Bradman, he was very much a self-taught player. He would see the ball early and play it late – none later, recalled Sir Leonard Hutton. He could place the ball with a marvellous precision and every innings was something from which experience could be garnered.

To his fellow West Indians of all classes and colour he made an appeal. The black masses, especially in Jamaica, saw in him the epitome of their expectations. He had achieved, taken his talent into the white man's camp and prevailed. The black and coloured lower middle class society saw, more articulately, that he made easier their own financial aspirations by his example. The path of many a teacher, civil servant, white collar worker and engineer seemed smoother.

No black cricketer matched either Constantine or Headley in these years but, in their wake, others followed. By 1939 they had pointed the way in which those of their race might make a living as cricketers playing in the English leagues or, as employees, command a job at home sufficient to enable them to play for country or colony within the context of the West Indies first-class programme. How West Indies cricket fared at international level is what we should now examine.

The 1923 West Indies side which visited England under the captaincy of Austin faced weeks and weeks of bitter weather which Constantine recalled:

Day after day we were positively shivering, playing for hours in the damp and drizzle with scarcely a ray of sunlight. It was difficult to appreciate what that really meant for us. I shall never forget that so-called summer! I recall miserable journeys in freezing trains from one damp hotel to another; dressing-rooms with their own private chills laid on, and afternoons in the field when it was impossible to pay attention because one kept thinking about overcoats.

Despite these conditions, by the end of June the side had won five out of twelve matches, though without exciting the imagination of the public. At Oxford, the University scored 390 for six wickets declared. After losing three wickets very cheaply, the tourists were in trouble. Constantine had to listen to some mild taunts in the Christ Church pavilion at the expense of his team. Rash promises of what would follow were made to critical undergraduate spectators. But the promises were fulfilled, runs were made and the match was eventually won by eight wickets.

It was the match against Surrey rather late in the year which aroused interest in the West Indies side. Surrey were dismissed on a good wicket for 87, Francis taking 5 for 31. The West Indies replied with 305, Challenor making 155. Warner, in the *Morning Post*, described him as 'good enough for any Test side'. Despite a Surrey revival (and a century by Jardine) the West Indies won comfortably by ten wickets and their reward was the invitation to open the Scarborough Festival against Leveson Gower's XI in their last game. Trailing throughout the match, the West Indies left an XI of England calibre a mere 31 to win but the two fast bowlers, John and Francis, secured six wickets, including those of Hobbs, Tyldesley and Chapman, for 19 runs before the batting side scrambled home. 'We felt we had put the West Indies far on the road to equality with England, Australia and South Africa,' Constantine wrote home.

The English press was generous to a side which had played in conditions so different from those in the Caribbean and noted the efficiency of fast bowlers who bowled at the stumps, the outstanding batting of Challenor and the fielding of Constantine. Yet the editor of *Wisden* could write six pages of Notes on the season without even mentioning the visit. It scarcely accorded with Constantine's optimistic letter. For men such as he the tour had been a financial struggle and the weekly allowance of 30s. did not go far when, for example, players were instructed on one occasion to give a 10s. tip to a waiter. It was cheaper to go for walks than to go sightseeing and Sundays were dull and lonely.

Early in 1926 an MCC side visited the West Indies and began in Barbados with a heavy defeat from the colony side. As in England three years earlier, Challenor's batting and Francis' bowling were the principal agents in the Barbadian victory. But, immediately afterwards, in the first representative match played in the West Indies, the MCC amassed 597 for 8 (Hammond 238 not out) and only rain saved the West Indies from impending defeat by an innings and possibly some 400 runs. At the close of their second innings, they were 21 for 6.

On the matting wicket of Port of Spain, a fair balance of bat and ball was achieved in all the three matches played in Trinidad, the MCC winning the representative game by five wickets. In the steaming heat of British Guiana, a heavy storm saved the MCC from defeat in the third match against the West Indies while the tour concluded in Jamaica with Robert Nunes, a white Jamaican lawyer, doing well for the colony in each of three matches, though distance had prevented him or any other Jamaican from taking part in the representative matches. *Wisden*, in its report, considered that the West Indies had 'made rapid progress'. The tour, though, nearly had dire consequences for English cricket since Hammond, stung by a mosquito in British Guiana, was dangerously ill for many months.

★ ★ ★

The first day on which a country plays at Test level is a landmark in its history. In pleasant weather, 22,000 people flocked to Lord's on 23 June, a Saturday, in 1928. They saw a fast bowling attack which presented few problems to Sutcliffe, Tyldesley, Hammond and Chapman and a day's play in which England scored 382 for 8. Yet, as the English press observed, the West Indies had not bowled badly and they had fielded splendidly. A total of 401 proved more than the West Indies could muster in two innings, however, only Joe Small making a half-century, against Larwood, Tate and Freeman.

Old Trafford and The Oval produced very similar results, and in the third Test the West Indies were close observers of what would be Hobbs' last Test century in England. Thus, in all three Tests they were beaten by an innings and a comfortable margin. As each match took its course, the spectacular victory against Middlesex at Lord's in 'Constantine's match' receded further into the background.

There was more than a hint that the match against Leveson Gower's XI would, as in 1923, allow the West Indies to leave with some honour. Edward Hoad made a century but a second innings collapse sealed their fate. It was a mirror of their performance in 1928 that the editor of *Wisden* could find no place for any of them in his 'Five Cricketers of the Year' but it also has to be said that they lost their Test matches to an England side on the crest of the wave who would, as good marines, leave their vessel in Australia a few months later to put the Australians to the sword four times running.

'Popular feeling prevailed in the Mother Country that it was a premature step to initiate the West Indies into the tenseness of Test match atmosphere,' wrote the Trinidad *Sporting Chronicle*, when the team returned home. *Wisden* took the same view: 'Everyone was compelled to realise that the playing of Test matches between England and the West Indies was a mistake', though adding a cautionary clause, 'whatever the future may have in store': in the late 1980s the cynic might feel compelled to use the same language, with the boot on the other foot!

The 1928 West Indians had in fact disappointed themselves

and their supporters. Much had been expected of Wilton St Hill, whose domestic reputation in Trinidad was enormous as a late-cutter, but nothing went right for him. Challenor, at forty, was not the bat he had been, nor Francis the bowler. Fast bowlers, as a whole, suffered from a plethora of dropped catches and the wicket-keeping of the captain, Nunes, was indifferent. C. L. R. James believed the best wicket-keeper never went to England. He was a man called Piggott who took the fast bowlers an inch behind the stumps. Of him, James wrote: 'Where he came from, what he did in the week, I do not know and never asked. He played usually in a shirt with coloured stripes without any collar attached. His place in history is that he was George John's wicket-keeper, and never was fast bowler better served. Piggott was one of the world's best wicket-keepers between the wars.' James and his contemporaries had no doubt that Piggott was the victim of the balance of colour in the pre-war sides so that he remained the obscure wicket-keeper who played for his club – Stingo.

Constantine was the only success of the 1928 tour. Apart from the Middlesex match, he took thirteen wickets, including a hat-trick against Northamptonshire and made a century in ninety minutes. He scored over 1000 runs and captured over 100 wickets, but the tour took its toll. Much was expected of him in every match, as it would be of Headley in a year or two. The critics applauded when he succeeded and accused him of playing to the gallery when he failed. He was not on particularly good terms with Nunes who, he believed, grossly over-bowled him. With the exception of Austin, very much Constantine's mentor, Constantine was critical of the white captains under whom he played and was one of the first to say that the West Indies would not realise its potential until there was a black captain. Sadly, in the games which mattered – the Test matches on which a West Indies reputation had to be built – he had fallen below the hopes and expectations of his countrymen. And, his biographer reluctantly concedes, at Test level he almost always would.

In 1929–30, for the only time, the MCC sent sides both to New Zealand and to the West Indies, each of which played

Test matches, though those against the West Indies were only given Test status retrospectively. Indeed, on 11 January 1930 England played two Test matches. While Voce and Rhodes were bowling to the West Indies, Duleepsinhji and Woolley were batting against New Zealand. The sun, in those days, never set on the British Empire nor, it seemed, on England playing a Test match.

It was no mean team which faced the West Indies at Barbados in January 1930. After two colony games and a Test in Barbados, Hendren had an average of 550 – only once dismissed! Even at the end of a long tour, it remained a healthy 126.14. Rhodes, in the sunset of his career, topped the bowling averages.

The Barbados Test was drawn, slightly in England's favour. Headley, brought by sea the one thousand miles from Jamaica, became the youngest man ever to make a century on his Test debut and Derek Sealey the youngest man ever to appear in a Test match. Headley's innings, Michael Manley has written in his *A History of West Indies Cricket*, was 'the first major statement of a genius' though it was Constantine whom the *Barbados Advocate* hailed as 'the only player whose performance had overshadowed all others'.

MCC tours in the West Indies had developed a pattern: two games against a colony then a Test match. In the Trinidad Test, after losing to Trinidad, England won by 167 runs, Hendren making yet another double century, a feat which he repeated for the fourth time against British Guiana a week later.

Georgetown, British Guiana – where Test cricket by England may never again be played, for political reasons – was the setting for the first West Indies victory, though the occasion did not win contemporary recognition. The West Indies made 471 in their first innings, Clifford Roach achieving a double-century and Headley a single one. England for the first time collapsed (for 145) against the West Indies fast bowlers. Headley made a second century and England failed by 289 runs to achieve a target of 617, Constantine taking 5 for 87. The match may be seen as prophetic of what would happen so frequently half a century later.

Constantine was not picked for the fourth Test in Jamaica.

As we have seen, Test match selection favoured the local heroes and Jamaica was a long way away. One may hazard another reason: he had not gone uncriticised for his tactic of bowling fast and short to a packed leg-side field. The England captain, Calthorpe, had made guarded references in a speech in Barbados, the English manager approached Constantine in Trinidad and he had agreed not to do so though he felt that Voce's eleven wickets included some balls which were intimidating. Both before and after the events in Australia in 1932–33, Constantine and his fellow fast bowlers were on the fringes of that great debate.

With the series all-square, the two sides came to Jamaica for a 'timeless' Test where Headley, the local hero, pleased his supporters with a double century. The West Indies faced a mammoth England total of 849, including 325 from Sandham. Only England's 903 for 7 in 1938 against Australia would eclipse the total. The West Indies were 600 behind on the first innings but drew the match. Calthorpe batted on unnecessarily long despite warnings of rain before he declared his second innings with nine wickets down, leaving the West Indies 836 to win. The West Indies were halfway there with half their wickets down and Headley's 223, when the Blue Mountains faded from sight and the rains came. The England party had to catch the banana-boat home and the match was left drawn: shades of Durban, 1939.

Headley's triumphant season – he made 703 runs for an average of 87.87 – has its own significance. He, rather more than Constantine, was becoming the focal point for a West Indian national consciousness in the 1930s. He was something different: the triumphant black batsman rather than black bowler and the West Indian public saw more of him than they did of Constantine. Jamaica, on the edge of first-class cricket, had provided someone with whom all West Indians could identify. He may be closely paralleled with Viv Richards whose achievements gave the Leeward Islands their first recognition and who, in his person, became a focal point for black endeavour and a national unification. What Headley did for the Caribbean in the 1930s, Richards did in the 1980s: the West Indies in the 1930s was a depressed collection of colonies near the bottom of the economic pit and, in the 1980s, a third-world group of nations struggling in a world which gave no favours: Headley and Richards were both folk-heroes.

Headley apart – and, up to a point, Barbadian recognition of Constantine – the series demonstrated the continuing insularity, not to say frailty, of the West Indies cricket scene. Twenty-eight players appeared in the four Tests while each colony supplied the captain for its home game and chose the team. Money was in short supply and it was a decision of faith to finance Headley's trips from Jamaica. White and black players alike found it difficult to get time off from work for so many matches against the MCC at colonial and representative levels.

Nevertheless, when the decision was taken to go to Australia a few months later, similar problems of identity beset the 1930–31 West Indies tourists. Players who had never met each other joined the ship at Jamaica. Not all knew G. C. ('Jackie') Grant, the captain, who came direct from his studies at Cambridge University to acquire his first experience of Test cricket and of leadership. To his credit, he learnt quickly and he would top the Test batting averages though Headley felt he was scarcely likely to challenge his opposite number, Woodfull, as a tactician. These early West Indies sides were unlucky in their timing: 1928 had been a bad year to take on England and 1930 was an equally bad moment to take on Australia. Bradman dominated an immensely powerful team. Yet the idea was good, much encouraged by Macartney; in execution it proved disappointing and financially disastrous, though instructive.

Grant was supported by the usual bevy of fast bowlers in the expectation of wickets which would suit them. In the first match the West Indies gave a strong New South Wales side a good run for their money, Noble writing in the *Sydney Sun* that one had to go back to 1914 'to recall such a sensational innings' as Constantine played. Yet the West Indies still lost and, when they came to the first Test, they had also lost to Victoria and South Australia. As in England, two years earlier, they then lost three Tests running, followed by a fourth in two dismal days at Melbourne. Totals of under 200 in six successive innings were a thorough disappointment to their compatriots back home reading their Jamaica *Gleaner* or

Trinidad Guardian. The fast bowlers had toiled with scant success on slow wickets with little life in them and the only crumbs of comfort had come from a Headley century and some fine spin-bowling from Tommy Scott. Everywhere they went the ground-fielding (but not always the catching) won praise, especially that of Constantine. But there was little with which to counter centuries from Kippax, Ponsford and Bradman and a harvest of wickets by Grimmett.

One must probe further: the Australians had studied their opponents and, in particular, the anatomy of Headley's batting. He was, they recognised, a fine off-side player so up until the third Test they succeeded in frustrating his play. Whenever he met Grimmett, he was attacked on the leg stump or just outside it. The cut, so effective and attractive a part of his repertoire, he had to discard, while the limitations placed on his off-driving had to be counterpoised by runs on the on-side. The decision taken, he changed his stance and set off to outwit Grimmett whenever they met. His reward was the century in the third Test, 75 against South Australia and another century in the fifth Test. Grimmett paid appropriate tribute: 'Headley is the finest on-side player in the world,' he commented at the end of the tour. Headley's Test average of 37.33 (better than Woodfull's) was hewn out of the hard rock of experience and self-discipline.

Headley's personal discipline – his colleagues recalled bowling persistently to him in the nets – was important to the future of West Indies cricket for the rest of the 1930s and it enabled them to end the tour with a flourish. New South Wales were beaten after the disastrous fourth Test and the West Indies entered their final match against Australia. It was said that Noble persuaded the Sydney authorities to give them a chance at the end of the tour and prepare a wicket more to their taste. The former Australian captain was, like Macartney, always their ally. The West Indies reached 332 for 2 before rain followed by hot sun made for a 'sticky' wicket. Grant declared at 350 for 6 (Martin 123 not out, Headley 105) and the Australians succumbed for 224. At the end of the third day, the West Indies were 124 for 5 – 251 ahead – and there followed a day of rain. On the morning of the fifth day Grant made the brave decision to declare (in another timeless

Test) and leave the Australians plenty of time to score the runs on another 'sticky' wicket. Everyone in the West Indies side sensed there was a chance to end the first series with some honour. At first, nerves triumphed over intent and two catches went down. Then, at 49, Woodfull skied a catch to Constantine.

Twenty-five years after this, I did a broadcast with Constantine, and I asked him to select a moment of crucial importance in West Indies cricket. He chose that catch:

Woodfull threw his bat at one from Griffith and the ball shot up to the skies straight over the wicket. 'Learie!' screamed the team at me standing in the gully. There was Barrow, the wicket-keeper with his gloves, as near to the ball as I was, but they called for me and I stepped forward from the gully. And as I moved to follow the catch more closely, I put my eyes straight on the solitary little scrap of sun and lost sight of the ball completely. For a desperate moment I could not find it. 'Woodfull!' beat through my mind. 'My God, Woodfull!' Never before have I ever been frightened at a catch and I hope I never shall be again. I went stone cold and my heart began to throb, but I grabbed at my cap, pulled it down over my eyes to shade the sun, and caught sight of the lost wanderer again. I opened my fingers wide high up in front of me and took the ball above my chin, so that if I had missed I should have had another chance below; but I held it safely at the first attempt and stood trembling.

The dismissal of Woodfull gave the West Indians their first breakthrough. Ponsford was caught by Constantine moments later, and Bradman went for 0. By lunch Australia had lost four wickets for 53. When Ironmonger was run out, the West Indies had won by 30 runs their first Test match against Australia, their first away from home, and the second in their history. It was a victory which did a great deal of good for West Indies cricket. Those who had encouraged the tour to take place felt, in the end, vindicated. The West Indies cricketers had been well received – any fears of rejection by a 'white' Australia immediately set at naught – and Constantine was delighted to have a portrait of himself placed in the Sydney pavilion. They returned home with the hope that Bradman would be seen in the Caribbean but this was not to be. Not until 1955 would an Australian side tour the West Indies.

It would be agreeable to be able to say that the public who wished the infant well at Lord's in 1928 came, five years later in 1933, to see a healthy and prosperous youngster. Sadly, that was not so: there had been natural growth but little maturity. As *Wisden* in its report on that year's Tests wrote, the West Indies 'did not convey the impression of being fitted temperamentally for matches of such an important nature'.

In their favour was an excellent English summer with sun on their backs and wickets to suit, though the absence of Constantine as a regular tour member – committed to Nelson in the Lancashire League – deprived them of his talents, personality and ability to draw the crowds. To a lesser extent the same applied to Francis. From the West Indies stud of fast bowlers came instead the Barbadian, Manny Martindale, who proved almost as essential to the team as did Headley. Grant was again captain and – whatever the rights and wrongs of a white captain chosen for colour and class – he was regarded as an outstanding close fielder, a sound bat, a thinking captain and a man who, wrote the editor of *Wisden*, kept up his men's spirits and made them popular wherever they went.

By the middle of June, with several handsome victories and only two defeats, the first Test could be approached with some confidence. England were bowled out for 296 and then the West Indies simply faded away, exactly as they had done at Lord's in 1928. Headley made a fifty but no-one else could cope against the England spinners and the match was lost by an innings.

Constantine was able to join the side for the occasional mid-week match and for one Test. It was in the train from Stoke to Manchester, after playing Staffordshire, that he and his colleagues decided (in his words) 'to give Jardine and his men a little taste of what they had been handing out in Australia' a few months earlier in the bodyline tour of 1932–33 (see Chapter 6). On the Saturday at Old Trafford,

in the second Test, the West Indies scored 333 for 6, both
Ivan Barrow and Headley making centuries. Headley's batting won wide praise – six and a quarter hours without a
chance. On the Monday, after their dismissal for 375, the
West Indies put their bowlers to work. Constantine and
Martindale bowled fifty overs between them, a large number
of which were fast leg-theory to a packed leg-field. Despite
the slow-paced wicket, Hammond had his chin cut open and
the man who stood fearlessly against the bowling was Jardine
who made his only century in a Test match 'never flinching
in the slightest degree' said *Wisden*.

Up to now R. B. Vincent in *The Times* had regarded the
controversy in Australia, rather like the death of Mark Twain,
as 'greatly exaggerated'. For the first time, he used the word
bodyline without inverted commas or a qualifying adjective,
and what he saw at Old Trafford he did not like any more
than he liked Jardine instructing Ted ('Nobby') Clark to bowl
in similar fashion in the West Indies' second innings. As for
the match, England finished one run behind on the first
innings, and the West Indies then made 225, leaving England
no time to bat. At least, for the first time in England, the
West Indies had not lost a Test match.

With heavy irony, the editor of *Wisden* thanked the West
Indies 'for showing us what an objectional form of attack this
kind of bowling can be'. He went on: 'The exhibition given
at Old Trafford confirmed opponents of it in their views and
caused hundreds who had open minds on the subject definitely
to turn against it. For this reason, the West Indies rendered
one great and, we hope, lasting service to English cricket'. It
also brought Warner's opinions out in the open at last in a
long letter to the *Daily Telegraph*. It was one of the occasions
when Warner chose to think of himself as a West Indian (on
nationality he could be ambivalent) and he was sorry that his
countrymen had had recourse to 'a type of bowling against
the best interest of cricket'. So, in a somewhat oblique way,
the 1933 West Indians helped to bring to an end this particular
chapter in the history of cricket.

In a converse way there had been up till now some coolness
between Constantine and Hammond and, perhaps, Constantine's bowling at Old Trafford was an aspect of this. Whatever

the problem had been, it was resolved after this match and something of a friendship developed between two men, similar in age and talent but different in colour and personality. Twenty years later, when Constantine sought and secured a professional appointment with an oil company, it was Hammond who was his principal referee.

Five matches later (three of them against minor counties) the West Indies came to The Oval for the third Test. Jardine was injured (though the MCC showed their continuing support for him by inviting him to be captain of the forthcoming tour to India) and Wyatt took over the captaincy, scoring 150 not out for Warwickshire against the West Indies on the day he was appointed. For the first time ever (and at The Oval, too) an England side had no Surrey player in it but the eleven secured a win by an innings in ten minutes over two days. Once again, the West Indies bowlers were let down by batsmen who found unfathomable the spin of Charles Marriott, playing in his only Test. Not even Scarborough and Leveson Gower's XI brought redemption and, as at The Oval, spin bowling proved the undoing of the West Indies.

The Test matches averages revealed how much the West Indies had depended on Headley. After his average of 55.40 the next player was Barrow with 23.83. Headley had also borne the burden of the batting on tour, making 2320 runs and scoring seven centuries. Martindale took 103 wickets and the orthodox left-armer, Ellis Achong, whose nationality gave the name 'chinaman' to the left-hander's googly, took 71. Contemporary opinion – and not just possible West Indies prejudice in his favour – put Headley on the same plane as Hammond or Bradman. The Australian Collins placed him among the four greatest batsmen of all time but, sadly, one swallow does not make a summer and the 1933 West Indies sailed despondently for home.

The literature on pre-war MCC tours to the West Indies is not extensive. There are agency reports in the British press rather than the accounts of travelling journalists, though many a sparkle comes from the lively descriptions to be found in the local papers. Cricketers who visited the West Indies have had something to say in their memoirs, none more entertainingly so than Kenneth Farnes in his *Tours and Tests*, a book of some rarity since the stock was bombed during the war. It appeared only a few months before the author was killed in a flying accident.

Farnes, a member of the MCC 1934–35 side to the West Indies, was delighted to be 'leaving England's chill grey December for sun-drenched coral beaches fringed by palms'. The MCC was led by Wyatt and it included Hammond, Leyland, Ames and Hendren; stronger in batting than in bowling, but deemed, said *Wisden*, 'sufficient for the occasion'. The amateurs in the party went at some personal financial loss. When Wyatt asked at Lord's what their expenses would be he was told by Lord Hawke that in his day 'amateurs considered it an honour to play for England'. Wyatt indicated that Farnes, for example, had forgone a term's salary at Worksop (about £100) and the MCC agreed to pay the amateurs £25. No-one made a profit though one of the better-off amateurs was able to fit in a trip to Miami by air while his colleagues sailed from British Guiana to Jamaica!

After two games against Barbados, in one of which Hammond made 281 not out and the better-off amateur 19, the MCC were ready for the first Test and so was the *Barbados Advocate*:

The 1934–35 MCC tour of the West Indies began on Saturday at Kensington Oval – the historic venue of many a dour struggle between the giant kings of the willow of a former day. Nothing was spared in preparation for the tour, and as a result every aspect was pleasing, and not even man was vile. Four thousand spectators looked on at the players, immaculately dressed in their silks and flannels, dotted here and there over the chlorophyll-coloured carpet of the outfield. And as if to crown it all, Nature was in her kindliest mood. The sun shone out in all his brilliance, while gentle breezes blew to lessen the heat of the rays. It was a typical tropical day, but all this was forgotten by the fieldsmen, who, like true sportsmen, delighted in the rivalry of the batsmen pitted against some of the pick of England's might.

In what proved to be a remarkable game on an uncovered wicket affected by rain, the ball had a mind of its own, skidding through or rearing up. The match was an exercise in tactics and a display of how to bat on bad wickets by two great exponents of the art, Headley and Hammond. After the West Indies had made 102 (Headley 44), England declared at 81 for 7 (Hammond 43). The West Indies lost six wickets for 51 before Grant declared with a lead of only 72. Wyatt sent in Farnes and Jim Smith, his two tallest men, to defy the kicking ball. Neither they nor anyone else accomplished much against the extremely fast bowling of Martindale, supported by Leslie Hylton. Hammond came to the wicket and, in Farnes' words:

> launched a fierce attack on the bowlers and smote the ball all over the field. It was an extraordinary innings for a Test match – but then the match itself was extraordinary – and all decorum might go to the winds. With the score at 69, Martindale, as fast as ever, began his next over. The third ball was not unlike the others but Hammond stepped out and lifted it clean over the long-on boundary for six, and the match was over.

Wyatt won the toss in the second Test in Trinidad and put the West Indies in. They made 302 and England then lost five wickets for 23 before recovering to reach 258. Eventually England were set 325 to win and Wyatt, as in Barbados, reversed the batting order, with much less justification – 'amazing and inexplicable', said the *Trinidad Guardian*. Although England held out till the second last ball, no-one made over 30 and they were beaten by 217 runs. When the game was won, West Indies supporters jumped down from the surrounding tree-tops in their excitement and the thirteen-year-old Jeffrey Stollmeyer had had his first sight of Hammond. Only four years later he would play against him.

The West Indies victory owed much to Constantine and Headley. Constantine had come out from England for the rest of the series and in this game he made 121 runs and took five wickets. Headley made 25 and 93. Neither would ever play a Test match in Trinidad again.

Wisden called the drawn third Test 'a somewhat featureless affair' and Farnes, who watched it, wrote that 'the wicket and the cricket were as lifeless as ever'. The two sides, all-square in the series, met in Jamaica. The West Indies batted for nearly two days and declared at 535 for 7. Headley made 270 not out and disaster struck England off the fourth ball of the first innings when Wyatt had his jaw broken in four places – 'by sheer pace and, let me add, scrupulously fair bowling', Farnes noted. Martindale took three wickets before the close of play and Constantine dismissed Hammond. From 26 for 4 overnight, England made a mild recovery with a century from Ames but eventually lost by an innings and 161 runs and the West Indies had won their first rubber against England.

Twenty-four hours later the MCC sailed for home in the banana-boat which had been loading at Port Antonio. Wyatt, in great agony and unable to speak, went straight from hospital to the ship. Like Hammond, nine years earlier, he was desperately ill on the voyage especially when septicaemia set in. Hammond had had no choice but to spend a year out of cricket: Wyatt, a man of outstanding courage, made a century against Surrey six weeks later.

In the light of later history, that Test match in Jamaica has its own interest. The West Indies had picked four fast bowlers and they were used for a substantial amount of the time so that batsmen had little respite. One of them, Martindale, was the leader of the pack, faster than the others and gathering all into a final devastatingly accurate delivery. Behind the bowlers lay at least one batsman, in Headley, capable of making the massive score. In the 1934–35 series, the West Indies fast bowlers took 47 out of the 64 wickets which fell and Headley's average was 97.00. By contrast, no England batsman had an average of 30 and the fast bowlers took 16 wickets between them. As the editor of *Wisden* observed: 'Our batting was generally at fault, breaking down against the concentrated attack of fast bowling' and the England bowlers 'did not at any time present the same difficulty to batsmen'. His words might have been written in the 1980s.

There was one further pointer for the future in West Indian terms. Grant, the captain, left the field in the fourth Test injured and Constantine took over the captaincy, even though

Grant's younger brother Rolph was playing. As when Hobbs, in similar circumstances, led England in 1926, the mould, if not exactly broken, was chipped. One day Hutton (but not Hobbs) would captain England as a professional and one day Headley (but not Constantine) would captain the West Indies as a black man; though Constantine would lead the Dominions against England in 1945 in a famous contest. The Test proved to be Grant's last match as captain of the West Indies and he left his homeland to devote the next forty years to missionary work in Africa – the C. T. Studd of the West Indies.

Grant would be succeeded as captain in 1939 by his brother, Rolph. It was an appointment which, in Michael Manley's view, 'showed a profound connection between the ownership of property and fitness to lead'. In comparison with the scions of the white business and plantation families, no claims could be made for either Headley or Constantine. On them the burden of responsibility, in playing terms, would fall and they would fittingly enough top the batting and bowling averages respectively both on the tour and in the Tests.

As a whole, the 1939 side bore some of the vagaries of selection associated with West Indies sides – Barrow was summoned from the United States where he had been working for some years and not playing cricket. John Cameron, the vice-captain, was picked on the evidence of his spin bowling at Cambridge University two years earlier and Hylton – not selected originally – was included because the Jamaican public raised his fare.

The early weeks of the tour went badly: results were poor, the weather indifferent and the receipts bad. As had happened eleven years earlier, it was the match at Lord's against Middlesex which caught the public imagination. The West Indies amassed 665 (Headley 227, Sealy 181, Stollmeyer 117) and defeated Middlesex by an innings and 228 runs. Constantine took 6 for 107: 'There is no man who can so completely bamboozle a batsman,' wrote The Times, though Constantine was not bowling as fast as in earlier years. A colleague, Bertie Clarke, recalled him as 'a graceful medium-paced bowler who secured his wickets by a subtle change of pace and by a beautifully concealed slower googly'. From this match onwards, the West Indies attracted crowds and they would take home nearly £5000 as their share of the Test match profits. It was just as well since the professionals in the party had been expensive. Constantine had sailed to the West Indies in March to negotiate terms before he had agreed to leave League cricket. He had secured £600 for the tour and the two other professionals, Headley and Martindale, were given the same.

The West Indies came to the Test matches with some confidence and fared not so badly. England were strong in batting: in the preceding ten months they had averaged 640 in a complete innings, while their opponents – Australia and South Africa – had averaged 351. It was to the credit of the West Indies that they lost only one of the three Tests (and with a bit more care might have saved it). At Lord's Headley made a century in each innings out of totals of 277 and 225, the pinnacle of endeavour for this quiet, unassuming and totally dedicated man who had accomplished as much for West Indies cricket as Bradman had done for Australia. In the same match, Hutton (196) and Compton each made centuries for England, who won by eight wickets, while Stollmeyer, with a half-century, gave indications of a talent which would blossom in the 1940s. He alone would survive to be in the West Indies side in 1950 which gained them their first victory in England.

The second Test at Old Trafford was reduced to virtually two days by rain and, in the sultry atmosphere of impending war, the two sides came to The Oval in mid-August. There were service uniforms among the crowd, an anti-aircraft gun on a tractor outside the gates and barrage balloons overhead. Hammond, the England captain, made an appeal for volunteers to join up and, as Constantine remembered, 'despite the glorious sunshine, one saw hard and frightened faces'. The three-day Test proved not so much a contest as a display of individual talent. Cricketers who had delighted the public in the 1920s and 1930s took their farewell though all those in this particular game would survive the war. Joe Hardstaff, stylist of his generation, made 94 in England's first innings of 352. The West Indies made 498: Headley got 65, Ken Weekes, a Jamaican left-hander whose Barbadian namesake would be remembered rather than he, made a century and there were 79 runs from Constantine. One paper called Constantine's innings 'a glorious hour of roman candles, rockets and giant crackers'. Even *Wisden*, soberest of reporters, waxed lyrical:

> It was a real joy to watch the carefree cricket of the West Indies on the last day. Constantine, in the mood suggesting his work in Saturday afternoon League cricket, brought a welcome air of gaiety to the Test arena. He revolutionised all the recognised features of cricket and, surpassing Bradman in his amazing stroke play, he was absolutely impudent in his aggressive treatment of bowling shared by Nichols and Perks. With an astonishing stroke off the back foot Constantine thumped Perks for 6 to the Vauxhall end – a very long carry – and helped himself to eleven 4's before he was last out to a very fine catch by Wood; running towards the pavilion the wicket-keeper held the ball that had gone high over his head.

This had been in the morning. In the afternoon the final act in Test cricket between the wars was played out by Hammond and Hutton, two of its finest performers, setting up a third-wicket record of 264 at 88 runs an hour. 'For a while we sat on the dressing room balcony,' recalled Compton, 'drinking the heady wine of Hammond and Hutton, and forgetting Hitler.'

Alas! Hitler could not be forgotten for long and the remaining matches of the tour were cancelled. Despite a telegram from the Sussex authorities 'Essential to play match tomorrow. Keep the flag flying', the West Indies departed from Greenock on the SS *Montrose*. Had they played Sussex, they might have boarded the next ship crossing the Atlantic, the SS *Athenia*, which was torpedoed. As for Constantine, he stayed in England and a few days after the Test match was filling sandbags.

In representative terms, 1939 is as much a watershed in the history of West Indies Test cricket as in that of the other Test countries. Though the elusive pimpernel remained – victory against England in England – their place in the firmament of

Test cricket had, in a dozen years, been indisputably secured. In terms of West Indies domestic cricket, the year 1939 has far less moment.

For much of the years before 1939 the West Indies had not been involved in cricket at international level, so that the game, at various other levels, had its own part to play in the Caribbean. The colonies had participated in a tournament since 1893 and during the period between the two wars this was dominated first by Trinidad or Barbados, with British Guiana becoming strong in the 1930s. Jamaica, by virtue of distance and because the banana-boat schedules simply did not fit, remained outside the competition and had to be content with the visits of the MCC and sides such as Lord Tennyson's XI in 1932 against which Headley made 344 not out. Tennyson's side lacked bowling and Headley made 723 with an average of 361.50 in three matches. As oil tankers became a part of the Caribbean economy, they were used to provide transport for Jamaican cricketers to take part in trials before the 1933 and 1939 English tours.

The inter-colonial tournament of the other three colonies was reported extensively in the local press and selection for colony conferred status, not to say stardom, on its recipient. Employers would be brave men who did not give leave of absence and ways would be found to help men who needed clothes or equipment. One such contest in 1922, at George-town, brought together the two Constantines, father and son, and Learie's uncle, Victor Pascall, in the same side. Trinidad made 359, after being 200 for 8, the last three men in the order scoring 92, 58 and 69 not out. Barbados replied with 673, Challenor and Tim Tarilton putting on 174 for the first wicket, and Trinidad lost by an innings. Barbados then successfully played the home side, British Guiana, and took the title. These tournaments would bring together some three dozen of the best cricketers in the Caribbean (save for Jamaicans) for nearly a fortnight and forge something of a West Indies cricket identity.

Fifteen years later, again at Georgetown, British Guiana were at last triumphant, beating both Barbados and Trinidad. In the final, Trinidad's 430 and 355 were insufficient for victory after British Guiana reached 627 in their first innings.

After such excitement, the colonial cricketer would be brought down to earth by returning to his Saturday afternoon club where he would find fierce rivalry.

No sight in the cricketing world can be as impressive as the vast Savannah in Port of Spain, Trinidad, where as many as thirty matches might be taking place simultaneously. C. L. R. James has seen the rivalry created by colour and class as essential in the understanding of the West Indies cricket achievement. When Shannon, the Trinidad club for black men with white-collar jobs, played Stingo, they met black men who might be labourers or unemployed. If Shamrock took on Queen's Park, Catholics played white or coloured men of wealth. Maple had brown-skinned men in the professions or trade. James, darker than most, was admitted to their ranks. Constantine, a Shannon player, as befitted a black law clerk, believed that the discipline of these clubs moulded him as a cricketer. When sides came from England and a Trinidad colony team was being picked, Shannon men would be there training on the coconut matting wickets in the Savannah. In Barbados, the rivalry of clubs such as the Wanderers, Pickwick and Empire was expressed in the same way. If all this seems exaggerated in its emphasis, one need only recall that English club cricket in the same period imposed similar distinctions created by accent, school and occupation. Only the question of colour was absent. Out of this many-splendoured thing – Caribbean cricket at the grassroots, in all its variations of colour, circumstances and wickets – West Indies cricket has drawn its strength and flavour. It has not ceased to be a joyous endeavour.

During the second world war, cricket there continued without much interruption. Problems of shipping and the threat of German U-boats made for transport difficulties but inter-colonial matches were played, though sailing to British Guiana was prohibited. In what was, in general, an era of high scores, the dismissal of Trinidad for 16 by Barbados in 1942 was very much the exception. Much more typical was a Triangular Tournament in 1943–44 when Barbados scored 650 for 3 in reply to Trinidad's 490 for 8. The feature of the Barbados innings was a world fourth-wicket partnership record of 502 between John Goddard, a future West Indies

captain, and the batting of the nineteen-year-old Frank
Worrell, who scored a triple century. Worrell's arrival on
the scene, together with that of Everton Weekes and Clive
Walcott, demonstrated that these three Barbadians were preparing to make a massive contribution to post-war West
Indies cricket, and to the aspirations of new emergent nations.
Great cricketers as they were, they were also men who were
among the finest examples of the new black leadership their
generation offered. Because there were three of them and
because West Indies cricket would achieve the maturity and
self-assurance it lacked before the war, markers were being
laid down for what would be accomplished in the first post-
war series against England in 1947–48, after which West
Indies cricket would scarcely know the meaning of adversity.
The lineage of Constantine and Headley would bear fruit.

5

THE ENGLISH COUNTY SCENE: THE 1930s

County cricket in the 1930s, against a background of the Depression and economic hazard, paradoxically flourished. Large programmes were fulfilled and some counties might expect to play up to thirty-six matches in the season, including a visit (or two) from the tourists, the MCC and one or both of the Universities. The professionals were being paid every day and more games meant more money at the gate. Surprisingly large crowds would watch the most pedestrian of encounters and a proportion of them came from the ranks of the unemployed. A day's cricket was cheap – a shilling, or sixpence after the tea interval – and a pleasant way to while away the hours of enforced idleness.

County loyalties were strong among all classes. Landowners and industrialists identified with the county which had made them, or their forefathers, prosperous and cricket would often be a beneficiary of their philanthropy. A few counties could attribute their survival to one man's pursestrings. People of modest means and those who were victims of the great financial drought of their generation expressed support for their county whether by membership, by their money at the gate or, less tangibly, by following the lengthy reports in the local press. Counties which perhaps should have ceased to exist as first-class sides with a professional staff remained, however precariously, in business. Loyalty to the county was also to be found in the players. Scarcely any ever changed their county allegiance and it was the knowledge that the same band of (more or less) local men would appear year after year, with infusions of new blood, that endorsed local support.

Gradually it became apparent that the counties were dominating the domestic scene rather less than in the 1920s. By 1932 the West Indies, New Zealand and India had joined Australia and South Africa in sending teams to play Test matches in England. Unlike in the 1920s there were visitors playing Test matches every year and counties were aware of increasing national demands on their players of ability while happy enough to take their share of Test match profits. Test matches themselves were brought closer to the public with the beginning of radio commentaries, news reel films and, at the very end of the decade, television.

Yet change was slow and to many scarcely perceptible. At the start of the 1930s fewer than three million households possessed a radio; television before the war remained the plaything of those living near Alexandra Palace who chose to indulge themselves, while the cinema's offerings on cricket on Movietone or Pathé News were tantalisingly brief and microscopically remote to the point of being worthless. There was no alternative to the 'real thing', and if circumstances precluded a visit to a Test match then the local county match was a very creditable consolation. Indeed, such a match as late as 1948 – the year of an Australian visit – attracted almost as large a crowd as a Test. Cricket up to 1939 seemed reasonably protected from economic reality and social change and the euphoria which greeted the return of first-class cricket in 1946 was out of step with the austerity of post-war Britain.

Yorkshire and Lancashire

Yorkshire cricketers were the aristocrats of the work-force in the 1930s: to be champions was the warp and weft of their experience and the title was theirs on seven occasions. Matched to individual talent was a deep team loyalty stemming from the leadership of Brian Sellers who created within the side a sense of total optimism so that, in a time of pessimism born of closures and unemployment which found very real expression in Yorkshire, cricket expressed the exact reverse. There is a parallel in the fortunes of Liverpool and Everton football clubs in the 1980s.

As senior professional, Sutcliffe continued to set standards on and off the field. Even in the wet summer of 1931 he

scored over 3000 runs and averaged 96.96. He was a man for
all seasons, wet or dry, in attack or in defence, for England
or for Yorkshire. In what was virtually Holmes' swan-song,
Sutcliffe partnered him to the tune of 555 runs against Essex
at Leyton in 1932 and then turned to the business of training
Hutton as Holmes' successor. 'Dare one suggest there is
another Sutcliffe at hand?' asked the *Daily Dispatch* at the
beginning of 1934. At the end of the season, J. M. Kilburn
would be writing in the *Yorkshire Post* that Yorkshire had
found 'a future Colossus who could be safely entrusted with
the task of regaining for England records which Bradman
had made his own'. Sutcliffe declared that Hutton was a
'marvel – the discovery of a generation' and for the first
(but not the last) time embarrassed the younger man by the
extravagance of his praises.

Hutton was commissioned to bat for Yorkshire and to join
a close-knit fraternity of players who might boast about
him to the opposition but concede nothing themselves to a
precocious youngster until he had served his articles. By
1939 he had scored over 11,000 runs for Yorkshire, Sutcliffe
declaring that he had only made 50,000 runs himself for
Hutton to eclipse the total one day. After Sutcliffe and Hutton
came Mitchell, Leyland and Wilfred Barber. No county could
match such batting in depth and in the 1930s twelve York-
shiremen were capped for England, five of them in the same
match at The Oval in 1938.

Yorkshire bowling in the 1930s was primarily entrusted to
Hedley Verity and Bill Bowes. Verity, in 1930, made much
the same impact within the county as Hutton was to do a few
years later. His place as Rhodes' successor – in the fine lineage
of Yorkshire left-arm bowlers – was assured once Rhodes had
watched him and pronounced 'He'll do!' He was faster than
Rhodes and brought the ball down from a greater height.
Helped as he was at the start by the wet wickets of 1930, he
soon became a bowler who responded more to the challenge
of a good batting wicket rather than one who revelled in the
gift of a bad one. Two sorts of partnership emerged: that
between him and Mitchell in the gully aching for the ball that
spun away, and that between him and Bowes as a bowling
partnership. Bowes' impact was not so immediate and initially

he was under contract as an MCC bowler. By 1931 Yorkshire were getting the better of the bargain, symbolised by his appearance for the MCC in Yorkshire in May and for Yorkshire v. the MCC in September. In the following year both men featured in *Wisden*'s 'Five Cricketers of the Year' and were picked to go to Australia in 1932–33. Bowes, with height and lift, was the fast bowler in the vanguard of the attack who might later finish off an innings as a medium-pacer.

Such was the side to whom victory seemed a matter of course. Kilburn saw them as players who were greater 'than the sum of themselves' – aggressive in fielding, astute in field-placing and equipped with batsmen able to set up huge totals and bowlers expecting to dismiss an opposition for less than 200. Symbolic of this was the month of July 1932 when Yorkshire seemed intent on pleasing all their home supporters. Surrey, undefeated, came to Sheffield and were vanquished, rather than merely beaten, Bowes and Verity taking eighteen wickets between them for ten runs apiece. Gloucestershire, despite 200 runs in the match for once out from Hammond, lost at Bradford. Headingley was the scene of Verity's greatest triumph when, in 19.4 overs, he took all ten Nottinghamshire wickets for 10 runs, and a match which was going against Yorkshire's way became a ten-wicket victory. At Harrogate the Indians were beaten largely due to Macaulay's bowling and Northamptonshire lost by an innings at Huddersfield.

By the end of the decade Norman Yardley, the future England captain, had come into the side and he and Hutton would make centuries in Yorkshire's match against Sussex at Hove on the eve of war. For the sake of Jim Parks' benefit, the game was seen to its conclusion on the afternoon of Friday 1 September 1939, and Verity took 7 for 9 in his last first-class match.

Then, one of the finest sides in the whole history of county cricket boarded a charabanc for home and an uncertain future. Verity would be killed, Bowes taken prisoner and Hutton, in training to be a Commando, would be badly injured. Despite such setbacks, Yorkshire returned triumphant in 1946. Hutton made a century in the first home match at

Headingley, the championship was again won and a successor to Verity was found in Arthur Booth who returned to the side after a fifteen-year absence. He topped both the county and the national averages. Ill-health made it a brief moment of glory but in the wings was John Wardle. It was a fine start to the post-war years, though a Yorkshire ascendancy would not be sustained and controversy and discord lay in the future.

Throughout these years the 'Roses' match remained the expression of Northern dourness, victory the occasional elixir to be quenched in moderation and without indulgence. One dreary May afternoon at Bradford in 1932, after rain had delayed the start, Lancashire's Eddie Paynter disdained such notions, hit Verity for four sixes and made 152 while the rest of the side fumbled and let Verity take 8 for 107. Lancashire's 263 proved more than enough, Yorkshire were dismissed for 46 and 167 and a result was achieved for the first time for five years. Frank Sibbles had a match analysis of 12 for 68.

Lancashire needed breaks such as this in the 1930s and real successes (such as the title in 1930 and 1934) were the exception rather than the rule. The great players of the 1920s never quite found their later counterparts and Paynter's was the only great name that emerged, a left-hander who averaged 84.42 in his seven Tests against Australia and, after a slightly hesitant start, scored 18,000 runs for Lancashire with a triple century at Hove against Sussex in 1937. He was a batsman who excelled in driving and in hooking, a defender on demand but an attacker by instinct. As a player, he responded to the big occasion.

Towards the end of the decade, Paynter would sometimes open the innings with Cyril Washbrook who knocked persistently at the England door which opened only once in his favour in the 1930s. Hutton's great post-war partner was penalised more than most by the years 1939 to 1945. Rather better served chronologically by the war was Sibbles who had retired from cricket in 1937 after taking over 900 wickets. He rose to the rank of major and the experience gained in administration and man-management led to later service on the Lancashire committee and to the chairmanship of the sub-committee for selection and player-welfare. He and his fellow bowler, John Hopwood, who became president of Lancashire in 1982, represented – as, indeed, did Washbrook (president in 1989) – the type of professional cricketer who was socially mobile and whose experience was drawn upon after his playing days were over. Lancashire were more ready than Yorkshire to recognise such qualities in their professionals, though Leyland was elected to the Yorkshire committee in 1946.

Washbrook brought a new dimension to the financial expectations of the professional with a benefit in 1948 which raised over £14,000 and which was organised through a committee. The sum itself stood unsurpassed for over twenty years – until inflation made a nonsense of all earlier figures – but the principle of careful planning and money-raising efforts over a summer was immediately taken up by other professionals, while insurance policies could be taken out against rain on the actual day of the benefit match. Unlike some professionals, Washbrook did not allow his benefit year to affect his form and his batting average of 92.73 for the county exceeded by almost 50 that of any other player; but good as the immediate post-war Lancashire side was, it lacked the resources to take it to the top.

In both Yorkshire and Lancashire, post-war enthusiasm for the game was immense and there were waiting lists for membership. 'The only time my husband ever pulled rank,' said one life-long Yorkshire supporter to me, 'was when he wanted to become a member of Yorkshire in 1946'; and added, 'There'd be 15,000 through the gate on a working day at Bramall Lane.' Yorkshire had over £22,000 in their accumulated fund and Lancashire raised, in the same year, £25,000 for reconstruction. Money values were substantially the same as in the earlier years – £450 a year was a good salary. Despite a war-damaged Old Trafford, economic recession and continued rationing, the wet summer of 1946 and the savage winter of 1946–47, cricket prospered and was popular, nowhere more so than in the great northern centres of the game.

Notts, Derbyshire, Warwickshire

Among the Midlands counties, Nottinghamshire were never quite the force in the 1930s which they had been a decade earlier. One of the by-products of the bodyline tour in

Australia (see Chapter 6) was its effect on their two famous bowlers. In the first place, both Larwood and Voce bowled less well immediately afterwards because of the heavy demands which had been made on them. Secondly, bad feeling arose in Nottinghamshire's relations with other counties because Carr, as captain, sought to employ the policies pursued by Jardine in Australia. Acrimony between committee and supporters completed an unhappy picture. By 1935 the dust had settled, Carr had been replaced, and Nottinghamshire's players' controversies were over; but there remained financial problems which the 1930s never resolved.

Larwood played until 1938 when he gave up the game on medical advice; 1936 had been a very good year in which he topped the national averages. There was press speculation that he might go to Australia again but it was as a player at county level that he ended his career. After the war, he wrote, 'nobody took a second look at the bespectacled man on Blackpool sands who sometimes bowled a rubber ball to his daughters'.

For batsmen, Nottinghamshire turned to the George Gunn and Joe Hardstaff of the next generation. George Gunn the younger made a century against Warwickshire in 1931 in the same match as did his father, while Hardstaff junior gave a glamour and stylishness to the game at both county and Test levels. He, like Washbrook, was someone whose career was severely hit by the war and who was thus deprived of a century of centuries. To a secure technique, he added fluency and individuality. Some cricketers are remembered only for their figures. Hardstaff is not one of them – the figures, 31,847 runs and 83 centuries, are only auxiliaries to his reputation.

Nottinghamshire cricket after the war fell into the doldrums. Improved conditions and wage-structures in the mining industry made cricket no longer an attractive alternative and an historic source of local recruitment for fast bowlers had ended. Some consolation for county supporters was the sight of Reg Simpson batting with Hardstaff – two stylists, the younger of whom would match the elegance of his batting by the tenacity of his leadership. Trent Bridge in the post-war years, with its modern, Australian-fashion scoreboard, bravely looked to the future while treasuring in its grand Long Room the pictures and trophies of its past. Behind the Radcliffe end, as many a broadcasting commentator remarked, could be seen the growing development of the city of Nottingham. But it would be the mid-1950s before players such as Bruce Dooland, the Australian leg-spin bowler, gave the county back something of its former glory.

The visit of the Nottinghamshire team to the little Derbyshire town of Ilkeston on a June Saturday in 1935 was something of an event, for it would be the only first-class match of the season there and 8000 people would set a record for the ground. It was a partisan crowd, for Ilkeston lay halfway between Derby and Nottingham and charabancs and cars had brought some of the spectators, while some had come from the nearby pit. They saw an even day's play with Derbyshire just nudging in front on the first innings. On the Tuesday, when far fewer people could be there, Derbyshire successfully chased 186 runs in two hours on a worn wicket and the performance was typical of the home side in the 1930s. They had been third in 1934, they would be second in 1935 and they would be champions in 1936 by being, as the County Report acknowledged, 'exponents of attractive cricket holding victory as the highest prize'.

They were not a team of 'stars' – Stan Worthington remains the only Derbyshire player ever to have scored a century in a Test match – but they possessed in Arthur Richardson one of the best of the inter-war county captains. They managed to pay a staff of about fifteen professionals, and in all departments of the game they had men of ability. As a recipe for success, it was enough.

The batting was in the hands of Dennis Smith, Arthur Alderman and Worthington, and the bowling in those of Mitchell and Copson. The Pope brothers, George and Alf, and Leslie Townsend were the principal all-rounders. Between them all these men played in only 22 Test matches between 1921 and 1948 so that the demands made upon the county were not great and a consistent unity was maintained. Without undermining Derbyshire's achievements in the 1930s, this gave them a considerable advantage over, say,

Yorkshire on whom the claims of Test matches were much more pressing.

Few grudged Derbyshire their success when the news came through to them at Wells on 28 August 1936 that they had won the title despite losing to Somerset that day. It was, wrote a local journalist, 'the greatest day ever in the history of Derbyshire cricket', and a long way from their seventeen defeats in seventeen matches in 1920. The spire at Chesterfield and the dome at Derby nodded their approval.

Warwickshire cricket in the 1930s is associated with Wyatt's captaincy until, in 1937, he was somewhat summarily removed on the recommendation of the county Executive Committee – ostensibly in the pursuit of a younger man. The outcry which followed Wyatt's dismissal surprised the committee and he was left in no doubt what both supporters of the club and the professionals thought about him. Eric Hollies, writing many years later, summed up their feelings: 'He was by far the finest captain of Warwickshire I ever played under. He was a great friend to the professionals and, although he didn't drink himself, he was always ready to buy a round. And if anyone began talking cricket the skipper would be there all night.' The relationship between the seemingly eternal secretaryship of Ryder and Wyatt as captain had been at the root of the problem: Ryder had found in Wyatt a man who would stand up to him.

Gerald Pawle, in his biography of Wyatt, has also indicated that Wyatt met in Sydney Santall, the chief coach, an obstructive and uncommunicative man to deal with. Setting aside these off-the-field problems, Wyatt forged a side which reached fourth in the championship on one occasion. He bore a large personal burden as a run-maker and an occasional bowler, besides setting an example to a side not immediately distinguished by its fielding ability. To all this was added his role through a substantial part of these years as an England captain and batsman. His success with England complicated relations with Ryder to whom the county was 'all'. Less talented amateur captains whose sights were set on purely county matters avoided conflicting strains on their loyalties. Wyatt was a big enough man to give total loyalty all round, Ryder not big enough to realise it.

Among the older batsmen still playing were Parsons, who occasionally acted as captain in Wyatt's absence and as forceful and attacking a player as ever, and Smith, willing to bat at no. 1 or no. 11 – but 'nowhere in between' he told his skipper. In support were Croom, Bates and Kilner – all sound players at county level who would help to ensure respectable Warwickshire totals. The problem was much more that of dismissing the opposition. Derek Foster represented the talented young amateur fast bowler unable to appear frequently, while George Paine was secured from the Lord's groundstaff. With the ability to top the England national bowling averages in 1934, Paine was, as a slow left-arm bowler, the one most likely to win matches for the county. Those two apart, Warwickshire could look distinctly thin in attack until the emergence in 1933 of Hollies as a leg-break and googly bowler.

To beat Yorkshire was the ambition of any county side. Warwickshire in 1934 at Scarborough must have had some expectations after dismissing them for 101 (Paine 8 for 62) only to have them dashed by their own dismissal for 45. Paine, with support from Hollies, then dismissed Yorkshire for 159 leaving Warwickshire 219 to win – the highest innings of the match if attained. Parsons was in charge and playing in his last first-class match (he was still playing cricket in 1960, at the age of seventy). Wickets fell and he went in to bat, as he related in old age, 'determined to go from the scene having beaten Yorkshire'. He attacked the bowling of Macaulay and Frank Smailes, reached the boundary fifteen times and made 94, being bowled just before Warwickshire clinched victory. The game had had its 'aggro' – one can too easily romanticise past encounters – and Parsons had complained at the perpetual chatter of the Yorkshire slips. 'Take no notice of t'bloody parson,' they had told Sellers, their skipper, and the war of attrition continued to the end. Of Parsons, *The Cricketer* wrote, 'his batting made it hard to realise that he was born in 1890'. The match had been a tough baptism for 'Tom' Dollery on his first appearance. He and Hollies belonged to the generation who would sow the seeds of future success and be the mainstay of the immediate post-war sides. The reward in 1951 of the title to 'an extraordinary team of ordinary cricketers playing purposeful cricket' was how Dollery, the professional captain, described their success; not an unreasonable epitaph on Warwickshire cricket as a whole in their better years after 1919.

Worcestershire, Leicestershire and Northamptonshire

All the other three Midlands counties, Worcestershire, Leicestershire and Northamptonshire, struggled to achieve much in the 1930s. Worcestershire had individual players of talent in Cyril Walters, Dick Howorth and Reg Perks. Walters, who opened for England on eleven occasions, was an exceptionally good secretary-player, neither role suffering by his occupation of the other. His batting in 1933 led *Wisden* to write that 'none of the heroes of a past era of Worcestershire cricket ever had such a brilliant season'. When he batted with Hammond in the Test against the West Indies at Lord's, he compared equally with the Gloucestershire player 'for grace of style and beauty of execution'. R. L. Arrowsmith called him one of the most beautiful stroke-players in the game. Symptomatic of his efforts for Worcestershire was a double-century against Kent in 1933 in a match which his county still lost by nine wickets. In 1935 he left the game – 'too soon', thought Arrowsmith.

Howorth joined the county in 1933 as a slow left-arm bowler with some ability as a batsman. Like many another there was no place for him at higher level while Verity played, and his England opportunities came after 1946. One of his great moments was in taking 5 for 21 against Yorkshire when the little ground at Stourbridge was packed to see the county's first defeat of the Northerners since 1909 (one of the rare instances when Hutton made a 'pair'). In a low-scoring match – no-one made 50 – Worcestershire won by 11 runs, Yorkshire's batting and the wicket simultaneously crumbling. Howarth ended his days in the Birmingham League, a little disenchanted with the first-class game but very willing to give of his experience on the county committee. Perks joined Worcestershire in 1930 and promptly dismissed Hobbs. He was a fast-medium bowler who took 100 wickets in sixteen consecutive seasons and became in 1955 the county's first professional captain and, like Howorth, ultimately a committee member. He was an immensely popular player who did much for morale and helped the county to finish seventh in 1939. The good relationship between the committee and the players was demonstrated in the willingness of the professionals to accept a voluntary reduction in pay in 1933, though Fred Root, in his memoirs, left his readers in no doubt that not much was left over by the time a man had paid for 'hotel accounts, taxi fares, flannels and cricket equipment'. The county's financial situation was eased a year later when membership rose by 500. The influence of Lord Cobham and of his son, Charles Lyttelton, who was captain in the four seasons before the war, was important in maintaining goodwill in these difficult years. The younger Lyttelton was a natural leader, as behoved a future Governor-General of New Zealand, who, in his term of office, made 44 runs for his own XI against the MCC tourists.

To the continuing contributions of Astill and Geary to Leicestershire in the 1930s was added the sparkling batting of the New Zealander, Stewart Dempster. Leicestershire gave the captaincy to Astill in 1935 – the first county to make such a formal appointment of a professional – and he rewarded them by taking the county to sixth place (their highest since 1905) although he was replaced by Dempster a year later. Dempster, already an established New Zealand Test player, had toured England twice before joining the county: batting and fielding such as his gave colour to Leicestershire cricket in what was otherwise a drab picture in the years immediately before the war. Lack of support from within the county brought this philosophic comment in the County Report for 1933: 'Victories were received without any enthusiasm and defeats with gloomy indifference'. As in the 1920s, Sir Julien Cahn helped financially and the devoted services of the Packe family – administratively and as players – helped to save Leicestershire from the threat of extinction. It was not a county without wealth but its landowners looked to the hunt rather than the cricket field for their leisure interests.

What Sir Julien Cahn did for cricket in a wider sense, Stephen Schillizzi continued to do for Northamptonshire cricket. Between May 1935 and May 1939 not a match was

won, and only Schillizzi's continued financial help and a
devoted committee kept the club in business. Nothing seemed
to go right. Their best batsman, Bakewell, after making 241
against Derbyshire at the end of the 1936 season, was so
severely injured in a car accident that he never played first-
class cricket again. Their best bowler, Clark, was often unavailable and declined in ability. With the appointment of
Robert Nelson as captain in 1938, the county secured a cricketer of much promise and a leader of distinction. He took
the side, wrote the secretary, somewhat bluntly, from 'a
disorganised rabble into a team impossible to recognise as
the same lot who had done duty before'. The hopes which
Northamptonshire might have entertained for Nelson's
long-term future were dashed by his death in the war. Yet
the picture of Leicestershire and Northamptonshire, so often
the two bottom sides in the championship in the 1930s, was
not entirely one of doom and gloom. A local 'derby' between
them would arouse much interest and 5000 were there on the
Whitsun holiday at Nottingham in 1939 to see a match full
of excitement. Half the Leicestershire side were out for 8
before lunch on the Saturday, the total finally reaching 134.
Dennis Brookes then made 187 and Northamptonshire enjoyed the luxury of declaring on Whit Monday at 510 for 8.
Bill Merritt, the New Zealander, took six wickets for 56
and Leicestershire were beaten by an innings and 193 runs.
Northamptonshire had broken the run of four years without
a victory. Nevertheless, few would have envisaged the role
they would play in post-war cricket, no longer a backwater
but, as Alex Bannister has observed, 'a modern centre of the
game, solvent, up-to-date, progressive'.

Gloucestershire, Glamorgan, Hampshire, Somerset

Of the western counties, Gloucestershire began the 1930s in
great style setting their cap at the title and very nearly achieving it but, after Beverley Lyon ceased to be captain in 1934,
they lost their way a little and despite the dominating presence
of Hammond they never secured the honour which has eluded
them since 1877. Among many exciting games none was
more so than that against the Australians in 1930. Playing

near enough the same side which had beaten England by an innings at The Oval twenty-four hours earlier, the Australians bowled out Gloucestershire for 72 on a wet wicket at Bristol and replied with 157. Hammond's 89 was the main feature of Gloucestershire's 202 made against a threatening Grimmett (who had often proved his downfall that summer). Australia's task of 118 seemed easy enough when they had reached 50 for 0, till wickets began to fall. As the news spread through Bristol, many thousands simply left work and boarded trams for Nevil Road and the gates were closed for the first time since 1888. Runs and wickets advanced in tandem: 73/5; 106/8; 115/9. When the totals were level, 14 balls were bowled before an lbw made the match a tie. Amidst scenes of great excitement, crowds followed both teams to the railway station to see them off to their respective destinations, Swansea and Canterbury. Hammond recalled a seething mob filling the streets and the railway platforms; it was a hysteria more associated with the world of football.

Hammond's contribution to Gloucestershire cricket of 33,664 runs for the county in twenty years and 504 wickets, goes without saying. In 1932, for example, he made twice as many runs as anyone else and his average of 60 was twice as high. Against Lancashire he made 264 and bowled 77 overs, being on the field for all but ninety minutes of the match. A year later, H. E. Roslyn, writing on the county for *Wisden*, wrote, 'Few, if any, cricketers of recent years have, during such a short period before the public, done so much as Hammond, not only for the county but for England'.

He was among the most prosperous of professional cricketers of his time and the first cricketer to be given a 'sponsored' car. Gloucestershire paid him £450 a year and he had a successful benefit in 1934 which raised £2500. Nevertheless, he found it hard to maintain the standard of living for which he craved – he dressed well, bought his suits in Savile Row, played golf with Bristol businessmen and was a welcome guest of the Duke of Beaufort at Badminton. The invitation to turn amateur and become a company director in 1937 at a salary of £2000 was not one to be resisted, especially as it opened the way to the England captaincy. In the rigid social context of the inter-war years, Hammond – a grammar school

boy whose father had been commissioned from the ranks –
found himself by circumstances (and even more by his own
shy temperament) fitting naturally into neither the ranks of
the amateurs nor of the professionals. Yet, as some of his
contemporaries have indicated, he was more sensitive about
such matters than he need have been. None of this detracted
from his cricket, though it allows us to see him as a man who
gave happiness to thousands without securing a fair share of
it for himself.

Despite the attraction of Hammond – if he was 'not out'
in the mid-day editions of the papers, the crowds on any
ground would increase in the afternoon – Gloucestershire's
finances remained a worry and membership was less than it
might have been. In 1933, for example, the club lost over
£3000 and it was a brave decision to raise a debenture loan to
buy back Fry's Ground at Bristol which they had sold to the
chocolate firm in 1915. In our age of inflation it is interesting
to note that they paid exactly the same sum in 1933 as they
had got for it eighteen years earlier.

Meanwhile a new generation of players was responsible for
much of Gloucestershire's success on the field, among them
Sinfield, Barnett and Goddard. Sinfield, an old pupil of
C. B. Fry's training-ship *Mercury*, was the stock all-rounder,
unlucky only to play once for England but with the wicket
of Bradman to show for it. After his cricketing days were
over he coached at Clifton College until they retired him;
then he coached at Colston's School, Bristol, until he was
well over eighty. On a Saturday in the summer term he
would get up at 5 am, do some gardening, get to school in
time to prepare the First XI wicket, umpire the school match,
tidy up and drive home at 10 pm. He was a delightful man
to talk to – he would even recall his grim, tough days as a
boy on Fry's training ship with pleasure and a laugh.

Barnett was an outstanding batsman by any standard –
John Arlott called him 'the most militant opening batsman
modern cricket has ever known' and it was perhaps his
misfortune (though equally his due) to find himself so often
compared with Hammond. Against Glamorgan at Bristol in
1934, Barnett's batting was 'little short of amazing' and 'he
punished the bowlers mercilessly' wrote *Wisden*. He hit six

sixes in his 123 while Hammond made 302 not out! Against Hampshire at Southampton in 1937, after both men had just returned from Australia, Barnett made a century and took 5 for 40. Hammond made two half-centuries and took 5 for 30! Barnett had been second in the MCC tour averages in Australia – Hammond first. Long after his cricketing days were over, Barnett would be seen in his home town of Cirencester occupied in the family business at an age when most men had retired from active life.

Goddard's 'second spell' as a Gloucestershire player – after a year at Lord's learning to bowl off-breaks – began in 1929 and lasted until the 1950s. In a side which lacked a pace attack, his task was to spin the opposition out with flight and a sharply turning ball, something he did with tremendous effect year after year. Against Kent at Bristol in 1939 he equalled the record of Verity in 1933 and Colin Blythe of Kent in 1907 by taking seventeen wickets in a day. His benefit match against Nottinghamshire at Gloucester was the last game of the 1936 season. Goddard bowled too well for his own good on the Saturday and Nottinghamshire were dismissed cheaply. Visions of a near-empty ground on the Monday haunted him until Hammond promised he would bat for a day, and did so with a triple century. Far removed from Goddard's worst fears, the Monday produced the largest crowd ever seen on the Gloucester ground.

Over and over again, one is amazed at crowd attendances for county cricket on working days – not all the time, or the national economy would have suffered, and not sufficiently often to let some counties balance their books – but to a modern generation which only watches Test matches or limited-overs games, an interesting phenomenon.

Immediately after that match, tragedy struck and Gloucestershire's young captain, Dallas Page, died from injuries in a car crash returning home. Basil Allen (for one year) and then Hammond were appointed in his place and continued Lyon's policy of going all-out for victory. Gloucestershire were seen as the most attractive side in the country to watch. Against Hampshire in 1939, by leadership and example, Hammond engineered a victory when lost time through rain had made it seem impossible: against Glamorgan he was less successful and, after two Gloucestershire declarations, Glamorgan scraped home four minutes from the end of extra time. In the Cheltenham Festival, Gloucestershire determinedly pursued a total far greater than any earlier in the match, only to lose to Derbyshire by one run. Cricket such as this made its appeal and, no doubt, contributed to Gloucestershire being able to raise the £13,000 – a considerable sum – with which to discharge their debentures. After the war Hammond had one more glorious summer with the county, then he was gone: a peremptory decision made the day after he returned from the less than successful captaincy of the MCC in Australia in 1946–47 and an era in Gloucestershire – and English – cricket had suddenly ended.

That victory snatched from Gloucestershire in 1939 did Glamorgan more good than Gloucestershire harm. What occasional success the Welsh county had in the 1930s owed much to the continuing performances of Turnbull and Clay. Turnbull fell on the Normandy beaches and Clay led the side immediately after the war. Bowling his off-spinners as effectively as ever, he helped in Glamorgan's successful onslaught on the title in 1948 under Wooller's leadership. He had been part of the entire panorama of Glamorgan's cricket ever since 1921. The side which finally won the title was almost entirely Welsh-born and one whose success was measured not so much by great batting or bowling as by outstanding fielding.

A triumph such as this brought a degree of economic security. Gate money, an Appeal and a profit of £10,000 gave Glamorgan the resources with which to launch coaching schemes throughout South Wales. The years 1921–48 had had their ups and downs – and mostly downs – but the future of first-class cricket in the Principality was assured.

As the 1930s moved on the Hampshire stalwarts of earlier years gradually moved out, though Mead played until 1936, completing over 55,000 runs and remaining in the game until the war as a professional on the Suffolk staff. His 182 not out for England against Australia at The Oval in 1921 was still a record against them on an English ground when he retired, though it was eclipsed four times in the 1938 series. Hampshire treated him well, paying him for a full season after he retired and arranging a public subscription. He was to be seen batting in club cricket during the second world war with one eye and within a year of losing the sight of the other.

No one approached Mead in ability and Hampshire became a side of good county players, one of whom, John Arnold, made a single Test appearance in 1931: enough to make him a dual international at cricket and soccer. Had the same side played regularly, Hampshire might have fared better than they did but too often a few professionals were supported by a changing variety of amateurs, none of whom matched the talent of Richard Moore, whose 316 against Warwickshire in 1937 remains the highest individual score for the county.

County cricket was the essence of the game to the supporters at Southampton, Bournemouth and Portsmouth, few of whom in those days would ever see a Test match. Loyalties to the county were, therefore, exceptionally strong and players such as Arthur 'Sam' Pothecary, Len Creese and Ossy Herman would be treasured for the guaranteed contribution of runs or wickets which they would make. Creese had an unusual background. His father, William, had gone out to South Africa as baggage man with the MCC in 1913–14 and stayed there. Later William's brother joined him and the two men virtually ran the club at Newlands, Cape Town, holding offices between them of groundsman, caterer and secretary.

After the war, Desmond Eagar – a surname totally expressive of his approach and interest – took over the captaincy, secured a bowler in Derek Shackleton and pointed the way ahead. It would be a long toil but not unfruitful in the end. The county of the Hambledon men and of John Arlott and John Woodcock deserved to prosper.

In the days when Somerset retained a rural charm of its own, such places as Taunton and Bath – almost outposts of empire to a Londoner – were centres where West Country people might go to shop, sell their wares in the market, absorb some culture or even enjoy a day's cricket. At Taunton, surrounded by the Quantock Hills and a range of spires and towers, the spectator could contemplate the beauties of nature and of mediaeval architecture. At Bath, he could ponder the elegance of Beau Nash or recall that cricket's early historian, James Pycroft, had played there and seen cricket affording to the professional player 'a merry and abundant, though rather a laborious livelihood, from the time the first May-fly is up to the time the first pheasant is down'. Thoughts such as these might not have been far from the mind of young Harold Gimblett as he thumbed a lift early one Saturday morning after missing the 6 am bus to Bridgwater. He was bound for Frome to play for the county, he informed the lorry driver who picked him up, though the man had his doubts.

The tale has often been told – by Gimblett himself and by David Foot, his biographer – of the summons to fill a last-minute gap in the Somerset side. They put him in no. 8 and Wellard lent him a bat. He went in at 2.20 and by a quarter to three he had made a half-century. The beer tent emptied and the wooden benches creaked with the crowd's excitement. Just after half past three he reached his century, in sixty-three minutes, and won the Lawrence Trophy for the fastest century of the season. On Tuesday evening they took him to Lord's where he made a fifty and talked to Patsy Hendren. He had come to stay, this mighty striker who forsook the family farm to be a professional, who had been sent to the local public school, who made over 23,000 runs for Somerset and whose 310 against Sussex remains a county record. In his cricket, like Pycroft's professional, he was 'merry and abundant': in life less so and David Foot has recorded the mental agonies which tormented this man to whom life gave no happy ending to match his cricketing beginning.

The Somerset schoolboys never quite made up their mind whom most to cheer – Gimblett or Wellard. Wellard, turned down by Kent with the jest that he was better suited to be a policeman, became the professional at the Weston-super-Mare Club in Clarence Park where holidaymakers, forsaking the beach, watched Somerset play its festival matches. He joined the county in 1929, hit twice as many sixes as Gimblett – a quarter of all the 12,562 runs he made. Twice he hit five of them in consecutive balls. His value was threefold, for he could also bowl a fastish ball with a vicious break-back or spin it with a slow off-break. Three times he did the 'double' and, against Hampshire in 1933, he made 77 and 60 and took ten wickets for 109.

Yet, at heart, Somerset remained a team primarily of amateurs with unusual names and initials – Robertson-Glasgow, Mitchell-Innes, McDonald-Watson and C. C. C. Case – with a small core of professionals such as Gimblett and Wellard, Horace Hazell, Bertie Buse, and the Lee brothers, Frank and Jack. Twice in the 1930s they finished seventh and in the first post-war season they aspired to fourth. By then another age was in sight: motorways to the West Country, overseas signings and an entrepreneurial approach which would change the image of Somerset cricket. 'Buy a ticket for the county lottery – keep cricket in Bath' greeted me as I entered the Pump Room one day in 1988. Gimblett had done his bit in the 1960s to advocate such changes.

Surrey, Middlesex, Kent, Sussex and Essex

It was at Old Trafford, in 1934, when Surrey played Lancashire, that Hobbs made what proved to be his last – and 197th – century in first-class cricket. He had never been a man of vaunting ambition; the quality of runs had mattered more than the quantity; but he had hoped that two hundred centuries might be something peculiarly his own. The occasion was Duckworth's benefit and Hobbs was fulfilling a promise to play. The century came in the first innings and a not-out half-century in the second. The warm-hearted Lancashire folk sent him on his way with 'Auld Lang Syne' and this much-loved man, the greatest English cricketer of his generation, took his leave of the North.

Throughout the first half of the 1930s, those who watched Hobbs bat were stealing cameos from an album of the past, but ones as rich and fresh as the day when they were first composed. The new decade was no more than a month old (in cricketing terms) when Hobbs batted with Hammond in a Test Trial at Lord's. The two came together about a quarter past four on Saturday 31 May 1930. They scored an unbroken century partnership and a huge crowd were part of an experience which had its own unique quality, while seventy miles away at Southampton Bradman was successfully securing the last 46 runs he needed to make a thousand runs in May. For a few minutes the three greatest batsmen of their times were simultaneously at the wicket. Nine years later, the mantle was handed on – Hammond would bat with Hutton at The Oval in a partnership of 264, drawing down the curtain on Test match cricket until a war had been won.

Hobbs ceased to play Test cricket in 1930 but for Surrey he continued to average over fifty in every year except his last and there was a double century against the West Indians in 1933. The county built entrance gates to The Oval bearing his name and made him a Life Member. Cricket had served him well but he had realised that for many a professional it was a struggle – 'a bare living for a few years, with nothing at the end; one saves a few pounds in the summer and spends them in the winter'. Some twenty years after writing this in his memoirs, he was knighted in Coronation Year, only persuaded to accept the honour when he was convinced that it would confer dignity on the profession and livelihood of being a cricketer and that it would please the South London crowds who had trammed, walked and queued so long and so often to see him – ordinary folk, without wealth as he had once been and into whose lives he brought lustre and goodwill.

'The Master' had gone but Surrey was not without its supporting cast whose autographs the incessant schoolboys, with their caps and ginger-beer, might claim. Jardine's captaincy was a brief one before cricket's great furore drove him from the game; Errol Holmes was Hobbs' last captain. He had played in the game at Taunton when Hobbs beat Grace's record; he had had to earn his living and he came back to Surrey in 1934, a latter-day Chapman, the amateur who gave gaiety to cricket, a man with whom Hobbs served on the Surrey committee. 'Remembering Errol with affection' wrote Hobbs on the copy of Ronald Mason's biography of himself which he gave to Holmes' widow. Separate gates to pavilions were not a frontier to friendships.

Holmes was in command when Surrey played Middlesex at The Oval in August 1937. As in the 1920 and 1921 matches between them, the championship was within Middlesex's grasp. Surrey still had Sandham together with Laurie

Lord's, 27 June 1930. England v. Australia, second Test first day: the flag-bedecked scene, and Airship R101 overhead. See Prologue.

a) Middlesex, County champions, 1920. Warner is captain in his last playing season; b) the triumphant Australian side of 1921; captain, Armstrong.

Sydney Cricket Ground, with its big new scoreboard — first Test of
1924-25 series against Gilligan's team, during last-wicket stand of 62 between
Oldfield and Mailey.

Cartoons, by Australian leg-spinner and journalist Arthur Mailey, of Hobbs
(left) and J. M. Gregory.

The young Harold Larwood and W. W. Whysall, both of Nottinghamshire.

The Lancashire side of 1926; Paynter, back row left, in his first season.

a) Hobbs; b) Sutcliffe; c) Warwickshire trio of Parsons (left), E. J. Smith
(wicket-keeper), and Wyatt

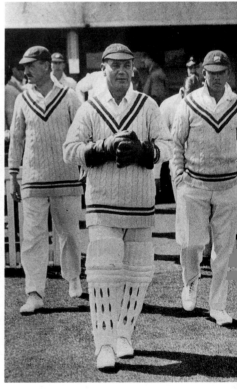

Kent and England: a) Chapman; b) Ames; c) the 1932 County side with
Woolley (far right) and Freeman (third from left).

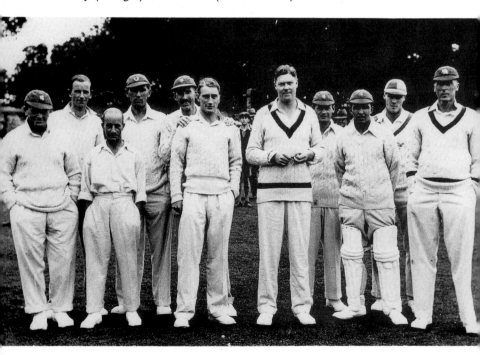

a) Hammond, in the famous 1928 photograph by Herbert Fishwick;
b) Woodfull; c) Ponsford.

'Bodyline' series, 1932-33: a) At Adelaide Woodfull loses his bat playing Larwood to leg; b) field set for Woodfull at Brisbane.

South Africa: a) 1929 team to England; b) the first win in a Test against England in England, Lord's, 1935.

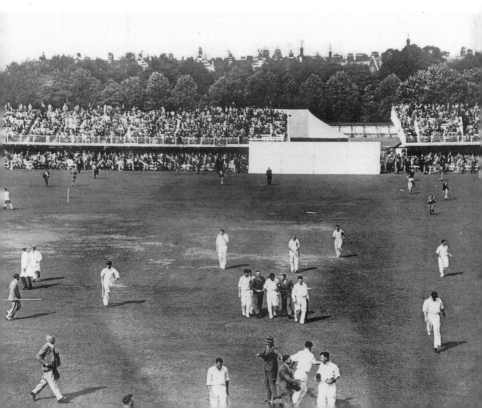

West Indies: a) Headley, one of the 'greats' alongside Hobbs, Hammond, and Bradman; b) the 1933 team to England.

India: a) the first team to play Tests in England, 1932; b) the fast bowler Amar Singh who made such an impression in 1936, as did c) Merchant (right) in 1936 and 1946, and Hazare (left) during and after the war.

The Oval, 1934. Echoes of 'bodyline' as Clark traps W. A. Brown in the second innings of the fifth Test, caught by Allen. Note who is keeping wicket — Woolley, at the age of 47, deputising for Ames.

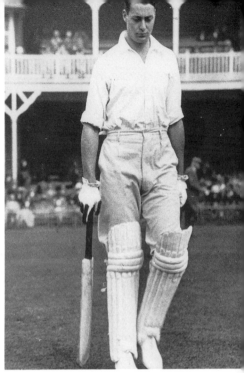

Two England fast bowlers appearing as batsmen: a) Allen, a genuine
all-rounder; b) Farnes, who was once asked to open an innings on a very
difficult wicket in the West Indies because he, and Jim Smith of Middlesex,
were the tallest men in the side; c) the early years of broadcasting —
Howard Marshall at Lord's. A 'glorious' day?

New Zealand: a) the 1937 team including, front row left b) Donnelly, photographed after the war. Walter Hadlee is on the right end of the back row, and the captain is M. L. Page.

Images of 1938: a) portrait of Hammond; b) photograph of Hutton; c) Bradman batting at Worcester.

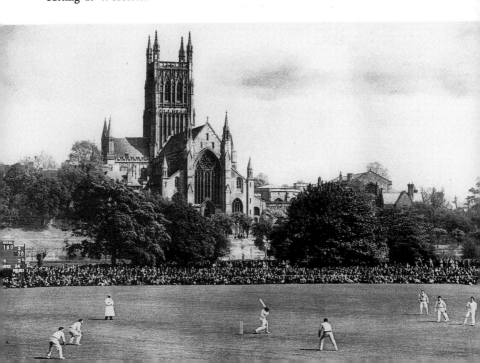

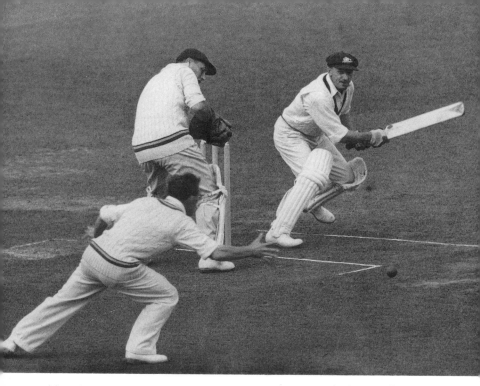

Bradman: a) photographed in 1948; b) scoring the hundredth run of his
hundredth hundred, 1947-48.

Fishlock. Bowling was principally in the hands of Alf Gover who bowled throughout the 1930s and a little after the war for fewer Test caps than he might have won. In 1936, he was the first fast bowler to take 200 wickets in England since Tom Richardson in 1897. Indeed, he was still bowling at his Indoor School in his ninth decade, still dispensing shrewd but kindly advice to cricketers, and their parents, of all ages and abilities, still accepting (as he ruefully said) that the public is really interested in batsmen, not bowlers.

Surrey in this match made 123 for 2 before Owen-Smith took five wickets without conceding a run. Surrey's total of 170 was 19 runs more than Middlesex could muster – Hendren, at the end of his career, and Compton and Edrich at the beginning of theirs, notwithstanding. Eventually, Middlesex were set 229 to win. Compton, shades of things to come, was run out and big Jim Smith, mighty hitter of sixes, John Human, a stylish amateur, and Jim Sims, a leg-break and googly bowler who could hit hard, saw them home. Thirty thousand people packed The Oval in a match which attracted more support than England against New Zealand on the same ground a week later. As for Surrey's future, Alec Bedser and Stuart Surridge took wickets for the 2nd XI in 1938 and the nine-year-old Peter May was making runs at his preparatory school in Reading. Unbroken success would come in the 1950s.

Three weeks after The Oval match in 1937, Surrey and Middlesex met again at Lord's. Yorkshire had virtually won the title and victory against Hampshire the same weekend ensured it. Central to the Lord's game was the last appearance there of Hendren, marked by a century. With his 57,612 runs and 170 centuries, he had been to Middlesex what Hobbs had been to Surrey and his departure diminished the number of players whose careers had begun in cricket's first Golden Age. In an article in the 1938 *Wisden* he wrote that the sort of cricket Middlesex played never failed to attract the public.

Much of that attraction came from the captaincy of Middlesex in the 1930s. Though Allen could never spare the time to be a regular captain and confined his leadership to that of England – before and after the second world war – Robins and Peebles successively were ready to take up any challenge so that from 1935 onwards Middlesex were third and then runners-up on four successive occasions – and again so in 1946 before securing a shared title in 1947.

Both Robins and Peebles were spin-bowlers and when they and Allen found time to play the Middlesex attack (with the professionals Smith and Sims) was among the best in the country. Contemporary opinion rated Allen not far behind Larwood in pace and accuracy – certainly worth comparisons being made and with an undoubted edge as a batsman.

Allen was at the wicket when Compton made his Middlesex debut in 1936, recommended by E. W. Swanton who had batted with him in a 2nd XI match the week before. Allen at no. 10 and Compton at no. 11 had put on 46 for the last wicket (their ultimate Test match batting averages 24.19, and 50.06 respectively) in a low-scoring match when Compton and the innings ended with a dubious lbw decision given by an umpire who could no longer resist the calls of nature. Before the summer was out, Warner was calling him 'the best young batsman since Walter Hammond was a boy'. Little more than twelve months later he made his Test debut against New Zealand and by 1939, when war came, he had established himself as firmly in the public mind as Hutton – lacking the concentration of the Yorkshireman in matches of less significance but offering judgment, skill and nerve (so wrote Warner) when circumstances demanded: above all, debonair, carefree and intuitive. His 181 against Essex in 1939 at Lord's led Charles Bray, the former Essex player and an astute critic of the *Daily Herald*, to compare him with Bradman.

In the opening match of 1937 against Northamptonshire, the Middlesex score-card for the first time bore the names of W. J. Edrich and D. Compton. At the end of the season they effectively topped the batting averages for the county and in the following season Edrich scored 1000 runs in May. When war broke out they were, as Altham anticipated, 'two young batsmen for whom the future may hold the most glittering prizes'. Their presence, with that of Robins in command, gave to Middlesex, as Swanton wrote, 'three scimitars in concerted action destined to cut down many adversaries'. Comparisons were constantly made with Hendren and Hearne. Of the later pair, Compton had the more natural ability. Both were fighters but Edrich – as befitted one who would be a wartime bomber pilot and win a DFC – the more pronounced one.

Robertson-Glasgow, in assessing their achievements, saw them as champions in the fight against dullness and commercialism, 'the inspiration and quarry of the young', and he shared with Swanton the view that they were happy philosophers in their cricket. Only in the matter of Australia was fulfilment awaited and sadly it remained true that the pair would never collectively present the threat to Australian bowlers that Hobbs and Sutcliffe had done.

It was in the summer of 1947 that Compton and Edrich demonstrated the apogee of their talent. In what was still a world of austerity and rationing, going to cricket was the great escape from bureaucracy and restrictions, though not from queues. For the editor of *Wisden*, 1947 was a year which bore 'comparison with any within living memory' and crowd attendances in many counties exceeded all known records. Nowhere was this more demonstrated than in the cricket Middlesex played, setting victory as the urgent objective in every match and achieving a result in all but two of them. In match after match, if they won the toss, 400 runs or so would be scored on the first day and three or four wickets taken; if they lost it, they would aim to be batting by late afternoon.

Triumphant as Middlesex were, they were not a two-man team. A match in 1947 illustrates this. When Edrich and Compton were absent on Test match duty, Jack Robertson and Sid Brown put on 310 for the first wicket against Nottinghamshire and the match was won by seven wickets. Robertson, unlucky to be an opening batsman at the same time as Hutton, had few England opportunities but he and Brown scored almost 4000 runs between them for Middlesex that summer.

The all-conquering Middlesex side of 1947 was a far cry from that of 1930 when thirty-three players had turned out and only three matches were won, yet there was common ground. The amateurs, Allen and Robins, spanned the years as did the professionals, Fred Price, the wicket-keeper, and Sims. Allen, with his debut for the county in 1921, played first-class cricket in virtually all the years embraced by this book.

An hour's journey on the Southern Railway took the cricket lover from the urban mood of The Oval or the urbane scene at Lord's to the rural setting of the grounds in Kent where rhododendrons embraced Tunbridge Wells; a deer park, the Mote at Maidstone; and the broad sweep of the North Downs, cricket at Folkestone. All enjoyed their Cricket Weeks in this most peripatetic of county cricket clubs but the Week at Canterbury at the beginning of August must be the epitome of all that lies close to the hearts of the Men of Kent or Kentish men. Tents whose flags denote municipal, theatrical and military associations; banks of grass and of flowers and a famous tree set within the field as shelter or shade to some lucky fielder; and the band of 'The Buffs' all give to the St Lawrence ground qualities uniquely its own.

There in the 1930s one might spy Jack Davies – he who had bowled Bradman for a duck when an undergraduate – taking wickets; Marriott effectively bowling his slow leg-breaks but with an action causing ripples of mirth to the uninitiated; Doug Wright with rather faster ones getting one of his seven hat-tricks. All three have their claims to fame: Davies became president of the MCC, Marriott took eleven wickets in his only Test match and Wright captained the county in the 1950s and played in thirty-four Tests.

For batting one turned to Ames, Arthur Fagg and Leslie Todd and for sparkling leadership as well as batting to Chapman, Bryan Valentine and Gerald Chalk. Valentine, in particular, was a batsman particularly able to profit by the off-spinners and in-swingers encouraged by the change in the lbw law in 1935. There was never a dearth of Kent amateurs of ability while the professionals, Woolley and Freeman, continued to perform for most of the decade. Woolley played his last game in 1938, ending with a record of 58,969 runs and 145 centuries – the equal in contribution and grandeur to Hobbs and Hendren. Freeman's career ended in 1936. He was a bowler whose statistics alone are impressive: five wickets in an innings on 153 occasions, seventeen wickets in a match twice, over 200 wickets in seventeen seasons, and 3776 wickets in his career, a figure eclipsed only by Rhodes.

Picture these men at Canterbury in the 'Week' in 1934 when Kent notched up 445 for 6 against Nottinghamshire at eighty runs an hour. Woolley got a hundred, Ames 99 and Freeman and Marriott put Nottinghamshire out twice for less than 300. Three years later Nottinghamshire got their own back when Hardstaff (after 97 in the first innings) scored a century in under an hour and Swanton watched it all sitting under a tree (not *the* tree) with a bag of cherries.

These were the years of Ames' contribution to Kent and England cricket as a batsman/wicket-keeper. Like Godfrey Evans a generation later, he was possibly a greater wicket-keeper for England than for Kent, for the big occasion brought out all his talents. Kent, through Freeman, gave him mastery of slow bowling. Vivian Jenkins of Glamorgan felt that when the pair dismissed him in the 1932 Canterbury Week he had joined an elect free-masonry: 'Annihilation when it came was brief and painless; a quick flick of the bails, a hopeless backward look and, from Ames, a tolerant, sympathetic smile'. He was a wicket-keeper without heroics, proficient without parading the fact. In 1932 he established a record of 64 stumping occasions in which a disturbed bail sent some luckless batsman on his way. Then he went to Australia, kept wicket to Larwood (a new experience, short-pitched bowling on the leg side) and returned in 1933 to have his most successful year as a batsman. He made over 3000 runs, topped the Test batting averages and, against Gloucestershire at Folkestone, scored 295. Since Gloucestershire lost by an innings and 294 runs (Freeman 11 for 60), one run from Ames would appear to have been enough. Instead, he gave an outstanding display of free-scoring orthodox batting against a strong Gloucestershire attack in which eventually everyone except the wicket-keeper was called upon to bowl. He would eventually be the only wicket-keeper to join the ranks of those who have scored a hundred centuries and he was still to be found batting for Kent as late as 1951 when Evans had long-since been established as his successor.

Ames was an outstanding example of those professional cricketers of his generation who made a major contribution to the game in later years. As a squadron-leader in the RAF during the second world war, he had acquired abilities in administration and man-management and these found expression as a manager of sides touring overseas in the post-war years. He served as an England selector on the MCC committee and as a Kent committee man becoming, in due course, secretary-manager and president. I recall the thoughtfulness with which he answered questions about the events of 1932–33 in Australia some fifty years later, and his shrewd and balanced judgments on the politics and relationships involved.

No mention of Kent cricket in the 1930s should ignore the role of Fagg. There was just the possibility that he might have secured a niche as one of the England opening pair but ill-health and lack of success when tried and, above all, the emergence of Hutton, meant that he remained a county batsman, scoring his 50s rather than his 100s for Kent until one match against Essex in 1938 when he scored a double century in each innings, a record unlikely to be equalled in the context of county cricket today, except perhaps in a four-day game. At the opposite end, one-day cricket lay in the future though both Gloucestershire and Kent displayed how it might be played to a packed bank holiday crowd in the Canterbury Week in 1932 after the official match had ended. Both sides fielded admirably and took the game seriously, yet Gloucestershire scored 194 in an hour (Hammond 69) to which Kent replied with 201 in 45 minutes, Woolley making 86 in half an hour. How well Hammond responded as a whole to one-day cricket, many matches during the second world war would reveal.

Kent were a joyous side to watch – how could they be otherwise with Woolley? – usually in the top half of the championship table, but never quite taking results with the seriousness that bred success. As Hubert Preston wrote of them in 1938, 'Defeat may have stung but it did not spoil the side or prejudice their attractive style'.

For three years between 1932 and 1934, Sussex were a side that dreamed dreams. They were second in the championship each year and beat Yorkshire three times running but ultimate success eluded them. Things might have been different had Duleepsinhji not been struck down with the illness which ended his career. In 1932 he captained Sussex and was one of the best batsmen and fielders in England. Nevertheless, the qualities which Arthur Gilligan had instilled remained. Only Yorkshire fielded as well as Sussex and their cricket remained, like that of Kent, joyful, no-one demonstrating this more than the younger George Cox. When he played, Sussex never gave up as, for example, when Yorkshire came to Hove in 1938. All seemed lost after Sussex had been dismissed for 77 and Yorkshire replied with 330. Defeat by an innings stared them in the face until Cox scored a century in an hour and Yorkshire had some uncomfortable moments before getting the 70 runs they were eventually set to win.

Jim Parks and his brother, Harry, continued the tradition of family links. Parks only once played for England, opening the batting in Hutton's debut Test against New Zealand in 1937. Like many another between the wars, he was the county player *par excellence*, good enough to score over 3000 runs and take over 100 wickets in the same year. Later, his son would play for both Sussex and England as a batsman/wicket-keeper, and his grandson for Hampshire.

To nearly two generations of followers, Sussex cricket also meant the Langridge brothers. James was a left-handed all-rounder, whose few England appearances take second place to thirty years of devoted service to the county and who, with John, enjoyed in 1937 the unique distinction of two brothers each making 2000 runs in a season. No player ever came as near to playing for England as did John whose 34,380 runs were virtually all made for Sussex and whose catching off his brother's bowling became a popular feature of the Sussex score-sheet: 'c. Langridge (Jn) b. Langridge (Jas.)'. Professionals such as these were the backbone of a county who were often able to call upon amateurs of talent, none more so than Hugh Bartlett whose century against the 1938 Australians, made in under an hour, matched a similar performance by him for the Gentlemen against the Players in the same year. Equally scintillating was the elegant South African batsman Melville, and the wicket-keeper 'Billy' Griffith. These were players to remember even though post-war Sussex cricket had a spell in the doldrums: someone in 1946 had to be bottom of the table.

Essex in the 1930s struggled financially. They began the decade with an overdraft despite an Appeal and the guarantee of personal loans by members. The wet summer in 1931 did not improve matters and in 1932 there was a distinct possibility that first-class cricket in the county would end. Fundraising and appeals at national level saved the day and the decision was finally taken to give up the lease of the ground at Leyton. Essex, in effect, found themselves a travelling 'circus', playing every match 'away', carrying around where necessary the equipment, including a mobile score-board, needed to mount a match at first-class level. From then onwards, circumstances improved and membership increased – a man might enjoy full Essex membership for £1.11s.6d. (£1.57) a year, and a lady for a guinea (£1.05p). Essex was not an area of great wealth and the county's struggle to survive in the years of the Depression was by no means untypical of the times. A limited number of good professionals was retained and the county were lucky in that they had several good amateurs. Even the device of a shared captaincy from 1933 onwards between men able to take time off respectively from business, headmastering and the Army (in the case of Tom Pearce, Denys Wilcox and John Stephenson) proved surprisingly satisfactory.

As part of their policy of travelling to various 'Weeks', Essex played at Brentwood in 1934. Kent chose the occasion to make the highest score in English first-class cricket since 1899 in reaching 803 for 4 declared (Ashdown 332, Ames 202 not out, Woolley 172). Essex valiantly replied with over 400 but still lost by an innings and 192 runs. Woolley was alleged to have met Hobbs at Liverpool Street Station on his way to Brentwood for Surrey's match and told him that there was a century there for the taking. Next morning 'Hopper' Read, an amateur, on his debut, bowled so fast and effectively that he took 7 for 35, including Hobbs' wicket, and Surrey were all out for 115. It was Essex' turn to make a vast score and their 570 for 8 declared (O'Connor 248) led to Surrey losing by the identical margin by which Essex had lost in the previous match.

Twelve months later Essex produced the sensation of the 1935 season at Huddersfield, bowling out Yorkshire for 31 and 99. The damage was done by Maurice Nichols and Read who took all twenty wickets between them while Nichols also beat Yorkshire on his own with a score of 146. It was Yorkshire's first defeat in twelve months. Fast bowling was the main feature of Essex in the 1930s. Nichols, first in England to the 'double' in five consecutive seasons, moved the ball into and away from the bat, while Read could be exceptionally fast. Opposing batsmen had little let-up, for the county also enjoyed the occasional services of Stephenson and of Farnes when the term at Worksop College ended. Farnes had never returned to banking and went up to Cambridge instead and became a schoolmaster. These two were the main wicket takers for the Gentlemen against the Players in the years just before the war. Stephenson's 9 for 46 against the Players in 1936 being among the most memorable of occasions in that fixture, while Farnes took 8 for 43 in 1938. At a time of much competition among fast bowlers, Stephenson was unlucky not to go with Farnes to Australia in 1936–37. From a great height, Farnes brought the ball into the bat and he was an awesome bowler when there was any life in the wicket. The brothers Peter and Ray Smith completed an attack which was always formidable and one of the best in the country.

Beside the all-round contribution of Nichols, Essex drew upon the batting of O'Connor, a temperamental player who found time, between moments of despondency, to compile nearly 29,000 runs and make 72 centuries. More than most, Essex were a county affected by the outbreak of war. They looked in 1939 a side likely to win the title some time in the early 1940s. When peace returned, they had suffered the blow of Farnes' death and a period of rebuilding was necessary, but initially, at any rate, the dual captaincy of Pearce and Wilcox continued.

County cricket in the 1930s had shared in the social and economic implications of the Depression. On the positive side, a cricketer might reflect that he was lucky to be in work when hundreds of thousands were not. On the negative side, he was playing a game in which survival and his wage-packet depended upon continuing personal ability and the financial security of his club. The Findlay Commission of 1937 did not even exclude Yorkshire and Lancashire from a grim picture of the fortunes of the counties. Cricket in the second world war did the game a great service, if only to demonstrate the options which were available and which would eventually be adopted as a means of attracting sponsorship and making the game commercially viable. It would not be cricket as an older generation had known it and by the 1980s some of the consequences of so much 'instant' cricket would be called into question.

There had been murmurings throughout the 1930s that the role of the amateur should disappear. Why should cricketers not become professionals instead of bankers, stock-brokers or even 'shamateur' secretaries, a correspondent in *The Cricketer* asked? Robertson-Glasgow, in the 1943 *Wisden*, believed that the hour was ripe for the 'sweeping away of anachronisms and the exploding of humbug'. The surprise is – together with the emergence of one-day cricket – that it took another twenty years to happen. County cricket, even as late as 1960, bore a surprising similarity to its position in 1920. Thereafter change would be rampant, competitions would proliferate and an industry born in which the old-fashioned three-day game was on the debit side of the county balance sheet and only valued as the professional training-ground for the players who would compete at international level. 'Cricketers do not expect anyone to watch the three-day game,' declared Peter Roebuck in 1985.

6

THE FIGHT FOR THE ASHES:
THE 1930s

One of the more memorable sporting photographs between the wars showed the *Graf Zeppelin* flying low over the Wembley Cup Final in April 1930. Not for a dozen years had a German airship been seen over British soil and this one came in peace. Somewhere in the vast anonymity of the crowd, caught in the photographer's lens, were the 1930 Australians, among them the cricketer whose performances would exhaust the vocabularies of journalists, confound the critics and secure the devotion of the English public. Don Bradman was taking a Saturday afternoon off to watch Arsenal beat Huddersfield 2–0.

The Australians were led by Woodfull, who would display the same quiet authority and imperturbable temperament as a captain which he had already done as a player. Leadership came naturally to him and disturbed him not at all: in later years he was a distinguished headmaster in Melbourne. Assured of his own outstanding talent he would, with Ponsford, establish a dominance in match after match on which his talented young batsmen could capitalise. In Alan Kippax's adaptability and Stan McCabe's driving, Australia had two of the outstanding batsmen of their generation. The potential many saw in Archie Jackson would sadly remain unfulfilled while dwarfing them all would be Bradman, Gulliver among the Lilliputians, as *Punch* portrayed him. Woodfull was less sure that his men would bowl sides out. Grimmett, whose flawless length and guile deceived the best of batsmen, was the only bowler who would take his place in cricket history. In the Test matches the continuing ability of Oldfield as wicket-keeper would be an important factor.

GULLIVER'S TOUR AMONG THE LILLIPUTIANS.
(WITH MR. PUNCH'S COMPLIMENTS TO MR. BRADMAN.)

Against Worcestershire, in what would become until 1972 the traditional opening match for the Australians, Bradman made a double century and Grimmett took nine wickets. In the next match, against Leicestershire, one made 185 not out and the other took seven wickets. The two men were establishing a supremacy they retained throughout the summer and by the end of May Bradman had made over 1000 runs and Grimmett had taken more than 50 wickets. Against Surrey Bradman had a particular point to prove. He had read Fender's somewhat disparaging remarks on him eighteen months earlier and he proceeded to score 252 not out on a soft pitch. Jardine fielded throughout the day, an experience filed away in his mind for possible future attention.

Bradman was by now an acclaimed hero and the crowds pursued him relentlessly after the match to The Oval tube station, on to the train, and to the entrance to his hotel at St Pancras. The Saturday proved to be the only day's play which the weather allowed in a dismal May. Bradman declared he found it difficult to sit huddled 'in front of a roaring fire' and then go out to bat, and the Australians were reported to be feeling so cold that heavy underclothing under flannel shirts together with two sweaters was of no avail. Despite such hazards, the counties were duly beaten when weather allowed, and the Australians came to the first Test at Trent Bridge full of expectations. 'Bradman v. England' announced the newspaper headlines.

England were again captained by Chapman and the selectors rightly pinned their hopes on the men who had served them well in 1928–29. And, if any of these failed, there seemed to be a strong supporting cast in players such as Walter Robins and Duleepsinhji. Public opinion was optimistic but Warner, for once not a selector, was less convinced and told his readers so in *The Cricketer*.

After England had made 270, Australia had by far the worst of the wicket on a pitch made difficult by hot sunshine after heavy rain. They were dismissed for 144, and ultimately faced a target of 429. While Bradman batted, the result was wide open and his dismissal for 131, by Robins, marked the impressive debut against Australia of the Middlesex googly bowler. A young member of the Nottinghamshire ground-staff, fielding as substitute, dismissed McCabe with a fine falling catch that turned the course of the match. Syd Copley would never play for England, only once for Nottingham-shire but his day was made, his photograph taken and his niche secured. Australia lost the match by 93 runs and Chapman, whose own catches to dismiss Woodfull twice were majestic, had won his ninth consecutive victory as a Test match captain. He had never lost, or even drawn, a Test, while never again would Bradman make a century in England and be on the losing side. For all England's victory, Fender, writing in the *Star*, had grave doubts about the retention of the Ashes.

The second Test at Lord's, on which the sun shone uncharacteristically all the time, brought the confirmation of Bradman as the outstanding batsman of his generation (see Prologue). Some went further: 'I left Lord's firmly convinced that he was the greatest batsman of all time', recorded the umpire Frank Chester. After their victory, the Australians went to Bradford, Bradman made only one, dismissed by the elderly Emmott Robinson with his first ball. The fourteen-year-old Pudsey lad in the crowd was made doubly desolate for Yorkshire lost by ten wickets. A few days later Len Hutton took the tram to Headingley for the third Test and watched Bradman amass 309 in a day, playing havoc with the statistics and the bowlers and reaching 334 the following morning. It gave the youngster something to beat eight years later while Fender ate his words of eighteen months earlier, writing that Bradman alone of his contemporaries could be 'brilliant without taking risks'. Cardus prepared a 2000-word essay on Bradman for his readers in the *Manchester Guardian* posing the thought that 'a number of Bradmans would quickly put an end to the glorious uncertainty of cricket'. As for the Test itself, Hammond made a century though he did little else in the series to set against his 905 in 1928–29 and rain made the match a draw.

The Old Trafford Test, again a match totally spoilt by rain, deserves recalling because of the appearance of the Oxford freshman, Peebles. With his first ball he missed Bradman's stumps by a whisker. When Bradman had made ten, Hammond made an uncharacteristic miss in the slips off Peebles, and four runs later a catch off him was taken by Duleepsinhji. 'Much has been written about this duel,' Peebles wrote later, attributing his success to Bradman's comparative inexperience of soft wickets. Peebles would only play against Bradman once more, in the fifth Test, and he never quite recaptured the skills he possessed in 1930. In a period of great spin-bowlers, he was briefly among the best. Arthur Mailey, mildly reproved by the Australian manager for giving Peebles some advice, replied that bowling was an international art: perhaps it was fitting that Peebles would one day become a chevalier of the Royal Swedish Order of Vasa.

So the two sides came to The Oval all-square and history repeated itself when the selectors dropped the captain for the fifth Test and Chapman experienced the same fate as Carr in 1926. Wyatt was appointed in his place – very much to his own surprise – and immediately there was a storm of press and public criticism. The debonair Chapman possessed the glamour to which the reticent, even remote, Wyatt could not aspire and the papers, looking to fill their columns in August, had a field-day. Chapman, rather unwisely, allowed himself to be interviewed in the *Daily Mail* under the caption, 'Why have I been dropped?' Hostile as was the reaction by official-dom to his interview, Chapman's remarks in the context of modern journalism were innocuous enough. The worst that one could say was that he showed a conceit entirely out of character. *Wisden*, with hindsight, believed that a place might have been found for both men: even if one might cavil at Chapman's tactics, no-one could dispute 'his inspiring influence in the field'. Fender was one of Wyatt's defenders and saw him as the better strategist. Letter-writers had fired off salvos, a fair proportion of abusive ones directed at Wyatt himself. Only when he went out to bat, with England 197 for 5, to face Grimmett for the first time in his life, did the cheers of the crowd assure him of support where it mattered. Ronald Mason was there: 'As Wyatt reached the wicket at the Vauxhall end, great banks of sound came volleying from the far side, volleying inexorably, answering and counter-answering the rise and fall of the volumes of sound'. Hugh Pickles was also there: a reluctant small boy taken by his father but, like St Paul on the road to Damascus, converted on the spot.★

Wyatt and Sutcliffe put on 170 runs and England's total

★ No greater cricket fanatic has existed than Canon Pickles, to whom Wyatt sent a telegram in August 1980 on the fiftieth anniversary of his 'conversion'. In 1988 the Canon, in his eighth decade, playing for the Oxford Clergy, performed a hat-trick.

reached 405. The innings bore strong comparison with that at Lord's and so did the Australian reply. Ponsford and Woodfull again got a century and a half-century respectively and Bradman again made a double century: 695 was near enough 700. Peebles took six wickets (not Bradman's) for 204. Australia's innings offered a pastiche which would remain sadly unique. Bradman and Jackson, in making 73, shared a partnership of over 200 and Jackson played his only innings of double figures in Test cricket in England. Already plagued by terminal ill-health, his batting was – the critics agreed – far below his worth.

England batted again and, in the closing minutes of a dark evening, Hobbs went out to bat with Sutcliffe. The Australians gave him three hearty cheers on what would be his last appearance against them and 20,000 Ovalites took their cue. He made nine runs before playing on and everyone knew that just as Bradman had begun one great chapter in cricket history another had now ended.

Next day it rained but Peebles did not spend it in vain. His hostess, Mrs (Plum) Warner, took him to Lord's where MCC's match with Wales was similarly rained off. She introduced him to Sydney Barnes who talked cricket to him in the pavilion. There was an unfortunate sequel: some reporter saw them together and conjured up an article for the *Daily Mail* on 'How I would bowl Bradman' by Barnes. Apologies were necessary all round. England were beaten by an innings and Australia had regained the Ashes. The Queensland left-arm bowler, Percy Hornibrook, had his brief hour of glory, taking 7 for 92. The Australians, and Hammond, caught the evening train from Paddington to Bristol for a match which would have its own special excitement (see Chapter 5, pages 152–3).

In bidding farewell to the 1930 Australians, the editor of *Wisden*, C. Stewart Caine, asked whether 'the ever-growing interchange of visits between England cricketers and those of the different Dominions' was good for the game. He meant, of course, the English county game. With considerable foresight he recognised that one day the other countries from 'those far-away lands' would provide as much excitement as the Australians and would endanger public interest in the county championship. Yet, without the counties, there would be no training-ground for England players to meet such visitors. He offered no solutions but he accepted, without qualification, that the visit of a touring side every year would be a permanent part of the England cricket scene. Caine in his day was one of the wisest of sporting journalists, a professional writer to his finger-tips, and a man to whom successive secretaries of the MCC and chairmen of selectors turned to for counsel and advice. Even that most stern and aloof of critics, Lord Harris, held his views in high esteem.

Australian success had been achieved by mammoth batting (five men averaged over 50) and by Grimmett's bowling. England's batting had been below expectations, especially that of Hammond but, in the end, the deciding factor had to be the performance of Bradman who made 974 runs in the Tests besides averaging 98.66 on the tour. He had defied all those who hinted that he might fare less well on English wickets. 'Even with four dictionaries at our elbows he leaves us gasping,' wrote one journalist almost with a sense of relief that his labours were over. At the end of the tour Bradman wrote a book to which Warner gave an introduction. As a contemporary judgment by a discerning observer, it has its own value in the hagiology on Bradman:

What were the secrets of his triumphal march through England? First, immense natural skill. Secondly, an idealism which urged him to learn everything he possibly could, and to profit by the lessons learnt. Thirdly, tremendous concentration of mind. Fourthly, physical strength. Fifthly, extreme fitness; and lastly, a cool, calm temperament. As to the actual technique of his play, he was blessed with a wonderful eye, steel-like wrists, and small and beautifully neat feet, which a Genée or a Pavlova might have envied, and which made him quite exceptionally quick in moving back or forward to the ball, every stroke fully developed, except, possibly, the straight drive, and, above all, an amazingly strong defence – which, as he says in his chapter on batting, is the keynote of all successful batsmanship in first-class cricket. His hooking of anything the least short was masterful to a degree; he missed nothing on his pads;

he off-drove brilliantly; but, above all, the cut, both late and square, was his chief glory. I have seldom seen finer or safer cutting – for he was always right on top of the ball.

In Bradman's success lay the seeds of all the planning and machination which preceded the visit of the MCC to Australia in 1932–33.

Politics *in* cricket and politics *and* cricket are two entirely different perceptions. Politics *in* cricket may be said to be as old as the game itself for in any institution there will be lobbying and soliciting. What political manoeuvring there must have been among those eighteenth-century enthusiasts, the Duke of Dorset and Sir Horatio Mann, as they sought cricketing-bailiffs for their estates who would win them matches and money by their prowess.

Politics *and* cricket used to keep their respective distances and only the sabbatarianism of some of the seventeenth-century Puritans brought cricket into conflict with the state. With the twin expansion of empire and cricket began the dialogue which married the two in a relationship over-sweet in its sentimentality but nevertheless integral in the development of both. Cricket, as well as trade, followed the nineteenth-century flag.

With the events associated with the bodyline bowling controversy in 1932–33, politics *and* cricket came face to face in an encounter which replaced fantasy by reality and the images of political imperialism and of cricket would both be tarnished in the process. This is not the place to give a detailed account of a controversy about which nearly two dozen books already exist. The enquiring reader, with a little time to spare, might turn to Laurence Le Quesne's *The Bodyline Controversy*, Ronald Mason's *Ashes in the Mouth* and *Cricket and Empire* by Ric Sissons and Brian Stoddart. *Wisden* for 1934 is also an authoritative source.

Fateful to the whole sequence of events was the appointment of Jardine as captain of the MCC tour to Australia. He had been the choice of Warner, once again chairman, and his fellow-selectors and one 'widely approved', wrote E. W. Swanton. In the opinion of the survivors of the tour in the

1980s (with almost all of whom I have had conversations), there was at the time no other candidate. He was 'the ideal man when selected' was the generous observation of Wyatt, whom he had displaced. Against the comment of his old schoolmaster at Winchester, the former England player Rockley Wilson, that 'we would win the Ashes but might lose a Dominion' may be set the pragmatic comment of Fender that Jardine was 'a man cast in the toughest Australian mould, à la Armstrong if you like'. The chairman of the selectors was appointed manager and so Warner found himself in a close but undefined relationship with a captain whose policies would drive him to the depths of despair. One paragraph from the many agonising letters Warner wrote home to his wife makes the point:

Nothing can compensate me for the moral and intellectual damage which I have suffered on this tour. Seventy-five percent of the trouble is due to DRJ's personality. DRJ almost makes me hate cricket. He makes it war.

To Jardine – and, indeed, to Warner – the whole business of beating Australia would stand or fall on the ability to contain Bradman. Warner himself had written in the *Morning Post* 'one trembles to think what lies in store for bowlers during the next fifteen to twenty years' and (more pertinently) 'England must evolve a new type of bowler and develop fresh ideas, strategy and tactics to curb his almost uncanny skill'. The MCC side contained, as its principal bowlers, Larwood, Voce, Bowes and Allen. By land and sea, Jardine laid his plans as to how the tactic of leg-theory might be exploited to its maximum advantage and discussions in a London hotel and on board ship established, in his mind, that Larwood and Voce would be the principal instruments of his policy. That something was 'in the wind', Australian journalists sensed when the MCC arrived in Australia.

Within a few weeks, an Australian XI played the MCC at Melbourne. Woodfull, the Australian captain, got hit on the head by a ball from Larwood. Its echo reverberated through the cricket world and, like the shots at Lexington in 1775, prefaced a colonial war. The picture told its own tale and the reporters told theirs. Londoners read in the *Evening Standard* of 'supercharged fast bowling' and in the *Star* of 'very dangerous stuff'; the one remark written by Bruce Harris who (then) did not know a great deal about cricket, the other by Hobbs who had faced Bowes just a few months earlier. If Jardine were setting out to soften up the Australians, he was succeeding. Before rain stopped play, Larwood had dismissed Woodfull and Bradman for a baker's dozen between them. What made it all so effective was Larwood's speed and accuracy and the need for the batsman to protect his body against the short-pitched ball. In so doing, the chances were high that he would be caught by the ring of close leg-side fielders.

By the eve of the first Test, Warwick Armstrong was using the word 'unsportsmanlike' in a cable to the London *Evening News*. The Test itself, at Sydney, passed off without incident despite a huge England victory. Sutcliffe, Hammond and the Nawab of Pataudi made centuries while McCabe's 187 not out for Australia was, said *Wisden*, an innings 'for daring and brilliance' not approached by another Australian throughout the series. By his use of the hook stroke he showed that bodyline bowling could be countered. England won by ten wickets but, with Bradman unfit to play, the Australian public was confident all would be well when he returned.

Not only illness had made Bradman's future appearances a matter for speculation. He had been at the centre of a controversy over whether he would be reporting the series for the press rather than playing in it. There had been a distinct possibility that all Jardine's plans would have been laid in vain – bodyline was for Bradman. As the London paper, the *People*, wrote: 'It now appears that the bogey man has been laid with never a ball bowled.'

To the relief of the Australian public Bradman was released from his contract to write. He had, as his biographer Irving Rosenwater observed, 'maintained a dignity and – as important – a loyalty to his contract that might, in different circumstances, easily have seen him stand down as a Test cricketer in 1932–33'.

It was in this atmosphere of high drama that some 63,000 Australians watched Bradman go out to bat in the second

Test at Melbourne. They gave him a reception – before he had faced a ball – eclipsing anything he had experienced in his brief career so far. Bradman took his guard, Jardine glanced at his field and Bowes ran up to the wicket. No 'golden duck' was ever made in such dramatic circumstances: Bradman dragged the ball on to his stumps as the crescendo of noise gave way to an eerie silence. 'Bradman, b Bowes o' heralded the cricketing world's press on the last day of 1932 and Movietone News captured the picture for posterity. Bradman's date with destiny awaited the second innings and the making of a century in which he threw down the gauntlet to Larwood and Voce. 1932 went out with a whimper: 1933 came in with a bang. Australia won the match comfortably enough but only Bradman had mastered the tactics of bodyline.

Back in England, rumours of Australian unrest at Jardine's tactics seemed to have little substance. William Findlay, the secretary of the MCC, wrote to Warner that it 'was difficult to discover here to what extent this leg-theory' was being used. It was an understandable view, for Findlay only got the occasional airmail-letter from Warner or Jardine and one finds it odd that neither used the telephone. The English press carried little beyond the guarded Reuter's reports and the usually bland comments from Hobbs in the *Star* and Bruce Harris in the *Daily Telegraph*. Things were different in Australia and Warner's Christmas was spoilt by attacks on him in the Sydney *Referee* which discovered that he had found leg-theory 'abhorrent in English county cricket' in the previous English summer, yet was seen to be doing nothing to stop it in Australia. The Melbourne *Truth* joined in with an onslaught on 'the hypocritical humbug of Captain Jardine and the guileless evasions of manager, Plum Warner' and in this taut atmosphere the two teams assembled at Adelaide for the third Test.

Soon after three o'clock on Saturday afternoon, 14 January 1933, after England had been dismissed for 341 (they had been 30 for 4), Larwood bowled the second over to Woodfull to an orthodox field and Woodfull staggered away from the wicket, hit this time on the heart. One over later, with a packed leg-side field, Larwood knocked Woodfull's bat out of his hand. Before the close of play, Bradman and McCabe had both been dismissed by Larwood, Woodfull had gone to Allen and the Australians had scored 109 for 4.

Such is the tale in barest detail. It says nothing of the antagonism of the crowd or of their booing and shouting. It does not convey the picture of the magisterial Jardine in his Harlequin cap and silk scarf coolly and determinedly placing his ring of leg-side fielders for Voce and Larwood. It ignores the genuine concern of English fielders, whom only a fence preserved from an invading crowd. It stands aside from umpires and fielders contemplating who could grab a defending stump quickest. It forgets the wretched Warner watching helplessly from the pavilion.

The denouement of the day's events has often been told. Warner walked the few steps from the English dressing-room to the Australian one. Little has changed there in the fifty years since: the masseur's bed stands in one corner of a room cluttered with the impedimenta of the cricketer's trade. Warner hesitated, knocked at the door and heard someone shout, 'Come in'. The place was full of young men, angry and upset at the chain of events. The frail figure in his panama hat and light suit cast a nervous glance around until he saw Woodfull. Various versions of the conversation exist. In essence, Woodfull said, 'I don't want to speak to you, Mr Warner. There are two teams out there; one is playing cricket the other is not. It is too great a game to spoil. The matter is in your hands'. Warner left to return to the English dressing-room, shaken, in tears and terribly upset. It was an image remembered by all who saw it. The shots at Lexington had given way to the battle of Saratoga.

On the Monday play was resumed and, late in the day, Oldfield was hit by a ball from Larwood. The batsman's personal exoneration of the bowler and the smile with which he walked off the field (so reported Hobbs) did nothing to heal Australia's wounds which had had a weekend in which to fester. By Thursday England had won the match by 338 runs. Larwood had taken 7 for 126 and Allen, who always refused to bowl leg-theory, 8 for 121. Before the match was over, the Australian Board of Control had dispatched a cable to the MCC containing the word 'unsportsmanlike'.

THE "LEAGUE THEORY."

MR. PUNCH. "COME ALONG, LET'S REFER THIS LITTLE SQUABBLE TO GENEVA."

There were three weeks before the fourth Test and during
that time there was immense activity off the field. The Australian Board of Control and the MCC exchanged cables while
the English press took up a standpoint almost universally
defending Jardine and attacking the Australians. *The Times*
saw such things as a 'craving for sensational news stories'

and, on the day on which Hitler reached 'the summit of his ambitions' by becoming Chancellor of the Third Reich, it urged Jardine to achieve his own ambition by winning the Ashes with 'such methods, allowed by the laws of cricket, as he considers most likely to win the game'. Cardus, alone of responsible English writers at home, expressed a contrary view in the *Manchester Guardian*: 'If this is how Tests are played, we would be better off without them'.

The stumbling-point in the exchange between the ABC and the MCC was the word 'unsportsmanlike'. Unless that word was withdrawn, the possibilities of playing the remaining Test matches seemed remote. To the debate by cable and press was joined that of the politicians. There is a great deal which may be said on this but two points may briefly be made: the Dominions Secretary in the British Cabinet, J. H. Thomas, would later declare that nothing gave him as much trouble while in office as the bodyline bowling affair; the Australian prime minister, Joseph Lyons, feared for the future of a £17 million conversion loan on the London Stock Exchange if English public opinion remained hostile to Australia. Nor, indeed, was the Australian Federal Government very secure – an uneasy coalition created by the effect of the world Depression which had hit Australia badly. It would, therefore, be hard political and economic facts as well as dialogue between cricket administrators which eased the immediate crisis and allowed the fourth Test in Brisbane to take place.

At the end of the first day's play Australia had scored 251 for 3, Bradman was 71 not out and Larwood had not taken a wicket. There was nothing different in Jardine's approach though the illness of Voce meant that leg-theory could only operate from one end. At the other end, Verity's slow bowling had confined batsmen to barely more than a run an over. To Australia's first innings total of 340, England had replied with 216 for 6 when Paynter was brought from his hospital bed with a temperature of over 100°F. Not out 24 overnight – and back in hospital – he returned in the morning to bat for a further three hours and finish with 83. His had 'certainly been one of the greatest examples of pluck and fortitude in the history of Test cricket', wrote Sydney Southerton, a verdict which no later critics would dispute. 'What about those fellows who marched to Kandahar with fever?' Jardine had replied when Warner doubted the wisdom of smuggling him out of hospital. Paynter's innings ensured England's marginal lead on the first innings. They then bowled out Australia – an unbalanced side with a long tail – for 175 and successfully pursued the 162 they needed.

The Ashes were won and some attempt was made to bury the hatchet. The press of both countries praised Jardine's leadership. The Brisbane *Mail* probably came nearest to a sound appraisal when it said 'whether the body theory is right or wrong one must admire Jardine as a skilled tactician and an exceptionally clear thinker about the game. He can have very few equals among England's captains.' *The Times* wrote, 'The biggest factor in England's success has been the captaincy of Jardine. He has beaten the Australians at their own game.' The sourest note again came from Cardus in the *Manchester Guardian*. Quoting Dr Johnson, he wrote of Jardine's philosophy of cricket, 'Knock the man down first and be compassionate afterwards'.

On the day England won the Ashes, Archie Jackon died in Brisbane. As recently as three weeks earlier he had made 77 in a grade match. Warner had visited him during the Test and he was asked to preach at the memorial service in Sydney, an invitation (he told his wife) 'which showed clearly that amidst all the trouble there was still some good feeling remaining'.

England won the fifth Test at Sydney by eight wickets. It was a match broadly free from incident although Bradman was hit for the first time by Larwood and Jardine himself was hit by 'Bull' Alexander, Australia's new fast bowler. The crowd cheered at this but they also cheered when Larwood, sent in as night-watchman, scored 98. Their applause, and their genuine regret at his not getting a century, emphasised the Australian attitude throughout the summer: Jardine, as the instigator of policy, was the target for attack; Larwood was only the paid professional instrument of that policy. Larwood later limped off the field with an injured heel, and out of Test cricket.

At a dinner given in Sydney by the New South Wales Government, the state premier declared that 'our visitors played cricket in the best tradition of the British people' and he expressed his 'appreciation of the sportsmanlike manner' in which they had played the game. Warner hoped that the 'little ruffles on the surface would be forgotten'. The jinx word 'sportsmanlike' or its kindred noun was being pushed to the front by all the speakers, almost implying that the more frequently it was said, the more it was wholly believable. The fact remains that the MCC left Australia's shores without a single member of the Australian team seeing them off and, in the analogous terms of colonial conflict, treaty terms would have to be worked out before the two countries met again. The speeches at Sydney had been no more than polite diplomatic exchanges.

There is a danger, amidst all the vortex of politics, of forgetting what the cricketers achieved. Larwood's 33 wickets cost him 19.51 each while the emergence of Bill O'Reilly, with 27 wickets for 26.81, heralded Grimmett's successor. The England fast bowlers took 71 out of the 99 wickets which fell: unusual for the times though it would be commonplace in today's cricket. Hammond scored exactly the same number of runs as Sutcliffe (440) while Bradman, with an average cut down to 56.57 still eclipsed all other Australians. The Australian batting figures as a whole showed the effectiveness of the England bowling. Hobbs told his readers in *The Star*: 'Larwood was the dominating figure of the tour because he made Bradman change his game. Larwood set the pace and Don followed it'. Yet Hobbs had also written that Bradman hit freely 'where others would just defend'. He alone of the Australians achieved any sort of mastery over the bodyline attack, something which his biographer, Irving Rosenwater, has demonstrated by an analysis of his runs in relation to the bowling of Larwood and Voce. In the opinion of Warwick Armstrong, 'Larwood conquered' and there is a sense in which Bradman himself might have agreed for he unswervingly held the view that the continuation of bodyline would have killed cricket.

The MCC departed for a fortnight in New Zealand, a mission of goodwill strangely resented by the Australian Board of Control who had consistently cold-shouldered the development of the game in the neighbouring Dominion. In fourteen months the Board would be sending

another Australian side to England and the long-term implications of the bodyline controversy needed to be hammered
out. Jardine had evolved a tactic which aroused unprecedented
bitterness compounded by its evident success and by its
physical threat to life and limb. The efficient and undeviat-
ing way in which he enforced his policy against the varying
voices of downright opposition, doubt and misgiving bred
hatred for the man and his device and fear for cricket and
its future.

During the summer of 1933, the University match between
Oxford and Cambridge and the second Test between England
and the West Indies, through the bowling of Farnes, and of
Manny Martindale and Constantine, gave the MCC Committee and the public at large a chance to realise the implications
of bodyline bowling and to relate that realisation to the
possibility that the Australians might not come in 1934. There
was much activity behind the scenes. Again, one must be
brief and the detail can be found elsewhere. The Australian
Board of Control sought changes in the (then) Law 48 governing the fairness of the bowler's delivery, and their representative in London, Dr Robert MacDonald, was able to achieve
assurances from an MCC special sub-committee sufficient
to satisfy his Board. At the Imperial Cricket Conference a
resolution was passed affirming that any form of bowling
which was 'obviously a direct attack by the bowler upon the
batsman would be an offence against the spirit of the game'
and Law 43, the law governing the powers of umpires, carried
an additional instruction on the definition of fair and unfair
play. Immediately after the West Indies Test, Warner, as we
saw in Chapter 4, broke his silence with a letter to the *Daily
Telegraph* which declared his opposition 'to this bowling
which has caused so much controversy' and he served on an
MCC sub-committee which drafted the recommendations to
umpires. All these decisions together with the introduction
of the new lbw(N) law in 1935,* may be said, in technical

---

* This law, experimental for two years, was confirmed at a meeting of
MCC in 1937 as Law 24. The batsman, by being out of a ball which pitched
outside the line of the off stump (as well as between wicket and wicket),
was denied the luxury of pursuing a negative policy of pad-play. The
bowler, for his part, was given the incentive to attack the off stump.

terms, to have ended the saga of the bodyline bowling crisis. Yet, in some ways, it was not so much an end as a beginning, for it heralded the dawn of a new world in which politics and cricket would become inextricably associated, in which the imperial bonds unifying cricket would become weaker and in which the role of the MCC would be ultimately diminished.

In the short-term, the scene was set fair – or reasonably so – for the 1934 Australians to come. Jardine had indicated in a cable from India to the London *Evening Standard* that he had 'neither the intention nor the desire to play against Australia' and a potential area of embarrassment was removed. The Australians arrived, and Jardine's place was in the history books in which he would occupy some formidable pages: the MCC's job was to resume a dialogue with the Australians and re-build bridges.

The series between England and Australia in 1934 may be looked at on two levels. There was the cricket itself, entertaining rather than enthralling, with grand displays of individual achievement rather than tense battles for mastery. And there were the distant rumbles of bodyline, gradually fading but not without an occasional sharp tremor during the summer. Significant figures on the English scene were discreetly absent: Warner had declined the invitation to be chairman of the selectors and confined his activities to what he wrote in *The Cricketer* and the *Morning Post*; Jardine was in the press-box instead of on the field; Larwood and Voce did not appear in a single Test though Voce's performance when playing for Nottinghamshire against the Australians caused bad feeling. He took 8 for 66 largely through a short-pitched attack and a leg-side trap and his absence through injury later in the match was widely felt to be a diplomatic reaction to an Australian protest.

Officialdom made every effort to welcome these 1934 Australians who confessed to some doubts as to how they would be received. The press and the film companies created wide public interest but in doing so began, as the editor of *Wisden* wrote, to lose 'all sense of proportion'. How players acquitted themselves mattered less than 'tittle-tattle of a mischievous character' so that the possibility of friction was never far from the surface. In the editor's opinion, it might have been better if the Australians had postponed their visit 'until the echoes of the cable fencing between the MCC and the Australian Board of Control had died away'.

Thus, without the leadership of Jardine or the bowling of Larwood and Voce, England, captained by Wyatt, took on an Australian side, again led by Woodfull, which would employ the spin bowling of O'Reilly and Grimmett as its main device. Together with the googly bowling of Leslie Fleetwood-Smith who did not play in any Test, these three accounted for sixty-seven per cent of the wickets taken on the tour.

The Australians' opening match against Worcestershire was almost a carbon copy of that in 1930 – a Bradman double-century, a fistful of wickets for Grimmett, and an innings victory. Grimmett took 50 wickets in May as he had done in 1930 but Bradman had, by his own standards, a less successful month. Other Australians made the runs which brought successive victories. However, at Lord's on a Saturday evening at the end of May Bradman played an innings superlative by any standards. Middlesex had batted until five o'clock with a century from Hendren. Woodfull and Ponsford were both lbw to Smith for 0 and Bradman came in at a quarter past five. Just after six o'clock he reached his half-century and by close of play at half past six, off the last ball of the day, he had scored a century. For sheer spectator-value, linked to the clock, it was an incomparable performance. With a double century by McCabe against Surrey in the next match, the Australians were ready for Trent Bridge and the first Test. There they fielded far better, batted in depth, depended on their slower bowlers and won by 238 runs. O'Reilly and Grimmett took nineteen of the England wickets between them while Farnes, the only really fast bowler in the England side, took ten Australian wickets. It was the match in which Arthur Chipperfield went into lunch on 99 and departed three balls afterwards on the same score. Cardus commiserated in the *Manchester Guardian*: 'Several batsmen have got a century in their first Test: how few, if any, have got 99'. Chipperfield's achievement was, indeed, unique but Cardus might have relished the quixotic fact that this proved to be the only Test between England and Australia between 1928 and 1939 which Australia won without the assistance of a century from Bradman.

The weather, as every cricket-lover knows, can dampen our spirits, ruin a long-awaited occasion and put to waste a day's budgeting. Yet, without its capricious nature, cricket would lose something of its charm and mystique. The second Test at Lord's in 1934 began under cloudless skies and for two days seemed destined for a rather undistinguished draw. By Saturday evening, England had made 440 and Australia 192 for 2. Then came a Sunday of rain followed by a Monday in which Verity reduced the Australian batting to something paltry and pathetic. First he ensured that they would have to follow-on despite a brave and undefeated resistance by Chipperfield whose 37, thought Cardus, was worth many a century. In the afternoon, in 22 overs and three hours, Verity put batsman after batsman out of his misery and left England victorious by an innings and 38 runs. Flight and length, a resilient turf, some bounce and the marriage of wile and guile spun the Australians to defeat in conditions which found them without experience or assurance. That victory was the first over Australia at Lord's since 1896. With perhaps three contests between the two countries at Lord's remaining before the year 2000, it has a fair chance of being the only English defeat of Australia at Lord's in the twentieth century.

Verity, in a day, took fourteen wickets and, in the match, 15 for 104, excelling the achievements of his fellow Yorkshireman, Rhodes, at Melbourne in 1904 who was present. So was the writer, Robert Lynd, who watched Verity's bowling, meditative and cunning, spinning batsman after batsman to destitution, not least Bradman:

> The ball shot high above his head and was lost for a time in the ether. The danger was that so many Englishmen were waiting for it. Wisely all but Ames stepped aside and Bradman was gone to a shout of joy that must have reached Australia.

All-square, the sides met at Old Trafford for the third Test instead of the fourth in the hope – declared the Lancashire authorities – that the sun would shine. It proved to be one of the hottest Test matches ever played in England with a Mancunian heat almost unbelievable and made even worse for the Australians because of a throat infection. So ravaging was this that diphtheria was suspected – scourge of pre-antibiotic days – and two of the team were dispatched to an isolation hospital after the match, the unlucky Chipperfield and the unfulfilled Kippax. The England public would never see the best of either of these players.

England amassed 627 runs, those that Hammond no longer seemed to be making being supplied by Hendren, Leyland and Ames. Hammond was a man with a sore throat, lumbago and an uncomfortable appendix. As was his sphinx-like manner, he kept his pains to himself, dismissed Ponsford, McCabe and Bradman and took catches that deserved to be preserved in the British Museum – so quipped the press which stood by him in his repeated batting failures in the series. He was worth a place, they all said, for everything else he did. A spectator at Old Trafford described fifty years later a piece of fielding which stuck in his memory:

This apparently half-asleep fielder instantly came to life and as the batsman went for a single, he spun round in a flash and raced after the ball, caught up with it, picked it up with his right hand and still running away from the wicket and without even appearing to look back and with an uncanny sense of direction, flung the ball back under his left arm straight into the hands of the wicket-keeper just above the bails and there was a run out.

To England's 627, to which Verity contributed an unde-feated 60, Australia replied with 491 and the brief second innings of each team (with an England declaration) were played out in that strange anti-climax which can come upon a great occasion – empty seats, pointless endeavour and the chance of opening batsmen (three of them) to strengthen their averages with not-out innings. From a match which faded to a draw, one image might be recalled: O'Reilly bowling one of the famous overs in Test match history sent back Sutcliffe, Wyatt and Hammond in four balls. Of the eleven England batsmen who came to the wicket in some seven hours, five appeared in as many minutes. At cricket's lower levels, the situation would have created a scramble for pads and gloves. And for the cartoonist to portray, there was an over from Allen with three wides and four no-balls. Cricket is joy or tribulation depending upon whom you are in the moment of elation or despair.

At this stage of the series the combined batting average of Bradman and Hammond was exactly 20. Neither man was in the best of health. Bradman had been unwell throughout the summer (and before) and one journalist described him as 'the wraith of the greatness we once knew'. The two greatest cricketers of their generation were striving to succeed in the face of an inquisitive, concerned and wholly sympathetic public. Bradman, but not Hammond, would put things right with over 300 runs at both Leeds and The Oval.

After England had made exactly 200 in the fourth Test at Headingley in as bad a display as you could see (thought *Wisden*), Bowes redeemed things somewhat by taking three wickets in ten balls and Australia were 39 for 3 at the close of the first day. The buzz of conversation in the morning was the news of Yorkshire's defeat by Warwickshire (see Chapter 5, page 149). Even when the day's play ended with Australia 450 runs further on for the loss of only one more wicket, Yorkshire's tragedy was the talk of the terraces until the evening newsvendors cried 'Yorks dismiss Kent' and pride was restored – even more so on the third day, when Bowes and Verity took all the Australian wickets with eminently respectable analyses in a total of 584.

The runs had virtually all come from Ponsford and Bradman (no-one else made 30). Bradman repeated the triple century he made on the same ground four years earlier. This time Hutton was not there to watch; instead, he was marshalling his forces for the debut century he would himself make in first-class cricket a day or two after the Test was over. Ponsford, with 181, was scarcely overshadowed and the two Australians set up a fourth-wicket record of 388 which has yet (1989) to be eclipsed by either country. Rain had the last word and once again the result of the Ashes depended on what happened at The Oval.

Throughout the summer the England selectors had seemed uncertain whom to select and this time the inclusion of Woolley, at the age of forty-seven, and Peebles, playing infrequently, in the squad of thirteen caused surprise. Woolley played, and had to keep wicket for the injured Ames in the second innings. Peebles was taking part in a cricket week at Kinnaird Castle in Scotland and received his telegram at breakfast after a Highland Ball. What he thought was a hoax was genuine enough, but an injury on the field just a few hours later put him out of the running. Instead, he went south to watch Bradman and Ponsford score at eighty runs per hour and put on 451 for the second Australian wicket, still a record to survive (1989) against all Test countries. Bradman's innings was chanceless. Fender thought him totally in control. There had been a seriousness of purpose which his innings in the first three Tests had belied.

England, for the first time, had three fast bowlers in the side and Clark, on a pitch which gave bowlers no help, bowled leg-theory with a packed leg-side field but, as *Wisden* recorded, 'it scarcely came under the category of what is known as "body-line"' (see plate 12). Cardus, the first journalist in England in 1932–33 to show real concern at what was happening in Australia, found no fault with Clark's approach: 'A wicket that has been tamed to quiescence gives the fast bowler the right to use his strength to get the ball higher than the middle of the bat.' Cardus thought the Australians would get 700, and so it proved. England, despite being nearly 400 behind on the first innings, were not required to follow-on and were eventually set a target of 708 runs to win. Set such astronomical scores there is little, cricket history shows, that a side can do. England crumbled for 145 and a series which the Australians had not really expected to win went their way.

The editor of *Wisden* felt that England were, in the end, a dispirited band at The Oval and remarked that scarcely a man, apart from the wicket-keeper, knew where he had to go in the field. The press attacked Wyatt's captaincy – he was never a man to court their favour – but the selectors stuck by him and invited him to lead the side in the West Indies in the winter. The word 'disagreeable' as an epithet on the series can be found frequently in correspondence and in the literature. It was 'short-hand' for saying that the bogey of 1932–33 had not yet been laid.

Peebles had his chance, after all, to play against the Australians when they were lured to Forres in his own northern fastnesses and he took 5 for 84. From Folkestone to Forres, via Scarborough, was a tidy journey, even for Australians

Small Autograph-Hunter. "HAVE YOU GOT BRADMAN?"
Smaller Autograph-Hunter. "NO, BUT I'VE GOT THE SIGNATURE OF A CHAP THAT HAS."

used to distances, and the party was weary and ready for home, having each earned £600 for their efforts. They went without Bradman on whom an emergency operation for an appendicitis was performed in late September and whose life, for a short time, hung in the balance. Public concern throughout the cricket-playing world over Bradman's health was acute. King George V was kept informed and the formalities were rushed through to enable his wife to catch a P. & O. liner to England. By December he was able to go home, starting his journey at Victoria Station. By chance Winston Churchill was there and the two had a brief conversation.

England and Australia, in the 1936–37 series, were under new leaders. Wyatt had been succeeded by Allen; two excellent men both of whom had considerable claims to the captaincy. On Wyatt's side it could be argued that he had had more experience as captain at both international and county levels, that he had played with more regularity and that he had been both a captain and vice-captain on overseas tours. On Allen's side it might be said that the MCC tour was intended to bury the bodyline hatchet once and for all. Wyatt had been (indeed still was) close to Jardine and had been his vice-captain, though he had scarcely been consulted, in 1932–33. Allen had not only demonstrably shown to Australians his lack of sympathy for Jardine's policies but he had, with his Australian family connections, been the one member of the MCC party who had remained popular in that country. Finally, it was openly accepted that Allen was very much a protégé of Warner, now once again chairman of the selectors and a man whose instinct it usually was to prefer leaders from the Oxbridge, south-of-England mould in which Wyatt had not been cast.

Woodfull had been succeeded at first in the Australian captaincy by Victor Richardson who led his country in South Africa in 1935–36. Bradman, unavailable for that tour, captained South Australia to success in the Sheffield Shield and leadership in no way inhibited his batting. Twelve months later he filled a State vacancy on the national panel of selectors and the Board of Control offered him the captaincy against

England. It was an appointment that he would hold until he retired. Nothing could have been more contrasting than the relationship between the England and Australian captains in 1932–33 and in 1936–37. Allen and Bradman would play squash and golf together and enjoy each other's company over a meal: a friendship still retained through correspondence fifty years later by the two cricketing knights and octogenarians. Allen's friendliness led him to create a happy team in which, as Ames recalled, Christian names were acceptable among everyone, while Allen himself was called 'Skipper'. As E. W. Swanton has pointed out, the need for a team which blended well on tour was even more important now that cricket reporters were accompanying the MCC in sizeable numbers for the first time, some of them more ready than others 'to peddle in gossip and controversy'. 'We were all four years too late,' observed William Pollock of the *Daily Express*, who took his wife and little daughter with him. C. B. Fry was paying his first visit to Australia and he would encounter that stubborn democrat streak which forbade even an ex-England captain from entering the pavilion at Brisbane because he was not a member. One reporter left at home to comment for his paper was Jardine whom the *Evening Standard* continued to employ. It seemed likely that influence at the highest political level was brought to bear to stop Jardine visiting Australia as a journalist.

Jardine may not have gone to Australia, but Voce did so after making a statement of apology to the Australians for past attitudes. Allen has left it on record that the question of selecting Larwood on grounds of ability was never an issue. In all, eight men who had toured four years earlier went again. It was a party probably not quite strong enough for the task in hand and weakened by a besetting frequency of injuries. As ever, runs from Hammond were vital and would have to be seen in relation to those which Bradman might make. Voce would prove the outstanding bowler, well supported by Farnes.

England came to the Brisbane Test with an indifferent record against the States and decried by the Australian press principally because of repeated batting failures. Three wickets fell for 20 and Hammond was out first ball – 'Nothing in pre-war years was as daunting to an England side as a Hammond failure,' recalled the writer Denzil Batchelor who was present. England seemed destined for defeat until Leyland made a century and Allen a vital 35, leading to a total of 358. England led by over a hundred after Voce, with 6 for 41, ran through Australia's batting. Allen played an even stronger role in the second innings and his 68 helped to set Australia a target of 381. A night of rain followed and in the morning Batchelor flew over the ground. It was difficult to realise, he reflected, that the 'deserted spot at the fag end of a suburban street, looking like a dirty khaki handkerchief, would become the focal point of an Empire's interest'. Difficult, but true, as Australia was routed for 58, Allen taking 5 for 36, and the press coverage in England and Australia almost rivalling the crisis created by Edward VIII's abdication in the same week. The Australian prime minister, Joseph Lyons, busy sending cables of support to Stanley Baldwin, found time to send a telegram of congratulation to Allen as well. For Lyons, prime minister since 1931, it had been a pleasanter relationship with cricket than that of 1932–33. William Pollock was sharing a compartment with Woodfull on the train journey south. Looking up from his Baroness Orczy novel, Woodfull remarked: 'You can't expect to bat on a bed of roses every time'.

Hammond came into his own at Sydney, as he so often did, and made a double century. The crowd, less vociferous than in earlier years, reserved their taunts for their own bowlers. Then it rained and Allen declared at 426 for 6 and bowled out the Australians for 80. As at Brisbane, there were three successive noughts on the score-sheet, one of which was again Bradman's. On a wicket which had dried out and rolled well, Allen had the courage to ask the Australians to follow-on and his decision was justified. Australia were dismissed for 324, Hammond taking 3 for 29, and England won by an innings and 22 runs. The best batting came from McCabe who gave more than a hint that the English bowling could be mastered. Allen accepted victory magnanimously and noted the element of luck in the weather; nevertheless, it was two-up at Christmas. Luck may have played its part, thought Robins the vice-captain, but he wrote home saying that the Australians had 'been gutless'. For the moment, Bradman had failed as captain and as batsman. What he would do about it as captain remained to be seen; experience had shown that a batting failure boded ill for someone sooner or later.

Melbourne Cricket Ground, on the first day of 1937, saw that great arena, intimidating and without beauty, packed with nearly 80,000 people. On a lifeless wicket, six Australian wickets fell for 130 before rain came. At lunch on the second day, with a mere 200 on the board, Bradman declared and sent England in to face the wickedness of a Melbourne sticky wicket. Hammond got 32 – one of his best innings ever, he would declare – and Allen declared at 76 for 9. Should he not have done so earlier? asked the press. Everything hung on the weather and, as Allen has said, 'I got the decision wrong because I assessed it incorrectly'. Bradman sent in his tail-enders first – 9, 10, Jack became 1, 2, 3 – and he and Fingleton eventually came together to set up a sixth-wicket record partnership of 346 when the hazards of the pitch had diminished. Bradman's score of 270 and the substantial victory by 365 runs ensured that he would retain the captaincy – for the vultures had been closing in and unflattering comparisons were being made between him and Allen. Luckily for Australian cricket, Bradman 'came good' at the right time and he would be a tactician superior to all of the England captains he would later meet.

England, in defeat, were still being rated the better side, as Hobbs told his readers in the *Star*, though Allen himself privately thought otherwise. Hobbs' own name invites a vital comparison with previous England XIs in these years: for the opening partnership of him and Sutcliffe had never been replaced by one of any substance and the fourth Test at Adelaide saw Barnett opening with Verity. That they did better than any other pair in the series only served to highlight England's problem. Indeed, Verity the batsman, Hammond the bowler and Bradman the batsman might be an oblique way to account for England's defeat. With no disparagement on the English pair, the prime role of each was to do the other's job. Verity, though treated with great respect, did not get a wicket though he took part in two sound opening

partnerships. Hammond took 7 for 87 in the match, including
the wicket of Bradman, but made only 59 runs in two innings.
Bradman made the double century which won Australia the
match – 'once more the master', wrote Cardus.

In the three weeks before the deciding Test, the captain
took a holiday – not the first MCC captain to do so on tour
and not the first to be criticised for it. At the end of February
England took the field for the fifth Test at Melbourne. The
Australian winter was fast approaching, in chronological
terms, but a temperature of 90° in the shade belied the fact.
At the end of a day in which Australia scored 342 for 3, victory
had effectively gone Australia's way. Bradman, McCabe and
C. L. 'Jack' Badcock all made centuries, while Ross Gregory
scored 80. Gregory, whom the English cricket public would
never see, came to England when war broke out and he, like
Farnes and Verity, would not survive it.

Against a total of 604, England might have made a sound
reply but a wet wicket on the fourth day reduced what slender
chance had been offered and the match was lost by an innings
and 200 runs. The Australian batsmen merited the palm of
victory as did the bowling of O'Reilly. Throughout the
1930s he bowled long and successful spells for Australia on
unresponsive pitches. Farnes took 6 for 96 and the critics rated
him the best bowler in the match. The other heroes were
Oldfield and Ames. It was not unfitting that in the last match
in which they would be opposing wicket-keepers – and
Oldfield's last Test altogether – they conceded a single bye
between them – one bye in 998 runs. What wicket-keeper
would not delight in a ratio of 1:500 in a match!

Bradman, as captain, had come from behind to win the
series and, as batsman, he had played with discipline in the
third and fourth Tests and with freedom in the fifth. In his
three massive innings he totalled 651 runs in eighteen and a
half hours without giving a chance. The whole enterprise had
been a triumph of willpower, decision-making and technical
skill. From 17,000 miles away Jardine wrote that he had
reinstated himself 'as the bowler's biggest problem'.

It was good that the final appearance of England cricketers
in Australia before the outbreak of war should conclude on a
note of extraordinary goodwill. Pollock called it 'the peace-

making tour: everyone was as nice as pie to everyone else. The players were on leg-pulling terms and the crowds didn't barrack'. Indeed, at Melbourne they cheered Allen, not three times but six. *The Times* spoke of the good feeling he created wherever he went. Hammond, not the most expansive of men, called it 'the happiest tour' of his life and he was the last person to worry, in personal terms, that he had made half as many runs as in 1928–29. Both he and Bradman topped the batting averages of their respective countries for, curiously, the only time as a pair. Australia, rather than England, had found some good new batsmen in Badcock, Gregory and (though not yet a Test player) Lindsay Hassett, but they lacked any fast bowling to match England's. As for England, the MCC tour had come a year too early for Hutton and Compton to demonstrate their talents and in the older men such as Leyland, who made a lot of runs, lay present pleasure rather than future joy.

Though no-one could know it, this was the last Test to be played in Australia for almost ten years. Bradman alone of the Australian side would be at Brisbane in 1946–47, while Hammond and Voce were the only two Englishmen to re-emerge there. In Australian terms it was therefore the end of an era in which the demonstrable loyalty of the Australian public to cricket had never been in doubt. Almost a million people watched the 1936–37 series and the average attendance per day in a Test match played in Australia against England increased from 19,918 in the 1920–21 series to 36,481 in the 1936–37 series. The graph of attendance in these matches rose steadily over the five series involved, despite the addition of the Brisbane ground – which lowered the overall average. These years were the hey-day of Australian enthusiasm for Test cricket. Safety regulations on crowd numbers and the attraction of other leisure sports meant that figures established before 1939 would never be matched in post-war years. It is worth looking at five factors which contributed to such enthusiasm: the increase of women supporters; the interest aroused by radio; the folk-hero role played by Bradman; the phenomenon of the Australian crowd; and the special appeal of the 'Fight for the Ashes'.

The interest of women in cricket and cricketers was noted by many commentators. They could be seen shelling peas for the evening meal, following the play avidly, and extending to players on both sides a hero-worship usually attached to film stars. Good-looking men were left in no doubt that their charms were admired, some reduced by comments to acute embarrassment. Kenneth Farnes in his *Tours and Tests* noted some of these things, being struck by the enormous number of women who followed cricket with great keenness.

Cricket broadcasting in Australia had begun with occasional announcements of the score during the 1924–25 series to listeners in Sydney. Four years later each city offered a ball-by-ball commentary when it was 'host' to a Test and by the 1932–33 series a national hook-up had been achieved. In the early 1930s there was some concern among cricket administrators that commentaries kept people at home but an Australian Broadcasting Corporation survey in 1933 showed that public interest in watching had increased, especially among women. As the Australian cities grew larger between the wars and people had to travel rather than walk to cricket, listening on the radio became a convenient alternative. The firms which manufactured radios were only too ready to link the sales of their products to cricket: 'Follow the cricket with a Tasma Tiger radio, £16.16s. Easy Terms arranged' was a typical advertisement.

During the 1930s there also developed the broadcasting of synthetic commentaries on the Test matches in England. Cables were received by the ABC every few minutes and a studio team in Sydney would create a make-believe ball-by-ball description with noise effects such as pencils tapping wood to simulate ball on bat and crowd applause. Obviously these bear no relationship to a discussion on crowd-figures in Australia except in the indirect way of keeping up public interest in the absence of Test cricket at home. In 1938, when television made its first appearance for London cricket followers, short-wave broadcasting was taking cricket 'live' to Australians in the cities and in the outback. David Frith has related the story of the aboriginal, listening in this way to Hutton's innings at The Oval in 1938, and asking 'How many'd this plurry fella make if he was batting in daytime?'

Despite the 'arrival' of radio, the overall conclusion must be that it fostered rather than hindered public attendance at Test cricket.

Dr Richard Cashman, the Australian cricket historian and academic, has examined the 'Bradman factor' and established that his presence (based on Sheffield Shield figures) brought an additional crowd of ninety-one per cent. The adulation given to Bradman knew no bounds. 'If he cut himself shaving' it would be front-page news, remarked one editor. Fingleton, often a critic of Bradman, recalled the train journey across the Nullabor Plain in 1932: 'Lonely men and women of the outback travelled many miles to catch a glimpse of this cricket magician'. These folk were merely voyeurs – to see him go out to bat was an extraordinary experience, said the *Sydney Morning Herald*: 'The crowd became very nearly hysterical at the sight of him, and directly he gets off the mark, you'd think he'd given away a million pounds'. His appearance, and that of English stars such as Hobbs and Hammond, was a major factor in attendance at Test matches and, as always, it was the batsmen rather than the bowlers who made the mass appeal, not least because of the size of the Australian grounds. Few spectators could appreciate at a distance the finer points of a bowler's art but they could see more easily the consequence of a batsman's skill. O'Reilly was the bowler who came nearest to public acclaim.

In the post-1919 years the Australian cricket authorities set out to win working-class support. The informative scoreboards on the major grounds encouraged statistical interest in what was happening although Farnes thought they created more interest in results rather than the game itself. Those who flocked to rugby at the Sydney Cricket Ground or Australian Rules Football at the Melbourne one were encouraged to come there for cricket at a different time of the year, though there was little attempt, no more than on English grounds, to make watching comfortable for them. Nevertheless, the cricket was not expensive: only at Adelaide were prices substantially raised in these years. There was money around for leisure in the 1920s and the late 1930s while during the Depression spectators – somehow – found the money to attend the drama of 1932–33.

The reluctance of Australian administrators to improve facilities in the 'Outer' spectator areas made for discomfort, even danger, which bred discontent and sometimes violence. The behaviour of the Australian crowd has attracted a greater mythology than its English counterpart. All MCC sides experienced the barbed wit of barracking to a greater or lesser degree and individual players reacted in different ways, while Australian cricketers were no more immune. MCC captains such as Douglas and Gilligan made a point of getting on good terms with crowds, the task no doubt made easier because Australia was winning. Jardine, of course, was the arch-enemy to all Australians, as they were to him. A hostility bred in 1928–29 took firm root in 1932–33 and the bitterness of the bodyline tour was heightened by Jardine's disdain and, one has to add, courage in the face of the Australian public. Englishmen whom the Australians took to their hearts included Hobbs and Hendren and, to some extent, Sutcliffe. All had their own ways of playing to the gallery if need arose. By 1936–37, barracking as a phenomenon, had declined and with the death in 1942 of Yabba, the most famous Australian barracker of them all, an era of earful crowd participation had ended. When, in the 1980s, I stood on what was left of the famous Sydney 'Hill' during a one-day international it was difficult to conjure up an image of those crowds who had harried players so much in the past. Today's modern arenas catering for family entertainment – at a price – and offering highly sophisticated technology in the video matrix scoreboards are a far cry from their down to earth, functional, predecessors.

Finally, there was a psychological and emotional appeal of Australians seeing cricketers from England. In this, the Fight for the Ashes had its own special quality and the low attendance figures accorded to the West Indians and the South Africans on their respective single visits to Australia in the 1930s demonstrate this. For Australia was still essentially a land of expatriates. William Pollock, who got to know the people well, found them 'terrifying, genuine and extremely loyal'. 'They loved to win at cricket but look out for a thick ear if you say anything disparaging about "home" in other directions.' Fender wrote in 1930: 'The Fight for the Ashes is important to the lives of so many people in Australia. It is not just a spectacle but a matter of imperial consequence'. England versus Australia between the wars seemed to matter more to Australians than to Englishmen. In England it was possible to find as much support for county cricket as for a Test match, while R. H. Lyttelton offered the most extreme version of this when he declared that he would rather see England lose to Australia than Oxford to Cambridge. His death in 1940 is a small, but not totally insignificant, landmark in our understanding of these years in cricket history.

Bradman was still the pivot of the 1938 Australians in England. Wilfrid Brookes, the new editor of *Wisden*, wrote that nothing seemed to disturb his equanimity while his 'influence and brilliant performances were extremely important factors' in the team's results. With him came some of those who would take Australian cricket into the 1940s and 1950s such as Hassett and Sidney Barnes. It was a side rather too dependent on O'Reilly as a bowler and its strength was essentially in its batting. Critics deplored the omission of Grimmett and Oldfield.

England were led by Hammond who had turned amateur at the end of the previous year. The claims of business had made Allen unavailable, though Warner pressed him hard to be a candidate. Hammond was a man whom Warner had long admired and of whom he would say in a broadcast at the end of the season, 'he was an able, inspiring and sympathetic leader'. Lord Hawke, a few weeks before his death, congratulated Hammond, a significant gesture in terms of his oft-quoted views on a professional captain. It is more pleasant to reflect on the captaincy of Hammond before the war than after it. Beset with personal worries, anxious about his own performance, in frequent pain, the post-war Hammond would, in Bradman's words, lack 'the leadership and tact required of an overseas diplomat'.

The customary Bradman double-century at Worcester – and thirty-five no-balls from McCormick – began the Australian tour and by the end of May Bradman (as he had done in 1930) had completed 1000 runs, in only seven innings. The Australians came to the first Test at Trent Bridge confident they would not lose if less assured of bowling their opponents out twice. The Test marked the debuts of Hutton, Edrich, Compton, Wright and Sinfield against Australia. Sinfield would bowl Bradman and be no more seen in such august surroundings. The other four had a part to play in the closing period of pre-war Test cricket and a larger one after the war. England, it seemed, had found an opening pair in Hutton and Barnett who scored 169 before lunch on the first day. Both men made centuries, Hutton giving, said *The Times*, 'a prim and proper answer to every question the Australians set him', while Barnett played the more spectacular and free-ranging innings. Paynter made a double-century and Compton another single one and England's 658 for 8 declared was their highest score ever against Australia. Wright celebrated his debut by bowling Fingleton with his fourth ball in Test cricket before the batting of McCabe dwarfed all other performances in the match. In an innings of four hours he made 232 and played one of the great innings of all time in Test cricket, causing Bradman to bring his players on the balcony to watch batting of a power and calibre, he declared, they might never see again. Nevertheless, Australia had to follow-on and centuries by Bill Brown and Bradman saved the day. In the end the match rather lost its point and dwindled to a draw.

The second Test at Lord's was played during a brief period of beguiling calm in the troubled European political scene. The newspapers carried pictures of the British and Italian fleets lying together in Valletta harbour, Malta. One caption read, 'Peace and strength blend in harmony: the friendliness of two great nations'. On the Saturday the largest crowd ever to come to Lord's led the authorities to reduce the playing area slightly so that spectators might sit on the ground and Hammond chose the occasion to score 240 in an innings which, said *The Times*, 'can seldom have been surpassed'. It was his finest hour. Never again in the atmosphere of stern, competitive cricket would he exercise such an unrelenting dominance and display such captivating elegance. His innings eclipsed all else in the match – Paynter's 99, Brown's double-century and yet another century by Bradman. For those who saw it, there was an image to take away and savour; a moment of happiness to recapture as world events took their course; a distant recollection to be won back from the depths of memory in the post-war years. Cardus caught the mood as well as anyone: 'More handsome cricket could not be imagined. He drove almost nonchalantly; the wrists were supple as a fencer's steel'.

Both sides had made over 400 in the first innings and this, with some loss of time through rain, led to a draw. The Test was portrayed by the Royal Academician, Charles Cundall – Lord's not yet dwarfed by surrounding high buildings; the old Tavern; the soft felt hats and flannel 'bags' of the spectators; a tranquillity capped by a clear blue sky and some benevolent white clouds. But the artist found no place for the innovation which had crept in with that very match: television cameras and the brave new world for cricket with implications undreamt of in 1938.

It rained every day at Old Trafford and, for the second time in the history of Test cricket, not a ball was bowled. Australia, by winning at Headingley, ensured the retention of the Ashes. Neither Hutton, Gibb nor Leyland was available, all three having been injured in a county match at Lord's on such a dangerous wicket that Warner made a plea for better batting gloves. Only Hammond (76) and Bradman (103) mastered the bowling in the Test, a low-scoring match played in gloomy conditions. The Australian spinners, O'Reilly and Fleetwood-Smith, took seventeen wickets between them. Little separated the sides in the first innings and Australia were eventually able to achieve a target of 105 with five wickets to spare. As a contest – which was closer than the eventual margin suggested and in which bowlers had a chance – it was perhaps the most interesting Anglo-Australian Test for many years, but the memory of it has given way to that of the fifth Test at The Oval.

Although the Ashes were not at stake, there was the possibility of drawing the series and, in any case, it would be the last occasion for four years when English crowds could expect to see an Australian Test side. With Europe (in Winston Churchill's words) 'confronted with a programme of aggression, unfolding stage by stage' many wondered, indeed, whether there would be an Australian visit in 1942. The real enthusiasts had set up camp the night before outside The Oval and by 6am there were long queues at each entrance. Although thousands poured in the moment the gates were opened, the all-night vigil had not been necessary and the ground was never full. It was, after all, the first day of the English football season.

Bradman, loser of three tosses running, lost again and Hutton and Edrich opened the England innings, Barnett rather surprisingly having been replaced. Yorkshire had five representatives in the side and there would be a Yorkshireman at the wicket the entire innings. Edrich was lbw at 29 and Leyland joined Hutton. Both gave a stumping chance and both were there at the end of the day. Leyland, in the last of his forty-one Test appearances, went on to make 187 and Hutton would eventually be dismissed for 364. He and Leyland established an England second-wicket record of 382 which still (1989) stands. Hardstaff made 169 not out and England declared at 903 for 7 and dismissed the Australians for 201 and 123. Both Bradman and Fingleton were injured, Australia batted with nine men, and England won by an innings and 579 runs – the greatest margin ever between the two countries. Such are the well-known statistics.

Hutton's innings fulfilled all the attributes of skill, concentration and endurance so often credited to him and he reached the pinnacle of endeavour. One by one he passed other records – Hammond's 240 at Lord's, Foster's 287 at Sydney in 1903, and Bradman's 334 in 1930. When he was finally dismissed for 364 he had batted for 13 hours and 20 minutes. Even the American newspapers joined in commenting on his performance and the poet and writer, Edmund Blunden, called it an innings, 'patient, serious yet charming'. *The Times* critic, Vincent, stressed that it had to be seen in the context of the timeless Test and that was the justification for its longevity – Bradman in 1930 had batted for half the time.

Two months earlier, at Lord's, Hammond had played an innings on a Saturday afternoon which had been superlative in conception and perfect in execution, essentially an experience for those who were actually there. Hutton's long weekend, from Saturday to Tuesday, caught the imagination of the country as a whole and gave as much pleasure (more?) to those who listened and read about it as to those who saw. 'Did you hear?' makes better table-talk than 'Did you see?' The Joneses, of course, saw; and their neighbours could not keep up with them. Everyone heard and, because everyone heard, Hutton had to live with their recollections. His 364 was for him both a milestone and a millstone and he was always conscious thereafter of his obligations to those who came to watch him. Hutton would never have to endure the burden of fame imposed on Bradman. No English hero in whatever sport had to face such a perpetual barrage of publicity as the public directed at Bradman. In light relief, when England were 770 for 6, had been the half-century made by the Yorkshire wicket-keeper Arthur Wood who saw himself as the right man for a crisis! He had been a last-minute selection for the injured Ames and a taxi from Nottingham had got him to London in the early hours of the first day of the match.

One takes one's final leave of the Fight for the Ashes in the 1930s with the sad picture of nine Australians marshalling 123 rather pathetic and nerveless runs against some particularly fine pace and swerve bowling from Bowes and Farnes. The Ashes themselves would remain in mythical Australian possession until 1953 when Hutton, in the role of captain, won them back after nineteen years. Bradman, in the *Wisden* of 1939, wrote a thought-provoking article which he called 'Cricket at the Crossroads'. He contrasted the Test at Leeds on a wicket which gave bowlers a chance with those at The Oval in 1934 and 1938 when runs were amassed but the sense of contest diminished: 'Wickets should be reasonably natural and amenable to some fair degree of wear'. Cricket, in 1939, faced the challenge of the 'Americanised trend demanding speed, action and entertainment value' and, in his view, must be 'hastening slowly' to meet the challenge. In his own country he detected the first hints of alternative sports making their bid for the public's attention. Cricket, Bradman concluded, could not be separated from the cold, hard facts of finance. It was the pragmatic judgment of a man as successful in business as in cricket and it came at a time when similar thoughts were being echoed by some of the younger and more forward-thinking county secretaries in England.

As for Bradman, the cricketer, his third tour of England – though ending prematurely through injury at The Oval – had been statistically greater than the other two. In twenty-six innings he had scored a century on every other visit to the wicket and he had become the first man to have an average of over one hundred in an English summer. His batting was deemed to be as fine as ever, perhaps rather more tempered to the needs of the moment than, say, in 1934. Captaincy rested lightly on his shoulders both on and off the field. Even when the runs were being piled on relentlessly at The Oval he remained in control with, wrote Altham, 'a courage and gaiety that alone sustained the side'. He was still under thirty when the Oval Test ended yet privately he was seeing it as his last Test match in England. Success and serenity, which was what the public saw, masked the strain imposed by responsibility and expectations. No hint of this was given by him at the time. Only an article in *Wisden* in 1945 by the Australian journalist A. G. Moyes disclosed what Bradman had had in mind. By then he had had several years of only occasional wartime cricket and, like Hutton, had been invalided out of the Services. He would, in the end, be there in 1946, when the Fight for the Ashes resumed. The man whose Test match batting average was 97.94 would raise it to 99.94.

7

NEW ZEALAND:
PERSONALITIES AND PERSEVERANCE

As a young man I used to play tennis with a crafty seventy-year-old whose grandfather, Captain William Hobson, took possession of New Zealand in the name of Queen Victoria in 1840, so 'new' in a way is that member of the Empire and Commonwealth. Two years later in December 1842 the Blues of Wellington beat the Reds before adjourning, reported the local paper, 'to the ship's hotel where they partook of a true Christmas dinner of roast beef and plum pudding'. The presence of the military during the Maori wars encouraged the game despite the occasional alarms as when Colonel McDonnell's troopers and rangers played each other. The fielders had carbines at the ready and the umpires carried the batsmen's weapons. These precautions were justified when a Maori attack swept the field with rifle fire in the closing overs of the game.

By the end of the century most of the more conventional hallmarks of cricket had become part of the New Zealand scene. Out of the swamp caused by an earthquake in 1855 came the Basin Reserve Ground at Wellington and the Domain at Auckland provided playing-space for dozens of cricketers; English and Australian professionals came to coach and cricketing schoolmasters took up appointments: George Parr and James Lillywhite brought teams from England and so did Lord Harris, Plum Warner and the MCC. The New Zealand Cricket Council was formed in 1894 and, a few years later, Lord Plunket, when Governor-General, donated a Shield for provincial competition.

In the last season before the first world war, New Zealand and Australia exchanged visits, both teams travelling to New Zealand, after the Australian tour, on the SS *Victoria* in

January 1914. Victor Trumper made 293 against Canterbury, sharing in a partnership of 433 for the eighth wicket with Arthur Sims, which is still (1989) a record in first-class cricket. Sims had arranged the tour and was playing against his own countrymen. As Sir Arthur Sims he would represent New Zealand on the Imperial Cricket Conference. A few days later Trumper made another double-century at Invercargill followed by 81 in an hour for the Australians against New Zealand. Just over a year later he died from Bright's disease. The New Zealand public had tasted greatness in seeing Trumper and their appetite for such talent would be fleetingly whetted and barely satisfied in the next generation or so.

When cricket resumed after the war, the New Zealand Cricket Council had a balance of £16 in the bank which did not prevent them endeavouring, though unsuccessfully, to persuade the Australian Imperial Forces to visit the country after their tour of England and South Africa. Instead, an Australian Colts side came in 1920–21 and two years later an MCC team led by Archie MacLaren. The New Zealand *Observer* welcomed 'this fine class of young and virile British-ers' but it was a rather older Britisher, the fifty-one-year-old MacLaren, who made the biggest impact. The local press, not to mention a somewhat inaccurate *Wisden*, billed the three internationals as 'Test' matches and in the first encounter MacLaren ended his first-class career with an undefeated double-century. Unfortunately his leadership of the party displayed a lack of tact. On arriving in Sydney, he told the press that 'some of the New Zealand players hardly knew the handle from the blade of the bat'.

During the 1920s New Zealand was visited by New South Wales, by Victoria and, in 1927–28, by a reasonably represen-tative Australian side with Grimmett returning to his native land and taking 74 wickets at 13 runs apiece in what proved to be the last visit of the Australians until after the second world war. The decision to send a team to England was taken by the New Zealand Cricket Council in 1927. The secretary of the MCC announced that it would be 'something of a sporting and educational trip, with no pretence of throwing down a gauge for testing its merits against the full strength of England'. Viewed in that light, the tour was a success. The

New Zealanders, led by Tom Lowry – who had played against his homeland for MacLaren's side – held their own against the less strong counties and showed themselves to be above-average club cricketers in the way they faced various opponents of less than first-class level. Decisive victories against the East of England, Norfolk and Durham, together with wins against Sussex and Derbyshire and defeat by Middlesex exactly express their performance. They were strong in batting and many a county failed to bowl them out twice.

On a cold and gloomy day before a sparse crowd they met the MCC at Lord's – rather nervous and stage-struck in the presence of players such as Chapman, Douglas and Allen. Catches went down and the MCC were allowed to make 392 in less than a day. The sun shone on the second day and Cecil Dacre played an innings of splendour: 'The most brilliant display an overseas batsman has given us since Trumper,' wrote the *Daily Telegraph*. 'Only a player of Hobbs' class could safely challenge comparison with him,' declared Vincent in *The Times*. He was a pugnacious batsman who hit the ball with both strength and skill. He had played his first first-class match for Auckland on Boxing Day 1914 (during the war) when aged fifteen, turning up at the ground in shorts. He and Lowry both made centuries and New Zealand reached 460. The MCC replied with 426 for 4 declared, Allen making his first century at Lord's. New Zealand had just over three hours to make 359 and they scored 224 of them to earn a draw. In a three-day match 1502 runs had been made, a record at Lord's. The match did a great deal for the reputation of New Zealand but cost them Dacre, who accepted an offer to qualify for Gloucestershire, the first of several New Zealand cricketers who would seek their fortunes in England. The Christchurch *Press*, while deploring Dacre's departure when New Zealand had so few cricketers of talent, accepted it as inevitable: 'Whether it is money that tempts him abroad or the love of glory, he is entitled to do what everyone else does in the presence of a unique opportunity'.

Nevertheless, it was Roger Blunt, rather than Dacre, whose performance on the tour won him a place in *Wisden*'s Five Cricketers of the Year. In all matches he made over 2000 runs and took almost 100 wickets. Although he was principally a batsman he was an effective leg-break bowler and it was as a bowler that he had first come to prominence as a schoolboy at Christ's College, Canterbury, playing for the First XI at the age of fourteen. He made his debut for Canterbury in 1918 and thereafter, for some dozen years, first for Canterbury and then for Otago, he was one of the handsomest and most successful stroke players in the land.

Three other players on that 1927 tour also made their mark. Stewart Dempster topped the averages, Kenneth James' wicket-keeping alone redeemed a bad fielding side, and Bill Merritt, a schoolboy who bowled googlies, took over 150 wickets. All three would, in due course, follow Dacre into English county cricket. Dempster first learnt the game at Wellington as a boy where a kindly groundsman at the Basin Reserve allowed him and his friends to practise from 6 am in the morning. As a player, he responded to the great occasion and statistically did more for New Zealand than for Wellington, averaging 65.72 in his ten Test matches. Later he would help struggling Leicestershire and strengthen the representative side of his native Scotland. Those from the Antipodes of Scottish ancestry would have served Scotland well between the wars: Hendry, Jackson, Dempster . . .

New Zealand could ill do with the loss of such cricketers but, for those with ambitions, financial or otherwise, there was limited scope at home. What first-class cricket there was centred around the Christmas holiday period. Walter Hadlee recorded that men would practise at the nets at 5.30 am and again in the evening so that work would not be affected. Nevertheless in 1928 the New Zealand Cricket Council expressed its concern that too much cricket spent on the Plunket Shield and on tours meant that first-class cricket would 'prejudice the business interests of young players'. Any less cricket and New Zealand, at first-class level, would not have survived and would, instead, have become the museum-piece which is the cricket of Philadelphia.

Luckily events turned out otherwise and the Cricket Council welcomed the visit of a strong MCC side in 1929–30, which embarked upon a programme of seventeen matches – enough to interfere with the 'business' life of many an aspiring

New Zealand cricketer. The MCC side was led by Harold Gilligan and included Duleepsinhji and Woolley. At the same time another MCC side was in the West Indies (see Chapter 4). In the parlance of the 1980s, the side which went to New Zealand would have been seen as an England 'B' team, and it was as the MCC, rather than England, that a team took the field against New Zealand on 10 January 1930. Subsequently (and by the time *Wisden* appeared), the New Zealand representative matches had been raised to Test level.

Perhaps it was as well that the New Zealanders were not aware of what they were contributing to the record books of Test cricket for, within an hour or so, they had lost seven wickets for 21. In one over Maurice Allom took four wickets in five balls, including a hat-trick, making the ball swerve in a strong wind. Blunt helped New Zealand to reach 112 and at the close England had lost four wickets for 147. On the next day it rained and when the match resumed both sides did little on a drying pitch but England had sufficient of a lead on the first innings to win by eight wickets in what had been less than ten hours' playing-time.

Woolley and Duleepsinhji made runs at the expense of Manawatu and Rangitikei before the second Test at Wellington. A contemporary photograph – rather unkind in terms of the overall public support for the game in New Zealand – shows the scene at the start to have been a far cry from Melbourne or Lord's: small boys sitting on a wall, a line of coupé cars straggled outside the ground, someone's bicycle propped up against the pavement and a modest crowd watching. Dempster and Jack Mills opened for New Zealand and the news that they were still together at lunch spread through the small city and brought many more spectators. By tea, both men had scored centuries and their partnership of 276 for the first wicket stood as a record for over forty years. From 339 for 3 at the end of the first day, New Zealand slumped to 440 all out. England were dismissed for 320 and eventually saved the game after being set an impossible target in the time remaining. A little courage might have brought an earlier second innings declaration by New Zealand and the victory at Test level for which they would have to wait nearly thirty years.

The third Test at Auckland was limited, by rain, to a single day and a fourth was hurriedly arranged for the following week on the same ground. In three days each side completed an innings, New Zealand replying to England's 540 with 387. As in 1927, a nucleus of New Zealand cricketers – Dempster, Blunt and Merritt in particular – had done credit to their country's cricket at first-class level and put them on the trade routes of Test cricket.

Although the MCC invited New Zealand to send a side to England in 1931, it was by no means certain the invitation would be accepted. The 1927 tour had lost money and New Zealand was in the depths of the Depression, made worse by the devastating Hawke's Bay earthquake. The Cricket Council took the decision to float a limited liability company to finance the tour and the public was offered 12,000 £1 shares at 6%, together with a lottery held in conjunction with the New Zealand Football Association. To save expense Lowry was appointed manager as well as captain, and this underlines his unique contribution to New Zealand cricket. His influence was as assertive as his size; his kind of leadership as aggressive as his play. Throughout his life he saw things on the grand scale, whether it was the horses he raced, the vast acreage in Hawke's Bay he farmed, the New Zealand Cricket Council over which he presided or the teams he captained. Command came naturally: as a schoolboy he captained Christ's College, Canterbury, at cricket and rugby. During the first world war he kept wicket, as a teenager, for Auckland and then departed to join what he saw as the infant and glamorous Royal Flying Corps. When the war was over he went up to Cambridge, became captain and played for Somerset in the vacations under the acceptable fiction that to have been born in Wellington (wherever) was a sufficient qualification. Into that county side with its share of eccentrics, wearing his Homburg hat, Lowry fitted well. Robertson-Glasgow chuckled to see him, declaring that he justified the entertainment tax on ground-admission.

Lowry had captained New Zealand in England in 1927 and now, in 1931, he was back again: there was no other contender. Once the 1931 party had arrived in England, he kept the books, booked the rooms, and made 1000 runs while the

Armstrong Siddeley Motor Company provided cars for the team. Before May was out, both Essex and the MCC had been beaten by an innings, the New Zealanders bowling out a strong MCC side twice at Lord's in a single day. Warner rather generously in the *Morning Post* compared this with the feat of the 1878 Australians who dismissed the MCC for 33 and 19 and won the match in a day.

On the first day of the Test match the London *Evening News* portrayed a scene more in the context of a festival week than an international at Lord's: 'Flags and flowers, pretty frocks, shrilly cheering schoolboys and veterans in sun hats provided the setting'. After the match the press was less patronising. Warner wrote: 'Bravo, New Zealand! With about one-sixth of the population of London, New Zealand holds sway as the world's rugby champions and in future must be regarded as a serious competitor for the cricket supremacy of the empire'; and the editor of *Wisden* said that 'from start to finish there was never a dull moment and, apart from the fine cricket played, the varying fortunes of a memorable struggle invested the game with special interest'. At the end of the first day, England were 190 for 7 in reply to New Zealand's 224. On the second day, Ames and Allen put on 246 for the eighth wicket, still (1989) a record partnership against any country, and England reached 454. On both sides the googly bowlers, Peebles and Merritt, had taken most of the wickets. New Zealand replied with 469 for 9, centuries coming from Dempster and Milford Page, and 96 from Blunt. *The Times* was fulsome: 'Dempster, Blunt and Page gave as brave an exhibition of batting as ever seen in a Test'. England, set 240 to get in two and a half hours, lost five wickets for 146 before time was called in what was a three-day Test match. There is a minor footnote: Jardine was the England captain and Voce bowled to a ring of close on-side fieldsmen. It did not do him much good, for he took 0 for 100 in the match but it led Warner, chairman of the selectors, to remark in a loud voice that Voce seemed to be 'bowling *at* the New Zealanders'.

The reporter in the Christchurch *Press* extolled his compatriots: 'The whole team made a notable entry into the lists of Test cricket.' The Lord's Test in 1931, rather than the 1929–30 series in New Zealand, was seen as a proper acceptance of New Zealand's arrival at that level and, with hindsight, it might have been better to have left things as they were for the summer – a gracious debut had been made. Hastily (and with tour finances in mind) two more Tests were arranged. Fifteen thousand people went to The Oval to see England overwhelm New Zealand, with centuries from Sutcliffe, Duleepsinhji and Hammond. Only James' wicket-keeping won any plaudits; Vincent in *The Times* thought him as good as Oldfield. Later, during the second world war, James 'stood up' to Alec Bedser in RAF cricket 'and I bowled better for it', Bedser recalled. Rain limited the third Test to an afternoon and a century by Sutcliffe.

As Lowry had so often said, the New Zealanders had come to learn so that even a partnership of 243 by Hobbs and Sutcliffe against them for Leveson Gower's XI was seen to be gleaning experience at close quarters. They returned home not down-hearted and their anxious shareholders were able to take a profit. Once again, the lure of the game in England lost them players whom they could ill afford to surrender. Merritt went to the Lancashire League and then to Northamptonshire, and the New Zealand Cricket Council (temporarily) disqualified him for breach of contract since those who toured had agreed not to play in England within two years. James later also went to Northamptonshire and Dempster's future was to lie with Leicestershire. *The Cricketer* believed that it was quite wrong for English counties and Leagues to entice New Zealand cricketers and Warner said so in an editorial in 1931: 'It has ever been the policy of *The Cricketer* to point out that England is not showing up in a good light when they cast covetous eyes on players from other lands. Surely a great and powerful country like this should stand on its own; attempts to attract cricketers from outside should be taboo'. Warner was running against the tide as, indeed, the 'import' of the Australian, McDonald, had shown, though the full impact of overseas players in English cricket would be a post-war phenomenon and a matter of particular controversy in the 1980s. As for New Zealand cricketers, Warner appealed to them 'to stick to what is now a very nice ship in the making' and he criticised Merritt 'for succumbing to the wiles of the tempter'.

Despite the limitations of finances and resources, and the

departure of players to England for good, New Zealand cricket retained a firm hold on its own public. The 1931 Test match at Lord's, for example, was linked to New Zealand by radio-telephone. Arthur Gilligan spoke from a telephone in the Great Central Hotel, London, to New Zealand and his report was then radioed across the country. Despite the smallness of the population and the struggle of its players to succeed at the highest level, cricket began to draw a support next only to rugby. In the 1930s it was not unusual to see a crowd of 25,000 at Auckland, a tenth of the urban population.

New Zealand, in three successive years, received brief visits from the West Indies, South Africa and England. The 1930–31 West Indies played one match at Wellington on the way to Australia and the 1931–32 South Africans, having lost 5–0 to Australia, found some consolation in inflicting an innings defeat on New Zealand at Christchurch. This was the first Test between two countries who so frequently met at rugby. The second Test at Wellington also went South Africa's way though the contest was closer and Giff Vivian, a left-hander, made a century. New Zealand and South Africa would only play each other seventeen times altogether in the history of Test cricket.

The MCC visited New Zealand immediately after the bodyline tour of Australia in 1932–33 and played two Test matches. At Christchurch England lost Sutcliffe and Paynter in the first two overs, Wyatt was run out cheaply and Hammond was dropped. Thereafter Hammond (227) and Ames (103) took command, putting on 242 in two and a half hours. Larwood had sailed home directly from Australia but his partner Voce made 66 and England declared at 560 for 8. A dust storm, bad light and rain saved New Zealand from likely defeat by an innings.

At Auckland Hammond made 336 not out, an innings which eclipsed Bradman's 334 in 1930 and which gave him his first triple century since one he had made as a schoolboy in a house match. Again, rain saved New Zealand from an innings defeat. Against both South Africa and England, they had faced teams which had played together over some months and the disparity between occasional cricketers playing a month after New Zealand's brief first-class season had ended and such opponents was understandably obvious.

While great players from elsewhere entertained the New Zealand public, New Zealand cricket itself did not advance in standard and, at Test match level, a first victory seemed as elusive as ever. The Australians planned to send a side in 1933–34 but several of the 'star' players dropped out and the New Zealand Cricket Council, fearing a financial loss of over £1000, cancelled the tour. The Australian *Labour Daily* criticised the Australian Board of Control for 'its disregard of duties to the game in the sister dominion and its rank parsimony to the players' – the main reason for withdrawals. The MCC, by contrast, recognised its obligations to New Zealand and 'in the best interests of New Zealand' sent out a side in 1935–36 under Errol Holmes which played New Zealand and Australia in that order of importance, was not committed to any Tests and was selected with New Zealand cricket standards in mind.

Just before the MCC left for New Zealand in December, they played an Australian XI at Sydney and the inclusion of Alan McGilvray proved the nearest the future radio commentator ever got to international honours. Once in New Zealand, the MCC spent four months playing all over the islands and taking part in four representative matches. All were drawn and three of them were reasonably balanced but some controversy surrounded the first at Dunedin. New Zealand were dismissed for 81, Read, the Essex fast bowler, taking 6 for 26. The MCC replied with 653 for 5. Then, in an unsuccessful effort to get the new ball sooner and so achieve an innings victory, the acting MCC captain, John Human, bowled an over of 24 deliberate byes and wides.

Between the second and third representative matches, the MCC played Taranaki at New Plymouth, under the imposing slopes of Mount Egmount. Hardstaff made a century and the local XI looked to be well beaten until an eighteen-year-old schoolboy called Martin Donnelly came in at no. 6 and made 49. During an interval, Hardstaff had given him some advice and the young man had carried it out. Taranaki saved the game and Donnelly would be picked to go to England in 1937.

Beneficial as the MCC tour was for New Zealand cricket, the expense made it a financial disaster and the New Zealand Cricket Council reported a loss of well over £3000. Among those who played against Holmes' MCC side for New Zealand was the twenty-year-old Walter Hadlee who scored 47 in the last of the representative matches. Just over a year later he was on a camping holiday when he saw a four-day-old newspaper and learnt that he had been selected to tour England with the 1937 side. His employers, the Christchurch Gas Company, agreed to let him go and paid him £37 which he left behind with his parents. The sum was half-pay for seven months, an interesting reflection on contemporary salaries. For the tour itself, there was a daily allowance of 8s., half the sum which the Australian players had regarded as too miserly a year or two earlier. Hadlee, although the allowance was 'meagre', remembered how happy everyone was – 'we were entertained and kept and it was the highlight of our lives'. Hadlee's was a typical view: tours of England were seen as a social attraction as much as a cricketing one. As representatives of one of the old white dominions the players were readily welcome in country-houses where golf, tennis and swimming were at their disposal and theatre seats were at once made available. All this was some compensation for it was never easy for players to go on tour. Those selected for the four tours to England between 1927 and 1949 came from a wide range of occupations – plumbers, electricians, carpenters, labourers, students, farmers, clerks and accountants and those with their own businesses. Employers sometimes had to be approached by administrators to release a man. The self-employed made their own sacrifices, others got either half-pay, or no pay at all, or had to find a replacement. The Cricket Council was ready, but only at a pinch, to make up for hardship.

In Hadlee New Zealand had found another cricketer who would be in the tradition of their finest players. He was elegant to watch and, when New Zealand came to England in 1949, he would captain the side with the precision and calculation that belonged to his profession of accountancy. By then the allowance was £1 a day and after the tour every player received a 10s. (50p) a day retrospective bonus. In order to tour at all, Hadlee had to find and pay a locum to work in the practice during his absence. He left the first-class game soon after his return home but could be found on the cricket field as late as 1976–77. By then, the cricket world knew his outspoken views on World Series Cricket (which he opposed) and on the return of South Africa to the Test scene (which he favoured). And there were Hadlee's sons, notably Richard who would be the first New Zealand Test cricketer to wear the mantle of a modern folk-hero and the apparel of sponsorship and the media.

Lowry was manager in 1937, with Page as captain. The two worked well together besides representing their country at the coronation of George VI – the usually casually-dressed Lowry having to don court dress, breeches and buckled shoes. Within three hours of arriving in London he had the side in the nets at Lord's and he had the foresight to let them be interviewed and seen on the infant medium of television. Not everyone in public life saw the potential of television. About the same time, Mortimer Wheeler, the archaeologist (and later a television personality), scorned an invitation and sent a minion to appear on his behalf.

At a welcoming lunch, Lowry reminded his audience 'not to expect too much from a group of amateurs', a remark to be set against the comment of the editor of *Wisden* some months later: 'It would be mere pretence to state that [they] fulfilled expectations'. New Zealand came to the first Test at Lord's without a win against a county and with much of their hopes pinned on the bowling of Jack Cowie. He was a man of enormous strength and energy (nicknamed 'the Bull') who could sustain line and length for long periods, just short of being really fast and with the ability to make the ball lift and swing away. Had he been an Australian, wrote the editor of *Wisden*, 'he might have been termed a wonder of the age'. Too much a wonder, indeed, for the new England opening batsman, Hutton, whom he dismissed twice in the match on his Test debut for nought and one.

That match also marked the debut in Test cricket of Donnelly who, in a brief career, would emerge as one of the greatest left-hand batsmen in the game. C. B. Fry found it difficult to rate any superior. Like Hutton he began at the very bottom with a duck. *Wisden* called him 'a "star" in the making' and he ended the tour with 1414 runs, one century and an average of 37.21. So far there had been promise rather than achievement; talent expectant rather than triumphant. Post-war cricket would see the best of him. In 1945 he made a century for the Dominions against England and for New Zealand against Leveson Gower's XI. The Parks at Oxford from 1946 onwards became a legendary place to see the 'elderly' undergraduate play every stroke in the game, especially a fearsome hook, and field at cover with consummate ease and agility. When winter came, Oxford watched him play rugby at Iffley Road and to his New Zealand appearances as a cricketer would be added one for England against Ireland at Dublin. There was a memorable and faultless innings of 162 not out for the Gentlemen at Lord's in 1947 and a double century for Warwickshire against Yorkshire in 1948. In 1949 all this talent was again given to New Zealand at Test level, with a double-century at Lord's before, all too soon, he left the game in 1950 to take up a business appointment in Sydney. Some thirty-five years later I met him there at a publishers' reception: the most striking figure in the room (like Bradman, the lack of inches did not seem to matter), elegantly dressed, with the grace of movement possessed by the top-class athlete and the charm and modesty his generation of cricketers remembered.

In that first Test match at Lord's in 1937 Hardstaff and Hammond made centuries for England and it fell to Donnelly to bat out successfully the last hour when only three wickets stood between New Zealand and defeat. Some 50,000 people had watched on three days and New Zealand had done rather better than their critics expected. Cowie had a match analysis of 6 for 167, a performance he would improve upon at Old Trafford with 10 for 140 where Hutton made the century that had been foretold on his behalf by so many for so long. England declared at 358 for 9 and New Zealand replied with 281 (Hadlee 93). There was a point at noon on the third day when England were 75 for 7 and New Zealand needed to get only three more wickets before pursuing a modest target of some 150 or so. Freddie Brown and Jim Smith thought otherwise: both smote mightily, Brown with a variety of bucolic strokes, Smith with simply one – a heave across the line of the ball. They put on 70 runs and were dropped countless times. New Zealand, instead, were faced with 265 in four hours, not impossible until Goddard spun them out on a turning pitch. 'New Zealand let the game slip through their hands,' was Howard Marshall's literal judgment in the *Daily Telegraph*. Dick Brittenden told his New Zealand readers that the final margin of 130 runs did his countrymen something of an injustice and gave little hint of the difficulties from which England had escaped in an hour of deplorable catching.

The third Test went marginally in England's favour but time and rain made a draw inevitable. Although the English press was critical of much of their own team's performance – 'England cricket lacks thrust and penetration,' wrote the *Daily Mail* – they fell over backwards to praise a New Zealand side which, honesty compelled some to accept, had fallen below the standards of earlier tours. They were, summed up *The Cricketer*, 'a singularly level lot' with the exception of Donnelly and Cowie. One critic saw them as too modest for their own good. On their return home (after playing in Australia), (Sir) Arthur Donnelly, the chairman of the New Zealand Cricket Council, made the somewhat pessimistic judgment: 'New Zealand is of no importance in the cricketing world at the moment'. The game had become 'so commercialised' (in 1937!) that he thought New Zealand would 'be very hard pressed' in the future to attract either England or Australia to the Dominion. The two Donnellys were not connected; Sir Arthur once giving a book to Martin Donnelly with the inscription, 'With sincere regrets that I can claim no relationship'.

Despite events, England's obligations to the needs of New Zealand cricket had never been in doubt nor would they be in the post-war years. Australia played her first Test match against New Zealand in 1946 (retrospectively recognised): that apart, there was some substance in Sir Arthur Donnelly's pessimism and it would be 1973 before the Australians again visited New Zealand, and two other Hadlees, Dayle and Richard, shared in New Zealand's first Test victory against them.

★　　★　　★

At home, New Zealand played little first-class cricket and it may be said that the distinction between first-class cricket and senior cricket has mattered more to statisticians than to players or, indeed, the public. The purist who followed only first-class cricket in New Zealand would be as ill-satisfied as the train-spotter who looked only for engines with 'names'.

What first-class cricket there was in the domestic programme in the years between the wars centred on the Christmas and New Year holiday period and a week in February or March. Auckland, Canterbury, Otago and Wellington competed for the Plunket Shield: between 1919 and 1939, Auckland were successful on eight occasions, to Wellington's six. One or two matches give something of the flavour of a competition which engaged, however briefly each year, some four dozen of the best cricketers in the land.

On Christmas Day 1930, Auckland met Canterbury at Christchurch. Auckland, expected to make a large score, were too replete with the traditional Christmas lunch of roast lamb to accomplish much and Canterbury did little better on Boxing Day. The real contest began on the third day when Auckland in blazing conditions fanned by a north-west wind reached a second innings total of 537. The principal scorers were Jack Mills and Malcolm Matheson. Mills was an elegant batsman, one of the first to make 5000 runs in New Zealand first-class cricket, and with the idiosyncrasy of batting in woollen underwear from neck to ankle on the hottest of days. Matheson was a medium-paced bowler and a future international rugby referee.

Canterbury were left 400 minutes in which to score 473 to win. There were two bowlers to fear, the Sussex professional, Bert Wensley, and the national boxing champion, Don Cleverley, but neither enjoyed the success they had done in the first innings and runs came throughout the day. People flocked in from the city as Canterbury approached their target and, with a few minutes left, they needed only 20 runs. Merritt swept a ball high over the stand and far beyond into someone's back garden. Spectators left their seats to look for it and the hapless owner lost his cabbages and peas before it was found. Five vital minutes had been lost as Canterbury scrambled for the final runs before achieving success on the stroke of six o'clock, long before the days of a guaranteed twenty overs from the start of the last hour.

Twelve months later, on the same ground, Otago were the visitors. Once again, batting on Christmas Day itself was more of a testimony to good cooking rather than to good coaching. Otago scored 161 and Canterbury replied next day with 472. Otago set about their struggle to avoid an innings defeat. Ted Badcock made a century: his had been an interesting career. After a Surrey trial before the war, he had become a regular soldier and left the Army in 1924 to coach and play in New Zealand. He had the appearance and urbanity of Herbert Sutcliffe, to which he added the talents of an all-rounder. After his dismissal, Blunt took command while no one else made many runs. With seven wickets down, Otago still faced defeat by an innings. The fall of the ninth wicket found Otago 94 runs ahead. They had fought well, everyone agreed, to reach 405, though defeat could not be long staved off. Bill Hawkesworth, the wicket-keeper, joined Blunt (who was 192 not out). Personal and national milestones were passed as Blunt reached a second century, eclipsed the New Zealand record of 256 and went on to become the first New Zealand cricketer to make a triple century. Not until 184 runs had been added for the tenth wicket did Hawkesworth succumb to a googly from one of the few balls Blunt allowed him to receive. Canterbury were left to score 279 in five hours and, with three wickets left and a comfortable margin of time, they accomplished their task. Although the game did not have a fairy-tale ending for Otago, it was a fine example of the variations of fortune which cricket, of all sports, can offer. Alas! New Zealand domestic cricket would see Blunt no more as he departed for his business career in England.

New Zealand's loss of players such as Blunt, and the lure of England, whether for business or cricket, had contributed to New Zealand's hard struggle for success at international level. One New Zealand writer, T. P. McLean, declared that the 'long uphill road would have been more easily climbed had Australia been a kindlier big brother'. The indifference of the Australian Board of Control between the wars was also an undoubted factor in handicapping progress in a country where more experience of the game at the highest level was essential. Indeed, a player would be lucky to have seventy-two hours of it per season in a domestic summer of Plunket Shield cricket.

All that is in contrast to the modern image of New Zealand cricket and some of the pioneers, men like Hadlee, Lowry and Page lived long enough to see their efforts rewarded. Dick Brittenden, the foremost journalist of New Zealand cricket, has expressed it another way: 'New Zealand may have had an unimpressive Test record but it had its full share of players with personality and imagination'.

8

INDIA: PRINCELY PATRONAGE

Indian cricket has possessed no more striking a figure than Bhupinder Singh, the tall, bearded, bejewelled and turbaned Maharajah of Patiala. Cricket at his Baradari Palace Oval was an experience to be savoured, whether watching elephants roll the wicket, searching for the Maharajah's pearl earring, seeing him striking sixes into the tent which sheltered his three hundred wives, or going on a deer-hunt before play and a big-game shoot afterwards.

The era of the princely patronage of cricket was a short one – a 'golden age' in its own way. For with their gold, princes favourably disposed to cricket could entice English professionals, lay out grounds, finance tours and employ in their retinues Indian players of talent. After the first world war the princes fostered cricket as a national rather than as an imperial activity, something for Indians themselves and not just as an adjunct of the Raj. Throughout the 1920s and 1930s – until Independence in 1947 pruned them of their wealth and bred the patronage of businessmen and bankers – the princes took the lead in Indian cricket supported by benevolent viceroys and governors who were content to see this as a natural consequence of what their own predecessors had done for the game at the turn of the century.

The motives of the princes were varied – a mixture of self-interest, pragmatism and altruism. Some were doing the 'princely' thing as eighteenth-century aristocrats in England such as the Duke of Dorset had done. Others pursued vainglory and the chance to play at a level above their talents. A genuine love of cricket and the opportunity to promote it joined forces with political opportunism among those who sought favour with the Raj or even looked ahead to the sources of popular support which they might need in a future

India. It is a debate where motives matter less than deeds. Cricket for Indians in India prospered because the princes filled the hiatus between the hey-day of nineteenth-century cricket-loving colonial administrators and the entrepreneurial patrons of the modern game.

Patiala, maharajah of a state in the Punjab, had inherited his love of cricket from his father. Having fulfilled all possible ambitions on the polo field, the elder Patiala turned to cricket in the 1890s and, as a demonstration of his new loyalties, invited Ranjitsinhji to join his personal bodyguard. The son – a man of political substance, a frequent chairman of the Chamber of Princes and a delegate to the 1930 Round Table Conference on India – took up his father's mantle with vigour. He brought English professionals of the calibre of Rhodes, Hirst and Leyland to his State and encouraged Indians of talent, such as Lala Amarnath and the Ali brothers, Nazir and Wazir, to join his retinue. Under his influence the Board of Control for India was established and a national team sent to England in 1932. He was wise enough to decline the proffered captaincy (unlike another prince in 1936) and instead enjoyed the pleasure of his own son's selection for India on genuine merit in 1933.

The prince who accepted the captaincy of India in 1936 was the Maharajkumar of Vizianagram. As a young man of twenty-six, he had successfully persuaded Hobbs and Sutcliffe to play for his side in India and Ceylon in 1930–31 after political events had caused the cancellation of the MCC tour. Like Patiala, he gave opportunities to Indians, notably Mushtaq Ali, and he poured his not inconsiderable horde of rupees into cricket. He had his critics, especially after 1936 when he returned from a disastrous tour of England with a knighthood. But when Independence came, he renounced the title and continued to serve the Republic of India as a member of the Board of Control for cricket.

A princely influence which bore fruit rather later came from the small state of Pataudi. The reigning Nawab in the 1930s was identified with English rather than Indian cricket until 1946 when he led India in the first post-war tour of England. His son, Mansur Ali Khan, would captain India in forty-one Test matches and be a symbol of transition from one India to another. Both Pataudis were highly talented batsmen. It was, indeed, batting which all the princes espoused. Bowlers came from the ranks of those to whom they gave patronage or employment.

The hospitality of the Indian princes was among the memorable recollections of many a cricketer transported from a grey English winter to the Arabian Nights' world of palaces. To the West Indian, Constantine, coming from Lancashire, the experience was especially profound. In 1934 he was invited to go to India to coach and to take part in the tournament in Hyderabad for the Nawab Moin-ud-Dowla Cup. He stayed in the Nizam's palace and 'was given a suite of rooms with gold couches, gold chairs and gold implements of every sort'. The wealth of the Nizam caught his imagination and he was made aware of a land of contrasts: within a stone's-throw of the palace were the teeming masses of India where men, women and children toiled, starved and begged. Constantine's native Trinidad matched India in neither wealth nor poverty. England in the years of the Depression had shown him poverty; now he saw wealth in the possession of Indian princes. Hitherto, he had interpreted colour divisions as a straight social and economic issue. England and India together made him realise how this was to over-simplify the situation.

Hand in hand with the patronage of the princes had gone the growth of cricket in the three great cities of Bombay, Madras and Calcutta. Lord Harris, during his governorship of Bombay in the 1890s, had encouraged the participation of Indians. Under his influence communal cricket became established in which the different creeds and races within India played each other. Before he left Bombay in 1895 the Europeans were playing the Parsees annually and by 1912 they had been joined by the Hindus and Muslims to form the Quadrangular Tournament, the Hindus being victorious for the first time in 1919. In 1937 The Rest, composed of all other communities, made it a Pentangular contest. Bombay set a pattern for Madras to follow where from 1915 onwards there was an annual fixture between Europeans and Indians.

Calcutta, however, with a cricketing tradition going back to the days of Robert Clive and the East India Company, remained – as late as the 1920s – exclusive. The Europeans played among themselves and co-operation with the Bengalis was discouraged. In what was very much a gesture by Europeans to Europeans, the Calcutta Club made the approaches to Lord's which led to an MCC side going to India in 1926–27. The tour illustrated the variety of the Indian cricket scene. After a series of matches in Bombay against the different communal teams, the MCC played All-India, a side entirely composed of Indians. The MCC scored 362 and All-India replied with 437. At the end the MCC were struggling with a lead of only 22 and five second innings' wickets down. Fifty thousand Indians had seen Indian cricket arrive! The English cricketers left Bombay amid tremendous demonstrations of popularity and boarded their train for the long journey to Calcutta punctuated by stops caused by monkeys on the track.

The scene at Calcutta was entirely different. European cricketers predominated and the opportunities given to Indians were limited as the programme of fixtures clearly illustrated. The MCC played a one-day game against the Anglo-Indians and Indians in Bengal, followed by a match on Christmas Eve against the British in Bengal. After a Christmas Day spent with local families, the MCC embarked on a match whose very title touches the traditions and service of a past era of empire – the MCC v. The Europeans in the East. Planters and tea-merchants, bankers and ICS men, army officers and shipping agents had created a side eight of whom featured in *Wisden*'s births and deaths. Alas! They had left too long the pleasant English county grounds on which they had made their modest names and proved no opposition for those who would bear back to England their good wishes.

Yet, despite this setback, the Calcutta Club selected seven of that same European side for the second representative 'All-India' match against the MCC and included only four Indians. The decision seemed strange in view of the achievements of the Indians in Bombay and it emphasised the European dominance of Bengal cricket. The MCC for their part selected the Maharajah of Patiala who had already played for them twice at Bombay and, as an elected member of the Club, was eligible. In the match itself, the MCC defeated

All-India by four wickets, owing most to Tate's match analysis of 10 for 106 and his innings of 58 and 12.

The exclusiveness of the Calcutta Club led to the only unpleasantness of the tour. The Calcutta authorities sought to distinguish between the amateurs and the professionals in their social invitations. Arthur Gilligan, the MCC captain, would have none of this and commented that Lord Harris, chairman of the Imperial Cricket Conference, had instructed him only to accept invitations for the party as a whole. The name of Harris, who had done so much to encourage cricket among the Indians in Bombay, was not so pleasantly received in Calcutta circles but Gilligan stood firm. He was not prepared to see the Calcutta Club regard his professionals as second-class citizens and he was also privately employed in discussions with prominent Indians which led to the setting up of the Board of Control for cricket in India. None of this could have pleased the Calcutta authorities whose days of monopolising the game in the sub-continent were clearly numbered.

At Patiala the MCC played the Maharajah's XI in between banquets, polo and big-game hunting. Rhodes and Leyland were in the prince's side as his current English professionals. Rhodes was on his sixth successive visit and he always took a fellow Yorkshireman with him. They lived in the pavilion and catered for themselves in local bazaars and markets. Wazir Ali was the Maharajah's 'local' professional and the century he made more than justified his place on the staff. After only one innings each – social activities prevented any more play – the MCC had to board a train to catch the ship for home. The sultry world of Maharajahs was set aside for cold, English grounds in April.

Men flung together for six months with endless travelling on the great railways of India were bound to make judgments on each other and on the world they encountered. Over fifty years later, three of them recalled for me that experience. To one of them, 'there never was a happier bunch of chaps than we were on that trip – Jack Parsons' experience of the country was a tremendous help on many occasions, especially when caste had to be considered'. 'He was able to protect his captain and colleagues from unwittingly fanning the flames of internal

discord,' commented another, referring to the tensions between Europeans and Indians which Parsons had seen in his
Indian Army days and which had intensified in the three years
he had been away from India. The third recalled a personal
sense of shame at India's poverty and at the mass slaughter
of game. All the players in the MCC party did much to
improve the current Indian image of the European. Among
the social consequences of the tour were exchanges of ad-
dresses and offers of hospitality to those, such as Nazir Ali,
who would be coming to England to study and to improve
their cricket.

Other consequences were significant. Within India the
game spread from its basic centres of the Presidency towns
of Bombay, Madras and Calcutta, and a few princely states,
to many places in the interior and especially in Hyderabad
and Bhopal. Gilligan on his return home recommended to
the MCC that India was ready to play at Test level. Lord
Harris had a few months earlier insisted that two Indian
delegates be allowed to attend the 1926 Imperial Cricket
Conference and by 1927 India had a Board of Control. All
was set fair for a start to Test cricket in 1930–31 until the
political disturbances of the period led to a postponement
until 1932. Hindus had opposed the idea of an MCC visit and
they also withdrew for four years from the Quadrangular
Tournament. Yet had the game not been demonstrably seen
as passing into Indian hands, it might have been not so
much a postponement as a cancellation. The forces of civil
disobedience and the voice of nationalism could have ended
a sport so identified with British authority and culture.

Scarcely anyone in the sparse Saturday crowd which greeted
the Indians in their first Test match at Lord's in June 1932
could have had an inkling of how close the visitors came to
not playing. At midday, with Sutcliffe, Holmes and Woolley
back in the pavilion for 19 runs, they were cock-a-hoop. But
eight hours earlier a group of them had refused to take part
and woken up the tour captain to say so. Cables to India and
back resolved the matter by a message of authority from the
Maharajah of Patiala.

The issue at stake was the captaincy: the Maharajah of

Porbandar was the touring captain. He was not a player of any ability, by first-class standards, but he met the conventions that no-one but a prince should be in charge. On grounds of health and ability, he stood down for the forthcoming Test in favour of India's finest player, Cottari Nayudu. But Nayudu was a disciplinarian and an army officer, besides being a commoner, and his appointment was resented by some of the players. Yet the troubles went deeper: the selection of the side and the financing of the tour had involved princely rivalry and even the Viceroy, Lord Willingdon, had entered the debate. The Maharajah of Patiala's offer to underwrite the tour was accepted by the Board of Control and fifty players had been invited to Patiala at his expense for trials. At the very last minute Patiala withdrew from the captaincy and the Board had announced the appointment of Porbandar instead.

All this belonged to the background of a tour in which India had come to the Test match at Lord's with only one county defeat. At the end of the first day's play they had dismissed England for 259 – a strong side with men competing for a place under Jardine to go to Australia. They made 189 in reply (Nayudu 40) and again took the first three England wickets cheaply but Jardine, forced 'to fight hard for every run', recorded *Wisden*, made an undefeated 85 and India lost the match by 187 runs. Individual players had done well: notably the tall fast bowler, Mahomed Nissar, who took 6 for 135, Amar Singh with four wickets and a free-hitting half-century when the game was as good as lost, and Nayudu himself. Amar Singh, moving the ball late, was rated by some critics as one of the best bowlers seen in England since the war. Altham thought the two Indian bowlers 'a nightmare to Holmes and Sutcliffe in both innings'. 'Here was unexpected sport,' wrote Cardus, 'England harried and worried by the latest aspirants to Test match distraction.'

A British public sublimely ignorant of internal conflict (and the tourists did not wash their dirty linen in public) was glad to have seen a side which won more games than it lost, fielded athletically, and put a cheerful face on the strain of day-to-day cricket. Nayudu won his place in *Wisden*'s 'Five Cricketers' on the strength of his all-round contribution to the tour. He made 1600 runs, took 65 wickets and played in every first-class match, as important to the morale of the team as Constantine had been to the West Indian tourists four years earlier. Nayudu would have a long career in Indian cricket, scoring a double century when over the age of fifty and playing his final first-class match, at the age of sixty-one, in 1956. He was an outstanding football and hockey player too and in later years much of his time was given to the administration of cricket.

The role of Lord Willingdon, Viceroy at this time, calls for some comment. He had already served as Governor successively of Bombay and Madras and he held the viceregal office at a time when the Nationalist movement was strong, Gandhi active and disorder prevalent. He stood to the left of many contemporary British politicians and civil servants in his view that the course of events in India should be understood rather than opposed. As Viceroy – and as a former president of the MCC – he sought to ease India's path into international cricket and to see that Indians themselves played a distinctive role in this. With the best of intentions, he interfered too much in taking sides in the contending princely factions. Patiala was never his favourite – 'a great overgrown puppy' – but Vizianagram certainly was and something of Willingdon's influence led to his being appointed captain of India in 1936.

Willingdon was a strong leader in a time of trouble, and so was Jardine who led the MCC side to India in 1933–34, hard on the heels of his Australian tour. Indeed, the two, Viceroy and Captain, clashed when the MCC played a match at Delhi. Jardine invited Patiala to play for the Club. Willingdon (and his wife) tried to persuade him to reverse his decision but Jardine stood his ground, declaring that the captain of the MCC would brook no interference from a Viceroy. That captaincy Jardine would very soon relinquish at his own request, but until he did so he remained the same iron-fisted and single-minded figure whom the Australians had encountered. The young Vijay Merchant thought him an 'object lesson to Indian captains'.

From an English standpoint the MCC did all that was expected of them. England won the first and third Tests and had much the best of a draw in the second. Jardine topped the tour batting averages while Verity took most wickets. The team met with one defeat – against Vizianagram's XI by 14 runs – and found themselves, to the point of monotony, playing against a cadre of the same opponents in match after match. The tour took more than the usual toll in terms of illness, injuries and general weariness. Five months travelling on Indian trains taxed the most dedicated player.

India were led in the Test matches by Nayudu (his military rank of major and his status as ADC to a maharajah being sufficient qualification at home). In the first Test at Bombay, England made 438 and made enough to win by nine wickets. The main feature of India's cricket was the century by Lala Amarnath and the exceptionally fast bowling of Nissar who dismissed Jardine but not before that advocate of pace had shared in a large partnership with Valentine. England again made over 400 at Calcutta in the second Test. India were forced to follow-on but batted long enough to deny England success. Merchant made his Test debut, scoring a half-century and embarking on a career of great distinction.

In the final match at Madras, the Indian batsmen, like many greater than they, found Verity on a turning and crumbling wicket rather more than they could manage. Not only did he take 11 for 153 but he shared in a partnership of 97 with Jardine and took the finest catch in the game. Patiala's son and heir, the Yuvraj of Patiala, made 24 and 60, qualities of batting which would, in the climate of the time, make him a possible candidate for the Indian captaincy.

Critics of the Indians declared that they were too easily mesmerised by great names: bowlers felt inferior when Jardine batted and batsmen diminished in stature at the sight of Verity. It was as well for India that the England team had been no stronger – nine of the MCC side who had come back from Australia declared themselves unavailable. Momentary consternation had been caused at Lord's by a telegram proclaiming, 'Selection of team a disgusting insult to India. Will recommend tour be cancelled unless more stars added' – until its origin was traced to a junior clerk in the Indian Telegraph Office.

These would prove the only official Test matches which the Indian crowds would see in the inter-war years and something should be said about the nature of public support for them and the game as a whole. The Bombay Gymkhana ground was packed – inside and out – on 15 December 1933 for the first day of Test cricket in India, with spectators sitting on wooden seats under the canvas roof of a shamiana or clinging to the tops of surrounding trees. The Bombay authorities allocated blocks of seats to different groups. Catholics, Parsees and Hindus each had their own Gymkhana as did commercial firms (shades of the present-day executive boxes), individual cricket clubs, colleges and schools. The public stand was a comparatively small section. It was a form of discrimination which produced a discriminating crowd, knowledgeable, enthusiastic, noisy but well-behaved. Spectators would only rush on to the pitch to garland a successful player. Members, of course, enjoyed the best facilities. When the Brabourne Stadium was built at Bombay in 1937 it offered them everything associated with a club charging substantial subscriptions. Some people went to cricket as part of the social calendar of the day. Others, Dr Richard Cashman has suggested, were there because their very presence 'at an event of high symbolic significance' conferred a spiritual blessing of its own.

Cricket at a less solemn level than Test matches could have a carnival spirit about it. Wise players participating in domestic matches responded to the mood and barracking of the crowd. The communal matches in the 1920s and 1930s lent themselves to banter between the different gymkhanas which did not always sustain its good humour. Gandhi believed that communal matches were a potential cause of racial tension and communal riots. Women, apart from the Europeans and some of the grander Parsee ladies, were scarcely evident before the 1940s.

Cricket commanded the supporter's allegiance only if he were either present or literate in the English language. *The Times of India* offered lengthy reports very much in the style of its English counterpart and directed at a readership of similar outlook. Readers were expected to appreciate that a batsman had displayed 'the effortless ease of a Lionel Palairet'. Publications and magazines appealing, in the English language, to a wider market were doomed to failure except for the monthly *Indian Cricket*. Commentaries on the Test matches of 1933–34 were broadcast for a few minutes of the day to small listening audiences while no reports of the two tours of England in the 1930s were sent home at all. *The Times of India*, through the normal reporting agencies, supplied the readers' wants. Not the least of the changes which Independence would bring would be a proliferation of cricket writing and broadcasting in both English and Hindi.

Just before the 1936 series in England, an Australian XI sponsored by the Maharajah of Patiala toured India. The main attraction was Macartney and the side was a blend of experience and youth. What was, in effect, an Australian Second XI was evenly matched against India in the unofficial 'Tests'. The Indian captaincy changed hands on several occasions, and throughout the season internal jealousies were undermining what little security Indian cricket at international level possessed. Quarrels among selectors, clashes between Bombay and Calcutta, princely jealousies, tension between Hindus and Muslims all came out in the open in the search for a captain to lead India in England a few weeks after the departure of the Australians. The Nawab of Pataudi was the first choice: despite his allegiance to English cricket rather than to Indian it was a reasonable proposition for he had both rank and ability. When he withdrew, Vizianagram secured the appointment for himself, for which he was suited by rank alone. He lacked the modesty which led Porbandar to stand down so often during the 1932 tour and he lacked the will or the capacity to blend men divided by creed, wealth, culture and language into a loyal and united band. Nayudu went as a member of a party which eventually numbered twenty-two players through calling on Amar Singh who played in the Lancashire League. There were three wicket-keepers, bowlers who never bowled and a captain of little ability who reserved a place for himself in match after match so that India effectively took the field with ten cricketers of first-class standard.

The English press, usually much more tolerant towards failure by the weaker tourists in the 1930s, pounced on India's troubles and players were soon forbidden to talk to journalists. All else, in a tour of disastrous implications for Indian cricket, paled in comparison with the punishment awarded to Amarnath. He was said to have thrown down his pads in a temper in the dressing-room at Lord's while waiting his turn to bat. In Vizianagram's view – and that of the manager, a retired Indian Army officer – he had to be sent home on disciplinary grounds. At a stroke India deprived themselves of their best batsman and drew unwanted attention to the faction within their ranks.

India came to the first Test at Lord's without Amarnath but with Amar Singh released by his League club. Allen, making his debut as England captain, put India in on a rain-affected wicket and bowled so well himself that they were dismissed for 147. Allen's 5 for 35 was bettered by Amar Singh's 6 for 35 and England made only 134. Allen getting a lot of pace from the soft turf again played the largest part in dismissing India for 93, and England won comfortably by nine wickets. This was the first Test match in which artificial means were used to dry the wicket.

A month later, at Old Trafford, Hammond returned to Test cricket after a spell of indifferent health. At once, as Howard Marshall told his BBC listeners, Hammond 'entered his kingdom again, fit and confident, master of himself and the occasion'. The 167 he made was the main feature of an England total of 571 in reply to India's 203. Yet India, in saving the game, emerged with credit. Merchant and Mushtaq Ali set up a record first-wicket partnership of 203 in the second innings, and made their contribution to a day's Test cricket in which a record 588 runs were scored. Merchant from now onwards was the leading batsman on the tour.

Hammond, with a double-century in the third Test at The Oval, was even more impressive than at Old Trafford. L. V. Manning, writing in the *Daily Sketch*, withdrew his opposition to the 'extravagant' entrance charge of 2s. 6d (12½p). England played a side drawn from those about to sail for Australia and the ten professionals and Allen were too good for an Indian XI which, however, never gave up. Typical of their rearguard action was an innings of 81 by Nayudu, after a severe body-blow, which averted an innings defeat. Hammond did not underrate the Indians whom he called 'very tough and worthy opponents' who would 'one day challenge England on absolutely equal terms'.

Yet the disappointment of the tour was evident: not enough batsmen had found form, while the bowling lacked the venom, and the fielding the accuracy of the 1932 side. Indian cricket, it was generally agreed by the critics, had declined in standard. The causes, many of them thought, were to be found in the factions and divisions which had been so obvious to English observers. 'The will to pull together was not often apparent,' wrote the editor of *Wisden*. Immediately after the tour Vizianagram flew home on the new Imperial Airways route to India possibly in the vain hope that he might forestall the proposed enquiry under Sir John Beaumont, Chief Justice of the Bombay High Court. The captain gave evidence as did members of his team when they reached Bombay by ship a month later. Anticipating its findings, *The Times of India* wrote that 'there was a strong feeling among most members of the team that Vizianagram was not successful as a playing captain'. The published report, in January 1937, went much further and blamed Vizianagram for 'forming his own party and not treating all members of the team with strict impartiality'. Nayudu was criticised for his refusal 'to co-operate in any way with the captain' and for 'holding himself aloof from the team', while the punishment meted out to Amarnath was held to have been too severe. Indian cricket had not been best served by the feudal structure which insisted on a princely captain.

A few months later Lord Tennyson's team arrived in India from England. Ironically, Indians could view an English side led by a nobleman while the sensible choice of Merchant as captain of India for all five unofficial 'Tests' reflected a change of opinion towards representative cricket at home. Merchant – neither a prince nor a soldier but a member of a Bombay business family – pointed to a future style of leadership in Indian cricket. Tennyson led a side of almost full England strength and the series ended in two victories each. Vinoo Mankad, at the age of twenty, dominated India's performance both in batting and bowling. By making a century and taking six wickets at Madras he helped India, for the first time, to defeat a touring side by an innings.

Despite Merchant's achievements, the lesson of captaincy was not yet entirely learnt. When the Indians went to England in 1946, the appointment of the Nawab of Pataudi as captain was an attempt once again to blend aristocratic authority with playing skill. Pataudi, who had never played for India but only for England, came out of retirement (and in poor health) to make a brave rather than a valuable contribution to India's difficulties at international level. He achieved little and relied heavily on the performance of Merchant, who scored over 2000 runs on the tour, and Mankad, who did the 'double'. The team did well enough against the counties but their form in the Tests was unimpressive. They lost the only Test to have a result and they found a new bowling adversary in Alec Bedser not at all to their liking. The tour was memorable if only for the last wicket partnership of 249 against Surrey in which Chandrasekhar Sarwate and Shute Nath Banerjee, nos. 10 and 11, each scored centuries, and for a match against Sussex in which the only four Indians who batted in the match all scored centuries.

On a bleak day in May the Indians came to Edinburgh to play Scotland. Vijay Hazare made a century, and the Reverend James Aitchison a half-century: the one, a prolific scorer for India, the other, Scotland's best post-war batsman. No matter that Sarwate's leg-breaks were far too good for my fellow-countrymen – I had seen my first first-class cricket match. More impressive than victory over Scotland, of course, was the defeat of the MCC by an innings three days later but the overall result of the tour, in a very wet summer, was disappointing. The domestic cricket in the 1940s in which batsmen prospered in India, and the visit of an Australian Services side just after the war, proved no preparation for the soft and slow wickets of England in 1946.

With the entry of the Hindus into the Quadrangular Tournament in 1912, the ideal of Lord Harris had been realised: a competition which would give the non-European players a goal, a place in their ethnic team, and a measurement of their standards against European cricketers. The result was to make cricket among Indians much stronger in Bombay than in Calcutta where, as Gilligan had observed, Europeans dominated the game. The Quadrangular Tournament matches were played at either Bombay or Poona. The decision was taken, after 1919, to play them in the Indian winter months when conditions were dry rather than in September which was often wet. Higher scores, better cricket, and matches brought to a conclusion, were the immediate benefits.

Among the Europeans playing immediately after the war was Parsons, who was serving in the Indian Army with the 7 Hariana Lancers as a squadron commander. Just before Christmas 1919 he was given leave to play against the Parsees in Bombay but his team was knocked out in the first round and he had to return at once to duty. Twelve months later he again made a long round trip by train to play in the first round of the competition, immediately afterwards going off with his regiment to Baghdad. In 1921 he was, at last, in a victorious team. In the first round a side containing himself, Fry, Rhodes and Hirst beat the Hindus by an innings and inflicted a similar defeat on the Parsees in the final, Rhodes making 183.

Parsee cricket had been established well before the war, but in the 1920s it was the Hindus who made the most progress. In the 1926 Final, played for the last time at Poona and temporarily switched back to the wet season in September, they met the Europeans. They were 60 runs behind after an innings apiece but, in soft conditions, did rather better in the second innings, owing most to D. B. Deodhar. The Europeans were set a target of 117 and the fast bowling of Ramji gave the Hindus a narrow victory. Few people of modest personal resources did more for Indian cricket, and Hindu cricket in particular, than Professor Deodhar. He made a century against the MCC in 1926–27 and was unlucky not to be selected for the two tours of England in the 1930s.

Popular as the Quadrangular Tournament was, it offered tantalisingly little first-class cricket and the Board of Control launched the Ranji Trophy in 1934 as a competition for the Provinces and the princely States. The Maharajah of Patiala presented a golden Grecian Urn as a memorial to Ranjitsinhji who had died the previous year. In practical terms, it meant that some 250 cricketers would play at first-class level each year instead of the fifty or so who met in the tournament.

The game was taken to a wide range of centres. Talent, as Professor Deodhar wrote, which 'was baulked owing to the narrow and vitiated field of the Quadrangular, found its right avenue and channel in the Ranji Trophy'.

Yet the large number of sides created problems. Standards between teams varied considerably – so much so that the first-class status of some teams was questionable. Walkovers were not infrequent whereby a team simply conceded defeat without playing. In 1937–38 there was the absurd situation of Hyderabad entering – and winning – the final without playing any earlier matches. The rules of the competition were far too lax in allowing players to change from one team to another. Despite this, to the Indian journalist N. S. Ramaswami, it was in these years that the first-class game in the country took root. The Ranji Trophy was the cement which held Indian cricket together, attracted huge crowds and was the nursery for its next generation of great players.

One of the first of these to distinguish himself was Hazare who helped Maharashtra to win the trophy in 1939–40. In an earlier round he had made 316 not out against Baroda at Poona and, in the season as a whole, his average was 154.75. Maharashtra were also successful in the 1940–41 competition, beating Madras in the final. Hazare, supported by Sriranga Sohoni was again the principal batsman. The success of a comparatively undistinguished side meant that other teams pursued their players and leading ones such as Hazare and Sohoni were attracted elsewhere. Cricket was never a livelihood and players went to towns and cities where they might be able to establish themselves in a job and achieve a measure of security.

The majority of those who played first-class cricket in India during the 1920s and 1930s did so essentially for fun and for the exercise of their talents. The princes and men drawn from the professional and business classes, such as the Nayudu brothers and Merchant, were amateurs in the mode of their English equivalents. The fast bowler, Nissar, for example, plied his trade in the same gentlemanly way as Allen had done in Australia in 1932–33, eschewing tactics which endangered the spirit of the game. If Merchant brought a more determined approach to batting than did many of his contemporaries, this simply put him in the same mould as, say, the Australian Woodfull or the South African Mitchell. John Arlott regarded Mankad as 'the first traditional cricket professional' to emerge in India in the sense that he was 'an unrelenting competitor as bowler, batsman and fielder'.

Financial support, in some way or other, was of course essential for the poorer men who played. This would be forthcoming in modest cash gifts, the supply of kit, retention on a prince's retinue or in the offer of a job. Amarnath was one of the poorest men in the game when he began, which makes his savage treatment in 1936 the more despicable. What could an immensely wealthy man like Vizianagram have understood about Amarnath's circumstances? Despite the set-back in 1936 – perhaps even because of the publicity it gave him – Amarnath soon made capital out of his abilities and followed Amar Singh into the Lancashire League where both men commanded almost the same popularity as Constantine. When the clubs retaining any of these three men played against each other, the gate money might well exceed £200, so that in three or four games a player's salary would be met. Amarnath, with a long career in front of him, would eventually become the first cricketer in India to receive a benefit. Others were less lucky and fell on bad times once the patronage of the princes had ended.

The outbreak of war in 1939 had no effect on first-class cricket in India though the tournament at Bombay was fast becoming an anachronism and would not long survive. The war years were a period of high scoring on pitches over-prepared and grossly in favour of the batsmen. Snippets of news would reach the outside world of yet another first-class record being broken. Scores of over 400 were frequent occur-rences. When Bombay met Maharashtra in 1943–44 they scored 735 after losing half the side for 90. Merchant made 359 not out, sharing in a record sixth-wicket partnership of 371 with Rusi Modi. Dicky Rutnagur, the Indian writer, has suggested that high-scoring became almost a matter of personal rivalry between the leading Indian batsmen copied, with less success and to the detriment of the matches them-selves, by lesser batsmen 'transcended by personal ambition'.

To join the batting achievements of Hazare, Merchant and

Modi there appeared a new star in Indian cricket in 1944–45 when Compton, stationed in the country on war-service, scored 249 not out for Holkar against Bombay in the final. It was, to say the least, a high-scoring match: Bombay made 462 and 764 (Merchant 278, Modi 151). Madras, who had only managed a modest 360 in the first innings were set 866 to win. Compton did his best, sharing in a last-wicket partnership of 109, and Mushtaq Ali made a century, but Bombay won by 374 runs. Twelve months later, Holkar reached 912 for 8 against Mysore. Six batsmen made centuries and there were seven century partnerships. Mysore, after following on over 700 behind, made a spirited fight before conceding defeat when their total had reached 560 for 6.

'C'est magnifique mais ce n'est pas la guerre': batsmen had triumphed on wickets that favoured them, especially at Bombay, and only Sarwate, a leg-spinner, had achieved much as a bowler; but India now faced the real world when the national side went to England in 1946 and Professor Deodhar fulfilled his ambition to visit England at last. After the tour it was his view that India's cricket needed reshaping. The choice of Pataudi as captain had been one last gesture to princely patronage and had ignored the claims of the new-style university and businessmen such as Merchant. Administrators needed to think in broad principles rather than let themselves be too much 'engrossed in the politics of administration'; more coaching and talent-spotting were needed; and there had to be a discipline and unity among players which transcended cultural divisions.

Deodhar returned home after the tour to a country which declared its Independence in 1947. From the outset politicians and officialdom gave a blessing to cricket as an expression of popular and national unity. The Ranji Trophy was not interrupted by the bitterness of Partition. Pakistan emerged as a separate country which would create its own cricketing tradition and keep within its borders the tall men from the North who had been India's source of fast bowlers. Fears that a game tainted with imperialism might disappear with the end of Empire proved groundless. Cricket flourished at the grass-roots and unprecedented crowds flocked to watch. As an indicator of change, the discredited Amarnath of 1936 was appointed captain in 1947 of the first Indian side to tour Australia. Leadership on tour had passed from the princes to a farmer's son who worked on the railways.

The age of the princes had been something of a Golden Age of Indian cricket. As Richard Cashman has written, after 1947 'princes were forced to prune their cricketing ventures, to dismantle their teams and to terminate cricketing appointments'. The new age beckoned and the currency would be distributed by the business and banking houses. It would prove, in the end, a worthwhile investment.

9

AUSTRALIA: LORD SHEFFIELD'S SHIELD

Of the eighteenth-century cricketers who played for Hambledon, only William Beldham lived long enough to be captured by the photographer. Of Henry Holroyd, third Earl of Sheffield, who gave his name and his money to Australia's domestic first-class competition, only two photographs exist. He had, so the historian of the Sheffield Shield, Chris Harte, tells us, 'a strong aversion to having his photo taken'. There also remains a cartoon (opposite) of a squat figure bearing a strong resemblance to a slimmed-down Edward VII. Curiously, one of the two surving photographs shows the king and the earl together.

In every other way the earl had been a generous man; cricket in Sussex at both county and village level, and especially his own ground at Sheffield Park, all benefited from his generosity as did Anglo-Boer War orphans, the poor and hospitals. He represented all that was best in nineteenth-century aristocratic paternalism. The Sheffield Shield arose out of his gift of £150 to the Australian Cricket Council when he took a side there in 1891–92. The presence of W. G. Grace brought big crowds to the three Test matches though the tour as a whole lost money. The great Australian boom of the 1880s was over and the public had to limit their personal expenditure while Grace charged Sheffield £3000 and the expenses of himself and his family! Sheffield, quite apart from making his gift of £150, finished up £2700 out of pocket. Chris Harte has demonstrated that there were many pitfalls between Sheffield's simple gesture and the launching of the competition. Some ten months after the original offer, the details of the competition were published in September 1892,

THE EARL OF SHEFFIELD.

though another eighteen months would go by before Uri Wanczewski, an early mid-European emigrant to Australia from Poland, and his son produced the handsome gold and silver Shield bearing the arms of the donor and of Australia. By then, Victoria, the first winners, and South Australia, the second winners, were each still awaiting the tangible reward for their efforts.

Colonial rivalry was acute – epitomised by the different railway gauges – and the eventual Federation of Australia in 1901 somewhat reluctantly accepted. The Sheffield Shield Trophy, which had taken 964 days from concept to conclusion, stimulated the competitiveness of the three colonies of New South Wales, Victoria and South Australia. By the first world war these three States, as they were designated after 1901, had all shared in winning the Shield, though by far the greater number of triumphs had gone to New South Wales and Victoria. Other prospective competitors, Tasmania, Western Australia and Queensland, all played first-class cricket but the extra travel involved, by sea and rail, made the three participants reluctant to accept them.

First-class cricket received a rapturous welcome when it was resumed in Australia some twelve months after the Armistice. The Australian Imperial Forces, after their tour of England and South Africa, finally reached home in January 1920 and made a triumphant tour of the States. Huge crowds turned out to meet them and to associate their return with that of all those who had fought in faraway places. At Melbourne 18,000 people and all the players stood bare-headed as the 'Last Post' was played in tribute to those Australians who would not come back. In this heady and emotional atmosphere, the great centres of cricket attracted and retained the immense following which would sustain the game through what proved a Golden Age for Australian cricket, to be endorsed by the achievements of an eleven-year-old who was in 1919 making his first half-century at Bowral.

Test cricket was popular in Australia (see Chapter 6). Some of the reasons for that popularity apply to the game as a whole: they are relevant to Australia, but not just to Australia. Cricket benefited from reaction to the horror and austerity of the first world war. Escapism was cloaked in many guises but men in white flannels was an acceptable one. The generation that would look for its weekly ration of Hollywood fantasy found an outdoor equivalent in seeing cricket as something with its own romantic glamour. Improved transport facilitated attendance and cricket was attracting a larger working-class support than in pre-war days.

Australians, in particular, had their own reasons for flocking to cricket matches. State loyalties were deep and rivalry, particularly that of New South Wales and Victoria, had almost the flavour of an international contest, with teams often of as near international calibre as made no difference. And there was a scarcity value: a Sheffield Shield match would happen on, say, ten days a year at any one centre. As many Sheffield Shield matches took place throughout the 1920s and 1930s as there were first-class matches in England in one single season. The public were not spoilt for choice and administrators were not greedy. Cricket might cost a little more than the cinema – or an Australian Rules Football match – but it remained basically cheap. Nor were the public seeking sophisticated comfort. Photos of the day demonstrate thousands standing to watch a whole day's play in cramped conditions that no modern spectators would tolerate. Only at Melbourne in the 1930s was there a significant improvement in the quality of accommodation. The sophistication spectators sought was in what they had come to see. Those who were not connoisseurs were, at the very least, enthusiasts and good cricket won their hearts. 'Bumper well-behaved crowds' Dr Cashman has declared and the evidence of his statistics and of the players whom he interviewed bears him out. Bill Brown, who played in front of many of them for New South Wales and Queensland, wrote that the Sydney crowd was 'caustic, critical but knowledgeable; it was vocal, humorous and had great insight; what they wanted was a sincerity of purpose'.

There is, of course, a negative factor to consider, more applicable to Australia than elsewhere. Before the second world war no other national sport – golf, tennis, swimming – really caught the public imagination, and less was on offer for individuals: people did not have swimming pools, tennis courts, cars, yachts, television sets and a thousand other amenities with which to entertain themselves. Sport, even in its very drabness, could appeal as J. B. Priestley brought out so poignantly in his *English Journey* in 1933. Cricket, the purist would fervently believe, was never drab, but players and officialdom in Australia did not have to work very hard to ensure that it was not.

In the unlikely surroundings of an American university campus I found myself involved, while writing this book, in a discussion on heroes. 'You needed them as much as we did in the 1930s: all that generation needed them,' said an American academic gently leading me from cricket to the achievements of 'Babe' Ruth, the baseball player and holder of a league record of 714 season home runs. 'Lindbergh . . .', my friend on the subject of heroes went on. It was time to introduce him to Bradman – who had sat beside Babe Ruth watching the New York Yankees play the White Sox in 1932.

The 'hero' role in which Bradman was cast throughout the 1930s does not even raise an area of debate. All Australia was conscious of it; he himself has written about the impact it made on him and how he coped; the evidence is legendary – expressed in print, anecdote, film and even a fox-trot 'hit' song. Richard Cashman's figures, as we have seen, demonstrate that the crowds at Melbourne and Sydney virtually doubled consistently throughout these years when it was known he would bat in a Sheffield Shield match. Few, indeed, were the opportunities to see him – in ten years he batted in Shield cricket on a total of forty-one days on the two grounds. No other person in any field of activity remotely approached Bradman in the public estimation. If one accepts the thesis that Australia – in the Depression years still a nation unsure of its identity – needed a folk hero, it was he.

In the immediate years after the second world war Sheffield Shield cricket retained its popularity but, with the retirement of Bradman, an era of support ended dramatically. Not a single Shield match in two immediate post-war seasons produced a really exciting finish, and it may be that the long tradition of unexciting finishes associated with these contests was no longer acceptable to a public seeking more instant excitement and immediate results. Powerful as New South Wales and Victoria both were, they had often inflicted very severe defeats on each other while South Australia (until

Bradman joined them in 1935) and Queensland became even more used to being buffeted by their stronger opponents. Many a match must have seemed lost or won within the first two days and spectators took their pleasure in watching individual performances rather than team achievements. Some figures make the point:

Margin of Victory

	Matches	Innings + 150 runs	Innings	More than 200 runs or 6 wkts	More than 100 runs or 4 wkts
1920s	81	9	10	24	5
1930s	125	11	9	34	14

Thus, in the 1920s, 53 per cent of the matches were decided by a very substantial margin and 59 per cent by a reasonable one. In the 1930s, the substantial margin had dropped to 43 per cent and the reasonable one to 54 per cent. Spectators, particularly in the 1920s, would be more than lucky to see a close result. Games were played to a finish in the 1920s and no limit was placed on the number of days.

Cricket in Australia had ended reluctantly during the first world war, partly because of a prevailing belief that the war would be a short one. The 1914–15 Sheffield Shield competition was seen to a conclusion and, in the very month in which the Gallipoli operation began, Victoria defeated South Australia at Adelaide. In a matter of days, Australian forces were landing at 'Anzac Cove'. When the bad news started coming through sportsmen were taunted for not volunteering. Victorian cricket officials replied by announcing that eleven Shield players and over 1000 members of Melbourne Cricket Club were serving, and that Australia's first Victoria Cross had been won by a Grade cricketer in the State. Nevertheless, it seemed wiser to cancel further cricket at most levels. As the deaths in action of cricketers were announced, all criticism was silenced. Among those killed were Tom Patton who had scored 408 in a world record stand of 641 for Buffalo River in Victoria and Albert Cotter who had played for Australia on twenty-one occasions. In December 1919 the Shield competition was resumed and from then until 1947 it was dominated by Victoria and New South Wales who won the title ten and nine times respectively. South Australia's best years would be when Bradman joined them in 1935. Queensland entered in 1926–27 but sixty years later were still seeking their first title. On the other hand Western Australia, who entered the competition in 1947–48, were successful on their first appearance.

Victoria

Cricket in Victoria was synonymous with the awesomeness of the Melbourne ground and the batting of Ponsford and Woodfull. Massive crowds filled the great Melbourne 'bowl' and they were offered scores of mammoth proportion. Turnstiles and scoreboards seemed to click in unison as Sheffield Shield cricket achieved a popularity unattained before or after in this Golden Age in Australian cricket. Huge scores were expected from both victors and vanquished. In the first two seasons after the competition resumed only once did no side score 400 in a match. The 600s, 700s and even an 800 were preludes to Victoria's extraordinary performance against New South Wales in the Christmas 'derby' of 1926. They became the first team to make a thousand runs in the competition and, by way of practice, had done so four years earlier against Tasmania – the islanders from Van Diemen's Land who struggled for so long to win mainland recognition. On Christmas Eve New South Wales were dismissed for 221. When the match resumed after two days' holiday, Woodfull and Ponsford saw Victoria safely to 375 in four hours before Woodfull left for 133. Hendry, who had come to them from New South Wales, made exactly a century before departing when the total was 594. There followed what, in other circumstances, might have been called a collapse and four wickets fell cheaply, one of them Ponsford's for 352 while Ryder, rather less successful, scored 295. Jack Ellis, the wicket-keeper, cried 'Long Live Victoria' (State rather than

Queen) as he brought the thousand up and his dismissal eventually ended the Victoria innings for 1107. Mailey, with 4 for 364, had kept up the morale of his colleagues with a host of witticisms which have become legendary: 'a pity Ellis got out as I was just striking a length'. Archie Jackson made an undefeated 59 in New South Wales' vain reply of 230. No-one took seriously the cartoon depicting a New South Wales fieldsman saying 'Wait till we get you in Sydney' but when the two teams met there, Ponsford, Woodfull and Ryder (780 worth of runs) were not playing. Victoria were dismissed, on a difficult wicket, for 35 – 3.16 per cent of their Melbourne achievement. Ponsford, with two more centuries before the season ended, became the first Australian to make over a thousand runs in a domestic season.

In what came close to being a 'two-horse' side of Woodfull and Ponsford in batting, Ryder – an immensely powerful striker of the ball – made a very good third, though his greatest contribution to Australian cricket would be as a selector for a quarter of a century after the second world war. Hendry was the principal all-rounder, an effective opening bowler who scored four centuries in the 1926–27 season alone. Bowlers had to be good to survive on the wickets prepared and the batting talent they faced. For two seasons after the war, Victoria enjoyed the services of McDonald. His best match for the State was his last one, against New South Wales at Sydney in 1922 when he took 8 for 84 in 21 overs – six of them clean bowled – to give Victoria both victory and the title. Thereafter his cricketing journey from Tasmania took him to Lancashire and a professional career.

In the 1930s, there emerged Fleetwood-Smith who, in a career of nine years, took nearly 600 wickets. His left arm spun Victoria to many successes, among them the 'double' against New South Wales in 1934–35 when, in the home and away games, he took twenty-six wickets. In that season the scores achieved by Victoria's opponents were reduced to normal dimensions, only one innings exceeding 400 runs. When Victoria resumed after the second world war new names such as Keith Miller and Bill Johnston would be their passport into the 1950s.

New South Wales

New South Wales, the State of Spofforth, Murdoch and Trumper, declared their future intentions against South Australia at Adelaide in December 1919. Bardsley, Andrews and Kelleway all made centuries, Mailey took 9 for 133 on a batsman's wicket, and their formidable strength in the 1920s would also include Macartney, Collins, John Taylor and Kippax as batsmen and Gregory and Hendry as all-rounders. With Oldfield behind the stumps there was little to distinguish them from a full Australian XI as, indeed, the 1920–21 MCC side found to their cost at Sydney when only one of the successful New South Wales side was not a current or future international. Such was their strength that Harry Rock could only win a place when a Test match made demands upon New South Wales, yet in Sheffield Shield cricket over three seasons in the 1920s he averaged 94.75 in six appearances.

The season of 1925–26 showed the New South Wales side at its very best: all their matches were won by huge margins and the game at Sydney against South Australia demonstrated the power of the batting. South Australia, not unusually in those days, fielded after an all-night train journey from Adelaide. Collins and Bardsley set the pace with an opening stand of 203 and the total of 642 contained four centuries. South Australia made no mean reply in reaching 475, both the Richardsons, Victor and Arthur, making centuries. New South Wales, in a match that would eventually last eight days, then made 593, Macartney getting a century and five others being not far behind. Set 761, South Australia had little fight left in them and lost by 541 runs. The aggregate for the match stood as a record until beaten by the timeless Test at Durban in 1939. A week later, New South Wales dealt almost as summarily with Victoria, Kippax making 271 not out.

In an age of prolific scoring, Kippax more than held his own. At Melbourne in 1928 New South Wales were 113 for 9 trailing over 250 runs behind Victoria when Kippax was joined by Hal Hooker late on Christmas Eve. They batted throughout Christmas Day and were not parted till noon on Boxing Day after establishing a world record tenth-wicket partnership of 307 which still (1989) stands. Kippax, reported

Wisden, batted 'with delightful ease and effect' while Hooker 'played fine defensive cricket'. Under the changed rules of the competition, matches from 1926–27 onwards were limited to four days, points were awarded for first innings lead, and this particular match was one of the first to be 'drawn'.

Among those who had disturbed the scorers to the tune of only one run in the huge New South Wales innings at Melbourne was Bradman. He was in his second season and he had forced his way into this powerful team by his spectacular performances in Grade cricket. He had made a century on his debut in December 1927 against South Australia at Adelaide; Ponsford, on the same day, scoring 437 against Queensland – a record which Bradman would eclipse.

Bradman brought a new dimension to Sheffield Shield cricket. In the two seasons before he went to England in 1930 he made a score of at least 50 in eleven out of fifteen Shield matches, and a century in six of them – and those centuries included 175, 340 and 452. It was at Sydney in January 1930, after an evenly balanced and low-scoring first innings by New South Wales and by Queensland, that he played an innings deemed to be utterly without fault. He was 205 not out on the Saturday evening and the *Sydney Sun* next morning described the scene for its readers: 'What a dramatic setting for any dashing batsman. A huge crowd that made the old green hill look black; grandstands around the ground parked with hero-worshippers; the band playing popular strains from *The Gondoliers*. What an incentive to make runs!' The other two hundred or so runs came on the Monday and he was left undefeated with 452 not out. Bradman has recorded his own satisfaction at the speed at which he scored and the generosity of his fellow-players, not least Ponsford.

New South Wales would enjoy Bradman's services for four more seasons and he would play for them between the 1930 and 1934 tours of England. In ten out of fifteen Sheffield Shield matches he made a century (at least): several were double- centuries. In the season of 1933–34, before going to England he scored, in successive Sheffield Shield matches, 200; 1 and 76; 187 and 77 not out; 253; 128. When New South Wales played Victoria in 1933–34 in the match to decide the Shield winners, over 32,000 people poured into the Sydney ground on Australia Day, 26 January, in the hope that Bradman would bat. Towards the end of the first day he did, and his 128 came in the final hour and a half.

Through all the run-getting of these years, New South Wales' bowling was served principally by O'Reilly. His Shield wickets were earned at 17.10 apiece, a magnificent return for a googly bowler on the pitches of the day. When he went with the New South Wales side to play South Australia at Adelaide in December 1937, Bradman was now an opponent. McCabe and Fingleton carried much of the burden of New South Wales' batting and both led New South Wales to the respectable total of 337. O'Reilly, with his own Irish blend of flight, spin and length took 9 for 41 and a further 5 for 57. Grimmett countered with a match analysis of 9 for 154 and one of the few Sheffield Shield matches in the period to be dominated by bowlers – the two best in Australia – ended in a narrow victory for New South Wales. Bradman's 91 and 62 represented 39 per cent of the runs made by New South Wales. However well the bowlers did, he was still a presence.

South Australia

When Sheffield Shield cricket resumed in 1919 South Australia had to live for some years on the legend of George Giffen and Clem Hill. Not until 1925 did they win a single match and many of their defeats in some twenty games were by very wide margins. In those high-scoring days runs themselves were not really the problem but it must have been disheartening to lose, for example, to Victoria on two occasions after making 543 and 518 in single innings.

Rivalry was keen and tough, and compounded by the distances teams travelled. The South Australia side, very weak in bowling, faced Victoria at Melbourne in the 1920–21 season and had over 1000 runs scored off them, Armstrong scoring 402 runs for once out. Play ended too late to get the night train to Sydney and this was boarded twenty-four hours later, allowing them a matter of minutes to take the field against New South Wales on their Eastern States tour. Their request to start a day later was refused and they fielded out for a further 800 runs, Bardsley making the first of two 235s he would make against them in the season. Rain saved South Australia from further humiliation, after they had made 191, though New South Wales claimed the match.

Victor Richardson, one of Australia's greatest all-round athletes, led South Australia and brought them to their first success since 1914 when they beat Victoria at Adelaide in November 1924. By then Grimmett had joined them from Victoria, to become one of the finest bowlers of his type of all time and, with George Giffen, to be one of only two Australians to take over 1000 wickets in first-class cricket without the benefit of playing for an English county. Grimmett helped South Australia to their first post-war title in 1926–27 and his bowling alone often kept at bay the vast scoring machines of New South Wales and Victoria. In the Christmas match against Queensland in 1934 he took sixteen wickets for 289 on a wicket which allowed batsmen throughout the match to average 46 runs per wicket.

'It was on Anzac Day 1935 that I arrived in Adelaide,' Bradman has recorded. That simple statement of fact would transform South Australia's cricket and would begin, for Bradman himself, an association which would last for over fifty years – as player, selector and administrator. He had come to Adelaide to begin a career as a stockbroker. Despite his new business responsibilities, he accepted the captaincy of South Australia and made an impact from the start. Clem Hill wrote at the time: 'His influence on the young South Australia side has been most pronounced. Keen and enthusiastic in everything he does, Bradman carries his men with him. In all my experience I have never seen a South Australian team to be so much on their toes.' As a batsman, he began with a century and in his first three innings made 727 runs, 357 of them against Victoria at Melbourne. His batting inspired others, particularly Badcock who also made a triple-century in the return match against Victoria. It was the batting of these two, together with the bowling of Grimmett, which enabled South Australia to finish the decade with a flourish – champions or runners-up in the last four seasons. Two matches, in particular, illustrate their contributions. In the 1938–39 season South Australia made 600 for 8 against New South Wales at Adelaide, Bradman (143) scoring the second of what would be a world record of six successive centuries and Badcock making 271 not out. Grimmett, with 11 for 175, ensured a victory by an innings. Twelve months later in the Christmas match at Adelaide against Queensland, the figures of the three men were similar. Badcock made 236, Bradman 138 and Grimmett took 10 for 195. The match has its own place in cricket history: South Australia made a record score of 821 for 7; war had broken out three months earlier but the Government, as in 1914, had allowed Shield matches to continue; two of the South Australia side, Ken Ridings, who made 151, and Charles Walker, the wicket-keeper, would join the RAAF and be killed.

After the war Bradman played only four more innings in Sheffield Shield cricket, two of them centuries. His energies were reserved for the Test matches and for his tour of England in 1948, from which he returned to play in a Testimonial match at Melbourne between his XI and that of Hassett. When he was 97 'he was missed in a manner that pleased the crowd' *Wisden* recorded – and he achieved his 117th and last century. The match was a fitting tribute to him and, without any 'engineering', ended in a tie. In financial terms it brought him £A9000. Three weeks later he became Australia's first – and only – cricket knight, played in a Testimonial match for Kippax and Oldfield and made a final Sheffield Shield appearance at Adelaide. It was again a reminder of the 'Bradman factor' that, when he had to retire from the match injured with a twisted ankle, the attendance at the gate fell away rapidly. No single name in Australian cricket would ever again command such crowds as he had done.

Queensland

Queensland entered the Sheffield Shield competition in 1926, reluctantly accepted by the Eastern States who disliked the extra travel involved, were critical of the poor standard of wickets, and unenthusiastic about playing matches in the tropical, even monsoon, weather of the early weeks of the year. Ideally, the winter months are best for cricket in Queensland. In the next twenty years Queensland had to be content with wresting third place from one of the other States. Yet there had been great promise in the very first match at Brisbane in November 1926. New South Wales were dismissed for 280 and Queensland led by 76 in the first innings. New South Wales under Kippax's example and leadership batted to much effect and set Queensland a target of 400. Leo O'Connor, the captain, batted throughout the fourth day for 191 and on the fifth morning Queensland needed 22 runs with two wickets left (including O'Connor's). They failed by only eight runs though they would win two other matches in their first year.

In an attempt to improve their fortunes, coaches were engaged: Andy Ducat of Surrey and James Christy, the South African Test cricketer, both spent a season with Queensland while Bill Brown was recruited from New South Wales, proving to be the linchpin of Queensland's batting for a few years in the late 1930s. In the 1938–39 season Brown made over a thousand runs in seven matches, a season in which Queensland were placed third and New South Wales, for the only time in this period, bottom.

An impact on Queensland's cricket as great as that of Brown was made by Don Tallon whose wicket-keeping career began almost in the cradle. He was behind the stumps for his school team at the age of seven, captain of Queensland schoolboys at thirteen, and a Grade A player at fourteen. He made his debut for Queensland when he was seventeen, witnessing his first Sheffield Shield match at the same time as he played in it. He proved equally valuable as a batsman and when Queensland met New South Wales at Sydney in 1938–39 he became only the second wicket-keeper in first-class cricket (the gap was seventy years) to take twelve wickets in a match. His non-selection to go to England in 1938 remained a mystery and smacked of selectorial preference for the 'fashionable' states. He toured in 1948 and became one of *Wisden*'s 'Five Cricketers of the Year'.

To watch Tallon was to see the unobtrusiveness of great art matched by sustained and dedicated concentration. When the inevitable chance came, he would leap like a panther to dismiss his quarry with a summary catch or stumping, the more impressive still if on the leg side. It was with the talents of Brown and Tallon, the bowling of Hornibrook, and the performances of visiting sides that the Queensland public had to be content until the days of Ken Mackay, Peter Burge and the players imported from other States and other lands in the 1970s.

The route to the top in Australian cricket has always been a democratic one based on the simple factor of meritocracy. The player of real ability travels quickly from the various levels of Grade cricket to the State, or even National side, even before he is twenty. In theory, it has mattered not whether his origins were rural or urban; his background prosperous or poor. In practice there have been restrictions depending on circumstances and ambitions. Cricketers in the Second Golden Age were technically amateurs in the sense that no player received an official salary or wage for playing the game within Australia. Nevertheless, success made inroads on the time a man could devote to his own job and career prospects so that decisions had to be made in which either cricket or a career took second place. Because Sheffield Shield matches in the 1920s had no time limit, a player could not tell an employer how long he would be away. Professional men, such as Ted à Beckett who was a lawyer and Rock who was a doctor, gave the game up early. Those in commerce, possibly as representatives, had more flexibility, for a sensible employer would take account of the marketing value of a man's name. Among those who were so employed were Badcock, Chipperfield, Fleetwood-Smith, Grimmett and McCabe. Players who eventually owned their own businesses, such as Oldfield and Kippax, enjoyed more freedom to play though this might not be achieved until towards the end of a playing career.

There were ways in which money was paid directly from cricket resources to players. Discreet payments in the late 1930s, known as 'retainers', certainly made the difference to a very few top players whom a particular State wished, in a literal sense, to retain. Coaching appointments financed Brown at Queensland and Grimmett at South Australia. Armstrong had been paid over £200 before 1915 as pavilion clerk at Melbourne Cricket Club and both Ponsford and Hendry were financed (though not nearly so splendidly) by similar appointments. Despite these limited opportunities, there were very few Australians who chose to throw in their lot with English professional cricket. McDonald, with both League cricket and county cricket, was the pioneer, followed by Arthur Richardson and Alan Fairfax. Only McDonald, of the three, played county cricket. To make the decision to play cricket professionally 12,000 miles from home was no easy choice, involving domestic upheaval. Both McDonald and Fairfax made their permanent homes in England.

Inevitably, real success – measured by achievement at Test match level – brought its rewards. Overseas tours meant a payment of some £500 or £600 – some compensation for months away from home and for leave of absence usually without pay. On the whole, as Dr Martin Sharp has argued – in his thesis on 'Professionalism and Commercialism in Australian Cricket during the 1930s' – the Australian first-class cricketers of these years proved socially mobile and may be said to have achieved higher rungs on the socio-economic ladder than did their fathers. Probably only Fleetwood-Smith faced real poverty in old age to which his weakness for drink had contributed.

Writing about the cricket which they played was seen by some players, but not the Board of Control, as a legitimate way to earn money. The Board, an authoritarian body founded in 1905, had frequent and acrimonious relations with players, not least in 1912 on the question of tour management. Friction, always there in the 1920s, came to a head after the 1930 tour of England when the Board censured and fined Bradman £50 for a 'technical' breach of contract by writing. A correspondent in the *Sydney Morning Herald* wrote: 'Who did the lion's share towards this great money-making tour – Bradman? He has done more here for cricket since his four years of first-class play than the Board has done since it was formed'. Bradman, by virtue of the reputation he enjoyed, was in a stronger position than others to challenge the Board head-on, and he did so in September 1932 just before the MCC visit: 'I have signed a contract to write newspaper articles, and I intend to carry it out. I must earn my living, and if cricket interferes with my living then I must give cricket up'. In the end, he was released from his newspaper contract and played in the 1932–33 series but the issue remained and would affect other cricketers such as Kippax. What the Board applied to journalism, they also applied to broadcasting. Dr Sharp has suggested that 'confrontation between players and administrators was diffused through the strength of the amateur ethos and the aversion of both groups to take action which might have jeopardised the stable and lucrative financial position'. A 'star' lost to cricket because of journalism or broadcasting might cease to be the 'star' in popular esteem and no-one – Board or player – would be the winner. Only Fingleton was regarded by the Board as an exception for he was a career-journalist and treated as a 'special case'. When not selected at Test level, though seen as potentially eligible, no restrictions were imposed on his reporting. Once his playing days were over, he became a distinguished parliamentary and political journalist.

In broader terms, relations between the Board of Control and the players were strained throughout the period and beyond. The Board's members were professional and businessmen of standing in Australian public circles but almost invariably without actual playing experience at first-class level. In retrospect, their attitude to players whose performances were the *modus operandi* of the whole exercise must be seen as bureaucratic and short-sighted.

While the Board might show little understanding of players, employers could sometimes be equally insensitive. Dr Sharp recorded an interview in which Alec Hurwood, an accountant and a Queensland player who toured England in 1930, revealed that he had to stand down after the first two Tests against the West Indies in 1930–31 because his employers would not release him nor would they permit him to captain Queensland in Sheffield Shield matches. These were the years of the Depression and Hurwood felt it more important to hold down his job. He had bowled extremely well in both Tests and had had a good season for Queensland. For a State that needed all the Test match opportunities its players could get, the attitude of his employers, General Motors Holden, seemed narrow-minded.

Whether a man might be allowed by his employers to play at Test or Sheffield Shield level was one thing: what he stood to gain or lose financially was another. Someone to whom playing first-class cricket was a handicap in making his way in business was Hunter Hendry who played at Test and Sheffield Shield levels from 1919 to 1935. He told me not long before his death in 1988 at the age of ninety-three:

My grandfather made his way in the wool trade of the late nineteenth century and my father became a grain merchant. I was sent to Sydney Grammar School and then I joined the firm of Westinghouse Brake Co. They gave a dinner when I was picked to go to England in 1921 but they didn't keep my job open for me. I lost a lot of jobs through cricket. Sometimes, later, an employer gave me leave but never with pay.

Hendry had no regrets: cricket had taken him to England, to Scotland (the home of his ancestors), South Africa and India, but he had not achieved the status or the security in business which he might have done and he provides a rare example of a decline in social mobility through cricket. His final word was about playing Sheffield Shield cricket on Christmas Day:

Of course we all wanted to be with our loved ones but playing for your State was a great honour, not a job. My boy, we would have done anything to be in the team. You just put up with it. Woodfull wouldn't play on Christmas Day because it belonged to the family.

As Hendry had indicated, employers were not willing to pay for work not done. He recalled getting 10s. a day expenses for playing in Shield matches. There was some variation but, in any event, these small sums, especially in the 1920s, were seen as mere honoraria. On a different plane were home Test matches where the sum paid had to be seen as more of a professional fee – £25 or so. The 'big money' came with overseas tours. Hendry had thought his £500 in 1921 just about broke even: ten years later Beckett could put his £600 aside for a deposit on a house. While hotels, travel and meals were separate, a player still had to support a family back home: tour money might represent twice, or even three times a normal annual income in the workaday world and could, at the very least, be seen as some compensation for the social, domestic and emotional fact of being away from family for some eight months. If the Australian Test player assumed a sort of professional status which the mere Sheffield Shield player did not, so be it. *Wisden* throughout the period continued to think otherwise and so did *The Times*: 'Mr Gregory bowled to Hobbs . . .'

The educational background of the Australian first-class cricketers of this period tended to have been at private schools rather than government ones and this owed something, as in England, to the coaching facilities available in the private schools. On the other hand, the universities were not a 'nursery' as were Oxford and Cambridge. Woodfull, Rock and à Beckett were very much the exception in being university graduates. Whether a man went to university or left school at fourteen, as did Bradman, was of little account in the correlation between his cricket and his professional or business career. Woodfull, with school holidays coming at the 'right' time in the year was able to play cricket, get leave to tour and eventually become headmaster of Melbourne High School, an orthodox career-structure in which his cricket was neither a handicap nor, positively, an advantage. His reluctance to talk cricket in his headmastering years suggested that a particular chapter in his life had firmly ended. Bradman, before he was thirty, made the decision to go to Adelaide and embark on a business career to which he brought to bear the same qualities of single-minded concentration which had been the hallmark of his cricket. Like Sir Leonard Hutton, his cricket ended at forty: both men pursued their business careers, and with success, for as many years as they had pursued their cricketing ones. In the end it was partly a man's temperament that determined as much as anything how he would tread the tight rope between playing Australian first-class cricket and earning a living.

Long after Bradman and his generation had retired the whole face of Australian cricket was changed irrevocably by the launching in 1978 of World Series cricket. The game was marketed and promoted in ways which satisfied the sponsors, attracted huge crowds (though at the expense of Sheffield Shield matches) and rewarded the players. Even in the post-World Series years, the rewards have seemingly come to stay and the barrage of one-day cricket in Australia, especially day-night cricket which suits the climate, brings – to a limited number of players – high returns. A survey carried out in Australia in 1987 indicated that two Australian captains, at the pyramid of cricket, earned ten times as much as the average annual working income. Top cricketers in Australia have become top professionals: essential cogs in a complex promotional exercise harnessing all the resources of contemporary technology. There is no turning back.

After watching cricket 1980s-style at Melbourne and Sydney where huge floodlights clawed the sky like giant tentacles, I spent a Saturday afternoon at Adelaide watching South Australia play Western Australia in a match in which crucial Shield points were at stake. A modest crowd of a few hundred had scattered itself in the stands or on the grass surrounds. Children played on the bank; families had picnics; the ABC man was speaking from his small commentary stand approached by an outside ladder; the press box consisted of a few rows of seats equipped with a telephone and some flagons of orange juice. It was all very English: Worcester in August or Somerset at Taunton. I sat watching the game with Sir Donald Bradman and, as we talked, a small boy sought his autograph. With a smile, the request was granted. I may not have been seeing Sheffield Shield cricket in its hey-day but I had seen something symbolic of it: the autograph-hunters still pursued the hero of that Golden Age of Australian cricket.

10

A SECOND GOLDEN AGE

'Cricket reform has always attracted the attention of the eccentric,' wrote Robertson-Glasgow towards the end of the second world war at a time of debate about the game's post-war future. He had, he admitted, little cause for worry: 'An interesting little battle ended in the rout of the "hustlers" and the triumph of conservatism'. He was right in identifying the heart of the controversy: the 'hustlers' in their plea for faster cricket and one-day cricket were using coded language for money. He would be proved wrong in his judgment that one-day cricket 'would empty the ground as surely as the rain'. Meanwhile, cricket when it resumed in 1946 was even less revolutionary in change than had been the two-day experiments of 1919. Those whom Robertson-Glasgow called 'honest, if deluded, zealots' were no match for the Establishment.

Yet it would be unfair to assume an utterly *laissez-faire* attitude upon the part of the cricket authorities in England. The MCC had set up a Commission in 1937 under a former secretary, William Findlay, which examined the financial problems of first-class cricket and called for more attacking cricket and for matches to be brought to a conclusion. During the war, a committee met under Sir Stanley Jackson which proposed changes of a minimal nature, none of which affected either the number of counties playing or the length of matches. Groundsmen were instructed to prepare fast wickets and concern was expressed at the extent to which they had been 'doped' before the war.

(Sir) George Allen had expressed a concern about this in an article he wrote in 1938. In his view, easy-paced wickets caused even the most menacing bowler to lose his sting and, in self-defence, adopt negative tactics. Groundsmen had advanced their skills. Gang-mowers and lawn sand came into popular use in the 1920s and relieved the tedium of cutting and weed-killing. There was more time to spend on studying the value of aeration and fertilisation in the preparation of soil conditioning. But increased knowledge could bring increased contrivance, and the over-watered wickets, with liquid manure and other forms of dope, had brought the lifeless conditions of which both Sir George Allen and the Jackson Report had complained.

Sir Stanley's report had made a positive recommendation that there should be a knock-out competition (of three-day matches), though it added that there were 'many practical difficulties'. Despite all the success of one-day cricket in war-time – and he himself had been responsible for organising much of it – Sir Pelham Warner's remarks at the Middlesex Annual General Meeting in 1942 conveyed the viewpoint of the majority and ensured that what had been good enough for 1920 (when he retired) would be carried into the immediate future: 'Do not be led away by the call for brighter cricket. It is a leisurely, intricate game of skill. We live in an age of speed and people are apt to think that cricket must be speeded up'. Robertson-Glasgow was on the side of the angels – though he admitted that his preference for three-day cricket was related to his preference for the three evenings which followed play: 'I should never have listened to nightly conversation on cricket, compared with which all books that have ever been written on sport are like cocoa and hot water'.

The Findlay and Jackson enquiries had been concerned with cricket in its English context – one aspect only of the MCC's obligations. Throughout the years covered by this book the MCC was both a private club and the executive body of the game. In its essential role nothing changed – it remained (as it still does) the custodian of the Laws of the game; it was responsible for overseas tours and Lord's was seen as the headquarters of cricket. Test matches were administered by Boards of Control and each country sent delegates to the Imperial Cricket Conference which had met since 1909 and with more frequency after 1930 as its membership increased, though the ICC in those days did little more than determine the dates of Test matches and 'rubber-stamp' MCC resolutions.

The one great trial which the MCC faced was the bodyline affair of 1932–33; almost a trial of Empire as well. Officialdom at Lord's had to think on its feet and politicians in both Westminster and Canberra had anxious moments. No other crisis emerged for either the MCC or the ICC though lurking in the shadows – never in the limelight – was the issue of colour. South Africa simply did not play against the new members of the ICC from 1928 onwards in whose ranks were coloured players. In the first Test against South Africa in 1929 England selected Duleepsinhji. The dozen or so runs he made in the match was perhaps the excuse for dropping him for the rest of the series despite a season in which he finished seventh in the national averages. E. W. Swanton has written that 'there was evidence of political pressure from the South African end' and of the distress it caused to Duleepsinhji's uncle, Ranjitsinhji, who had experienced something of the same thing himself.

Not until the 1960s would the 'd'Oliveira Affair' bring the racial issue out into the open by which time the Imperial Cricket Conference was becoming an anachronism in its title – in 1965 it became 'International'. As for the MCC it would eventually have to share power with new bodies such as the Cricket Council and the Test and County Cricket Board. From 1947 onwards Empire gave way to Commonwealth. Neither Lord's nor Westminster could be seen any longer as the fulcrum of imperial authority and the duet of cricket and Empire had played its last tune.

The years of Cricket's Second Golden Age avoided change as much as anything because cricket sustained its popularity. At international level it was still a rarity, unchallenged by the fiesta of international competition which sponsorship, air travel and package tours of supporters brought to a later generation. Despite the misgivings with which the editor of *Wisden* had viewed the arrival of new countries on the Test scene, they brought a certain magic to the game. By comparison with today when every Test cricketer is virtually known to every other through constant meetings in Tests, one-day internationals and on the English county circuit, cricketers of the Second Golden Age were often strangers to one another and certainly to the watching public. Every cricketing country was touched by the excitement of players arriving from another land perhaps with distinct cultural differences or bringing to the descendants of emigrants a whiff of the land of their forebears. A Test match or the tourists playing against county, colony, province or State, was an event to be cherished for its infrequency, and undiminished by familiarity. Only the drama of 1932–33 in Australia may be used as an instance of a touring side being sent on its way in no doubt about the low esteem in which its hosts held it. Yet even then, when Anglo-Australian relations were at their lowest, the *Sydney Morning Herald* compared the imperial bond through cricket to 'hooks of steel'.

Domestic cricket as much as Test cricket had a strong following. Crowds, still without the intrusion of television into their homes to set standards of excellence, were content to watch the fortunes of some lowly county, the aristocratic combat of Oxford v. Cambridge or Auckland v. Otago.

The social expectations of spectators everywhere were not high. The great majority sat on uncomfortable benches or stood, often exposed to the elements whether hot or cold. The game remained reasonably priced – even cheap – and the whole structure of cricket was shored up by the evidence of countless lovers of the game for whom the long day of travel and watching was one of pleasure, appreciation and fellowship.

The players were not unaware of these perceptions. Many felt a sense of obligation to the crowd and, according to individual temperament, would show it by some piece of buffoonery, the signing of autographs or exchanging quips over the boundary fence. Batsmen who were 'stars' were aware that they should make runs because people had come to see them. Yet with obligations went a sense of fun. Len Hutton, in a phrase he half-regretted later, once declared that the game was not played for fun in the sense that A. P. Herbert told the House of Commons, 'People are not here for fun'. But Hutton enjoyed his cricket and retained a zest for it right to the end and few men had more fun out of politics than APH. At one end of the scale was the guileless fun experienced by the South African, Ronnie Grieveson, who simply wanted the 'timeless' Test in 1939 to go on and on; at the other, there was the utter dedication of the Yorkshire professionals Wilfred Rhodes and Emmott Robinson whose universe was cricket and who grudged a Sunday on which they could not bowl.

To the first-class cricketers of the Second Golden Age fun prevailed. Like the spectators who watched them, the players did not have high expectations. The watcher no more expected to be cossetted in comfort than the player take home a silken purse. There was never much money for the run-of-the-mill English professional. Cricket, one of them wrote, lifted him and his fellows 'for a period from the rut of the commonplace and gave them in their palmy days an entrance into realms far above their station'. It was a remark heavy with Victorian undertones in its acceptance of social distinctions. Sutcliffe would have given it little credence although even he thought it better to decline the Yorkshire captaincy rather than cause embarrassment to some of the Committee. Hammond, by choosing his friends among the amateurs, distanced himself from his fellow-professionals and found it a financial struggle to keep up standards of dress and entertaining in the social ranks to which he aspired. To a young professional like Hutton, success meant being able to get married, when he was twenty-three, and to buy a house without a mortgage, though the purchase owed more to a benevolent patron than to his Yorkshire wages. Wages were, indeed, the normal way to reimburse professionals. When Parsons returned to professional cricket after his career as an Indian Army officer, his county made a special exception to allow a cheque to go to his officer's account with Cox and King's. Touring sides would wonder at all these very English distinctions and be mystified when they entertained the MCC in their own countries containing players who were neither MCC members nor permitted to walk within the portals of Lord's. Touring captains, such as Gilligan, Tennyson and Allen did much to reduce discrimination among players travelling together for months.

In essence, the capped English professional cricketer was seen, in his own country, as among the aristocrats of working-class society while those who displayed an independence of attitude, social ease, business acumen and cricketing talent would move into a middle-class milieu. Sportsmen will always be distanced to some extent from conventional social judgments and, as J. M. Kilburn observed, the professional cricketer of the 1930s 'held a high ranking in sport' even in the sombre economic climate of the times.

One can exaggerate, and much of this must be seen in the perspective of public attitudes. Players were appreciated for their talent and liked for their personality, irrespective of whether their initials appeared before or after their names. The triumphant Yorkshire side were fêted throughout the county with golf courses and theatre tickets, there for the asking.

These were still the years of the amateur. From the Indian princes downwards, there were those rich enough or independent enough to play first-class cricket; the sons of business houses with, for a few years, indulgent fathers; those who found ways and means to play at some personal sacrifice or those who simply put cricket above climbing the rungs of their chosen occupation. It became less possible in the 1930s as the effects of the world-wide Depression began to bite.

No-one seriously suggested that the status of the amateur might change and a variety of conventions, perks and quirks distinguished the amateur in England from his fellow professionals. He would use different hotels, dressing-rooms and railway compartments. He might, for example, if he played for Warwickshire in the 1920s, drink what he liked at lunch-time while his professional colleague might spend no more than ninepence on drink. The second world war made a nonsense of much of this – there was a wartime game in which the participants included Aircraftman P. A. Gibb and Private N. W. D. Yardley and Major Sutcliffe, H., and Second-Lieutenant Verity, H. – but the fact remains that it would not be until the 1960s that the distinction between amateur and professional disappeared. Whatever the labels and the order of initials, cricketers were recognisable figures featured in lurid colours on cigarette cards, in the tabloids or fleetingly glimpsed by the cinema news reels. They flourished in an age of increasing press publicity and the evolution of broadcasting.

Those who reported upon first-class cricket knew that they had a duty both to their editor (since continued employment depended upon his good favour) and to the public. Neville Cardus has told of his summons to C. P. Scott, the editor of the *Manchester Guardian*, for supposedly describing the 'wrong' arm when Woolley was batting. On being informed by Cardus that Woolley was a left-hander, Scott declared he would never criticise a specialist member of his staff again. Nevertheless, such editorial regard kept young journalists on their mettle and Cardus was left feeling the offender for having led the great man into error. Editors, after all, decided who reported tours and the preference for Bruce Harris to E. W. Swanton to go to Australia in 1932–33 probably deprived the English public of a quicker insight into what was happening.

As for the public: reporters were aware that they were expected to give a portrait of a day's play for those who might not know the scores when the paper arrived on the breakfast table the following morning. Much of the reporting was generous both in quantity and in attitude. Compared with a later age the press was more ready to create heroes rather than to destroy reputations. Even when he was going through a very bad patch in 1934, the journalists, as a whole, stuck by Hammond. Because his batting failed, they were at pains to praise his bowling and fielding, for which 'he was worth a place alone' said the *Daily Mail*. Hutton was 'spotted' early, particularly by J. M. Kilburn in the *Yorkshire Post*, and he was praised to the point of embarrassment in the national press, only *The Times* offering more sober, and even caustic, judgments.

Those who had played the game at first-class level might be employed either on a regular basis or under contract to report a tour. C. B. Fry was the doyen of a distinguished group of English players which included Warner, Jardine, Fender, Gilligan, Hobbs and Robertson-Glasgow. Warner, for years, depended on journalism for a personal income. He had learnt the trade before 1914, sometimes reporting on matches in which he had himself performed well. It was not unreasonable for him to write, anonymously of course, in *The Times* that 'Mr Warner played a faultless innings of 150' when it was probably true! After he retired in 1920, this particular conflict of interest disappeared (he would have others) and he was a faithful correspondent for the *Morning Post* from 1921 to 1932. His writing was at once factual (if sometimes mildly inaccurate) and historical though there were times when the reader got an essay on great players rather than the 'evidence' with which he might confront his colleagues on the 7.40 to the office.

Much more than Warner, it was Cardus who pioneered the art-form of an essay, closely followed by Robertson-Glasgow. Cardus drew heavily upon the imagery of music (Beethoven for preference) while Robertson-Glasgow turned to the classics, especially Virgil. Musical analogies and classical allusions could enhance the word-picture being conveyed of a dreary day between the showers at Southend, Lancashire doing battle with Yorkshire at Old Trafford or Gimblett smiting the attack at Taunton. Cardus gained followers in abundance and his reports in published book-form were among the successes of the comparatively small cricket book market of the day. Players to whom cadences and hexameters were as remote as playing cricket in Alaska might grumble or chuckle, as the mood took them, when they saw their names in some Cardusian or 'Crusoeian' flight of fancy but, on the whole, they welcomed the publicity he gave them. Sir Leonard Hutton has remarked that these were the two cricket writers who appealed to him most, and on whom he tried, in a modest way, to model his writing for the *Observer*.

Cardus *was* the *Manchester Guardian* so far as its cricket readers were concerned but for a few years in the 1930s he had a colleague making his own claims. C. L. R. James was a Trinidad journalist writing on cricket and laying the mental foundations which would produce his post-war classic *Beyond a Boundary* in which he crystallised his ideas on the evolution through cricket of a national West Indian identity.

Cricket writing in *The Times* was in the hands of Dudley Carew and Major R. B. Vincent. Both were typical of a generation of writers who turned their hands to many sports.

Vincent, for example, was primarily a golfing and rugby man. Neither attempted flights of fancy but offered their readers a detailed account of a day's play which stands the test of time. If the reader, fifty years later, wants to know exactly how Bradman was bowled by Bowes, the chances are he will be told. Whether or not a particular match is reported (apart from the obviously great occasions) depended on whether an editor could spare a reporter.

The 'nationals' might fail to give more than the cricket score-sheets supplied by the Cricket Reporting Agency but the 'provincials' would often supply the deficiency. Cricket was well served by provincial journalists. Typical of the dedicated writers who would travel around with county sides writing lengthy reports upon their doings was A. W. Pullin ('Old Ebor') of the *Yorkshire Post* who worked to the last, dying on the bus to a Test match at Lord's in 1934. In his early days his 'copy' was dispatched by pigeon from various Yorkshire grounds. Men such as he and his successor, J. M. Kilburn, and many another provincial journalist, wrote with shrewdness and authority and they were vital in sustaining the links between the players and the public. Even cricket at County Second XI received plenty of coverage. When I first met Canon Jack Parsons just before he was ninety, I dared to doubt a very old man's recollections of a double-century on his debut for Warwickshire Second XI. The files of the *Birmingham Post*, in considerable detail, soon confirmed his achievement!

The amount of first-class cricket played in England meant that a great number of journalists found employment. In the other cricketing countries particular writers built up a reputation, among them Louis Duffus in South Africa, Ray Robinson in Australia and Dick Brittenden in New Zealand, and – among the players – Arthur Mailey. Jack Fingleton was the professional journalist who happened to be a very good cricketer.

The distinction between good press-reporting and what makes literature must be blurred. Cardus wrote with an eye to publication in a more permanent form and his was the cricket prose which commanded the largest support in his time and which (despite the revisionists) stands examination in our own. Warner – no mean trafficker in cricket writing himself – was flattered to receive the great man's accolade in a private letter: 'through your pages come the glow of nature, civilisation and courtesy' – a commentary, perhaps, on both men. A. G. Macdonell in one book and Hugh de Sélincourt in several, wrote fictional cricket classics set outside the first-class game which were the stuff of romantic escapist literature, while the two great chroniclers and historians, F. S. Ashley-Cooper and H. S. Altham, published seminal work which consolidated decades, almost centuries, of cricket's history. The famous series in which different authors dealt with 'The Fight for the Ashes' belonged to a period before instant reporting supplied every known fact about a Test series between England and Australia. Cricket writing remained selective: not until the 1970s would come the plethora of authors whom a later generation of enthusiasts kept in business.

Of the writers in Cricket's Second Golden Age, E. W. Swanton would still be writing in 1989. Sixty years earlier he had embarked on a career which took him to the top of his profession – and it is his sheer professionalism which is his hallmark. To sit beside him at some match is to have observed a man who watched the game carefully, made notes and prepared a piece which would declare his mastery of the game's technique, be fair but penetrating in his judgments, acerbic if needs must, and – with the ease of a novelist – pass backwards and forwards in time. He would put a match or an incident in its historical context and offer some conjectures on the future for a team or a player. If something needed to be said without beating about the bush, he could be relied upon to do so with judicious impartiality and measured tones. Swanton was on the edge of the first-class game as a player, wryly observing that he would have liked a few years with Middlesex to see how he might have done.

At the very end of this period, the young John Arlott left his policeman's beat for the press-box to make his own magisterial contribution to cricket journalism. Both Swanton and Arlott won distinction in the related medium of broadcasting. Swanton, in measured, deep tones, becoming something of a specialist in summarising a day's play. Arlott, in a voice that seemed to evoke the cricket of Hambeldon and Hampshire, made poetry of his prose and gave a word-portrait of those who, as with Cardus, were always very close to being his own perpetual heroes.

No-one in 1919 had ever heard a cricket commentary but the technology which made broadcasting possible was known and the basic patents necessary for its operation were being secured, primarily in America, by business interests. The British Broadcasting Company (later a Corporation) was formed in 1922 and one of the earliest broadcasts on cricket was a talk in 1925 by Plum Warner on 'Prospects for the Season' for a fee of eight guineas. Twelve months later, as chairman of the selectors, he gave a talk on the eve of a Test discussing the team he and his colleagues had selected against the Australians and he was involved in the discussions which led to the introduction of 'eye-witness' reporting on county matches in 1927; he and Canon F. H. Gillingham being the BBC's first performers. The art of commentating came to be associated with the names of H. B. T. Wakelam, Michael Standing and Howard Marshall and in the 1930s their voices were synonymous with the presentation of first-class cricket in England. In 1939 the series between England and the West Indies brought the first sustained ball-by-ball commentary. Elsewhere, the impact of wireless on huge countries such as Australia and South Africa brought cricket to those who might never expect to see a first-class match in their lifetime.

Broadcasting between one country and another developed more slowly because of commercial and technical difficulties. In 1928 Warner gave the first cricket broadcast (though not a commentary) from England to Australia and the 1932–33 series was relayed through Paris from Australia. Swanton broadcast the MCC tour of South Africa in 1938–39 back to England.

During the war some one-day games in England had time allocated by the BBC and a feature of Learie Constantine's important weekly broadcasts to his native West Indies – ostensibly on the British war-effort – were his remarks on how West Indian XIs were performing against wartime sides such as London Counties, the British Empire XI, the Dominions, or an England XI.

After the war Constantine continued as a commentator – 'the equal of anyone else and superior to most', remarked a colleague. By then the voice of Alan McGilvray was becoming familiar: a symbolic link between Australia and England first heard during the bitter British winter of 1946–47. Gradually the structure of large commentary teams was built up and the immediate post-war voices were those of Swanton, Arlott and Rex Alston. They were joined by what H. F. Ellis has called a 'mighty cloud of witnesses' as experts and statisticians trooped in to air their opinions and figures and ensure that silence would never be golden.

On the other hand, silence on television was sometimes a virtue and commentators had to learn when to let the picture tell its own tale. Television in Britain had begun in 1936 and two years later the cameras were at Lord's for the first time to record the Test match against the Australians. Wakelam did the first commentary and was lucky enough to have Hammond's great innings of 240 to talk about. Two months later he was at The Oval to comment on the screening of Hutton's 364. After a total close-down during the war, television took some time to re-establish itself. By 1948, when the Australians came again, there was a British viewing public of millions able to watch on their black and white screens snatches of play, though it would be 1950 before a Test match outside London was televised. What might be accomplished and the relationship between television and sponsorship – not to mention World Series cricket – lay far in the future.

All the attention which cricket received from what we have learnt to call 'the media' was bestowed on a game which Lord Harris called (significantly in 1931 rather than a year later) 'more free from anything sordid, anything dishonourable than any game in the world'. In an ideal world it was a contest between bat and ball in which it was as essential to see a man dismissed as to see him get runs. Conditions would allow the ball to come on to the bat with an even bounce off a firm pitch so that strokes could be played with assurance and confidence. For the bowler, there would be the expectation of sufficient pace in the wicket to give him a chance, while the effect of rain or the passage of the match into its later stages might allow the spin bowlers to come into their inheritance. In many ways this simple philosophy prevailed whether applied to the black marble tables in Australia, the natural soils of England with a deep-rooted growth of grass or the matting wickets elsewhere. When concern arose that batsmen were making rather too many runs, the laws were changed to make the stumps slightly larger and to give the bowler a greater opportunity to secure an lbw decision.

Both batsmen and bowlers in the first-class game profited from the absence of any demands made upon them to play one-day cricket. In the stock phrase, nos. 5 and 6 in the order had time 'to build an innings' while a bowler was constrained neither by limitations on the number of overs nor upon field-placing. The modern devices designed to give high drama and constant action in a game in which money is the prevailing force would have found no abode. Perhaps in this lay the essential difference between then and now. No game stands still and an observer from (say) 1949 would say of cricket in 1989 that batsmen had things less their own way, that bowlers lacked variety, that fielders were more athletic and that more time was wasted.

So there ended an age that had been golden because of its personalities and because of its appeal. Cricket in the Hammond–Bradman years drew the crowds for the ferial days as well as the festal ones. Albeit the counter-attractions were fewer and the pace of life was slower, yet they went to the cricket when they might have stayed at home. The game had a pleasurable purpose about it: not yet shackled by the bonds of commerce. Even the recognition of a day-to-day English county championship does not deny the thesis that first-class cricket had a rarity about it. Test matches had an infrequency which sustained their glamour; visitors were exciting guests from faraway lands; Sunday was a day of rest.

It is all relative. The past has perfection and the present seems imperfect. The past cannot hurt us and the present can bruise. Only politicians tell us we have never had it so good: cricket-lovers are more ready to proffer such judgments on generations other than their own. Old men watching, praise the virtues of those they saw when they were boys. Gold Medals are for winners of Man of the Match awards – instant glory. Golden Accolades are for Ages – Times remembered.

EPILOGUE

1949 marked the departures of Hammond and Bradman. Even the youngest of those who saw them bat can now contemplate taking their grandchildren to Lord's or the Sydney Cricket Ground to watch stars born in the 1960s. One or other was playing throughout cricket's 'Second Golden Age'. After the war each offered a postscript to the game they had adorned in the 1920s and 1930s.

'See him while you can,' *Picture Post* told its readers in 1946 when Hammond was making what proved to be his last circuit of the county grounds. He was top of the batting averages, his 84.90 far ahead of the younger generation. In the autumn, against his own better judgment, beset with domestic problems and in frequent pain he took the MCC to Australia. He had little personal success and England lost to immeasurably stronger opponents – as in 1920–21 Australia's post-war recovery far eclipsed England's. Sir Robert Menzies, the Australian prime minister, declared 'that it was part of the eternal justice of things that Walter Hammond should play at least one great innings every Test series' but it was not to be. Many critics thought he was often unlucky to be out just when all seemed to be going right. As E. W. Swanton observed, 'His very last stroke in Australia looked worth four runs but he was marvellously caught by Lindwall twenty yards from the bat'. His final Test innings was played in New Zealand and he left the field with 79 to his credit and an average, in 85 Test matches, of 58.45. A few days after returning to England he announced his retirement and the greatest all-rounder in the period of cricket's Second Golden Age passed suddenly, unobtrusively, even furtively, from the scene. He had between 1920 and 1947 scored over 50,000 runs and taken over 700 wickets.

At the end of their careers, it was Bradman rather than
Hammond who had the breaks. After the incident of the
disputed 'catch' at Brisbane in the first post-war Test between
Australia and England, he brooked no opposition and –
in contrast to Hammond – enjoyed a Roman triumph. At
Brisbane he went on to make 187 and at Sydney 234, setting
up with Barnes a record for all Test countries for the fifth
wicket of 405. He came to England in 1948 to be garlanded
by a public who, if they could not see him play, would crowd
the railway stations, hotels and streets. He would say of his
reception at Leeds that it was the greatest he had ever received
in the world and it was at Leeds that he made his final runs
in Test cricket. Australia needed 404 to win on the last day
on a worn wicket taking spin. Bradman went into bat at one
o'clock when the Australians were 57 for 1. In just over four
hours Australia had won the match and Bradman had made
173 not out to give him an average in Test matches at Leeds
of 192.40. His average overall in Test matches would be
99.94, that elusive .06 being denied him by the googly with
which Eric Hollies dismissed him for nought in the final Test
at The Oval.

Australia had brought to England in 1948 a team as great
as that of 1921 and *Wisden* bestowed all its five places, as
cricketers of the year, to members of the team. Yet, within
a side of outstanding talent and of men younger than himself,
Bradman still dominated. He led the field in averages, aggregate and centuries. With 200 runs and one century more to
come when back in Australia, he would end a career in which
he had made over 28,000 runs and scored 117 centuries – one
in every 2.88 innings.

Elsewhere in the cricket world in the late 1940s new names
were appearing and fresh ground being broken. India played
Australia for the first time and learnt, as England had done a
year earlier, what it was like to be caught on a Brisbane wicket
after rain. The West Indies played India also for the first time,
George Headley becoming the only one of the really great
batsmen of his generation to play in a Test match in the
sub-continent. In New Zealand Bert Sutcliffe, master of all
the strokes and especially the off-drive, was making stacks of
runs in the Plunket Shield and in South Africa the younger

Nourse was eclipsing the record Currie Cup aggregate set up
by his father. Colin McDonald was making an impressive
debut for Victoria and Keith Miller was dominating the
cricket played by New South Wales. In the Far East, the
Asian Cricket Association was formed to 'spread goodwill
and fellowship' among its cricketing founder members –
India, Pakistan, Ceylon, Burma and Malaya. Finally, on 5
March 1949 Sir Donald Bradman scored 30 runs for South
Australia on his home ground at Adelaide. It was his last
appearance in first-class cricket and with his departure
cricket's Second Golden Age may be said to have ended –
'Cricket,' wrote Ray Robinson, 'was like a room with the
light switched off.' But others would soon switch it on again,
including a West Indian schoolboy then aged twelve: Garfield
Sobers' 365 against Pakistan in 1958 would eclipse the Test
match 364 of Hutton as well as the triple-centuries of both
Hammond and Bradman.

APPENDIXES

A. Test matches played between 1920 and 1948
B. Winners of domestic tournaments and championships, 1919–1949: the County Championship; the Sheffield Shield; the Currie Cup; the Inter-colonial Tournament; the Plunket Shield; the Bombay Quadrangular and Pentangular Tournaments
C. Select Bibliography
D. Select Index

A. TEST MATCHES PLAYED BETWEEN 1920 AND 1948

Date	Series	No. of Tests in series
1920–21	Australia v. England	5
1921	England v. Australia	5
1921–22	South Africa v. Australia	3
1922–23	South Africa v. England	5
1924	England v. South Africa	5
1924–25	Australia v. England	5
1926	England v. Australia	5
1927–28	South Africa v. England	5
1928	England v. West Indies	3
1928–29	Australia v. England	5
1929	England v. South Africa	5
1929–30	New Zealand v. England	4
1929–30	West Indies v. England	4
1930	England v. Australia	5
1930–31	Australia v. West Indies	5
1930–31	South Africa v. England	5
1931	England v. New Zealand	3
1931–32	Australia v. South Africa	5
1931–32	New Zealand v. South Africa	2
1932	England v. India	1
1932–33	Australia v. England	5
1932–33	New Zealand v. England	2
1933	England v. West Indies	3
1933–34	India v. England	3
1934	England v. Australia	5
1934–35	West Indies v. England	4
1935	England v. South Africa	5
1935–36	South Africa v. Australia	5

1936	England v. India	3
1936–37	Australia v. England	5
1937	England v. New Zealand	3
1938	England v. Australia	5
1938–39	South Africa v. England	5
1939	England v. West Indies	3
1945–46	New Zealand v. Australia	1
1946	England v. India	3
1946–47	Australia v. England	5
1946–47	New Zealand v. England	1
1947	England v. South Africa	5
1947–48	West Indies v. England	4
1947–48	Australia v. India	5
1948	England v. Australia	5

B. WINNERS OF DOMESTIC TOURNAMENTS AND CHAMPIONSHIPS, 1919–1949

The County Championship

1919 Yorkshire
1920 Middlesex
1921 Middlesex
1922 Yorkshire
1923 Yorkshire
1924 Yorkshire
1925 Yorkshire
1926 Lancashire
1927 Lancashire
1928 Lancashire
1929 Notts
1930 Lancashire
1931 Yorkshire
1932 Yorkshire
1933 Yorkshire
1934 Lancashire
1935 Yorkshire
1936 Derbyshire
1937 Yorkshire
1938 Yorkshire
1939 Yorkshire
1946 Yorkshire
1947 Middlesex
1948 Glamorgan
1949 { Middlesex
       Yorkshire

The Sheffield Shield

1919–20 New South Wales
1920–21 New South Wales

287

1921–22	Victoria
1922–23	New South Wales
1923–24	Victoria
1924–25	Victoria
1925–26	New South Wales
1926–27	South Australia
1927–28	Victoria
1928–29	New South Wales
1929–30	Victoria
1930–31	Victoria
1931–32	New South Wales
1932–33	New South Wales
1933–34	Victoria
1934–35	Victoria
1935–36	South Australia
1936–37	Victoria
1937–38	New South Wales
1938–39	South Australia
1939–40	New South Wales
1940–46	*No competition*
1946–47	Victoria
1947–48	Western Australia

The Currie Cup

1920–21	Western Province
1921–22	Natal / Transvaal / Western Province
1923–24	Transvaal
1925–26	Transvaal
1926–27	Transvaal
1929–30	Transvaal
1931–32	Western Province
1933–34	Natal
1934–35	Transvaal
1936–37	Natal
1937–38	Natal / Transvaal
1946–47	Natal
1947–48	Natal

The Inter-colonial Tournament

1921–22	No result	Port of Spain
1922–23	Barbados	Georgetown

1923–24	Barbados	Bridgetown
1924–25	Trinidad	Port of Spain
1925–26	Trinidad	Georgetown
1926–27	Barbados	Bridgetown
1928–29	Trinidad	Port of Spain
1929–30	British Guiana	Georgetown
1931–32	Trinidad	Bridgetown
1933–34	Trinidad	Port of Spain
1934–35	British Guiana	Georgetown
1935–36	British Guiana	Bridgetown
1936–37	Trinidad	Port of Spain
1937–38	British Guiana	Georgetown
1938–39	Trinidad	Bridgetown

The Plunket Shield

1921–22	Auckland
1922–23	Canterbury
1923–24	Wellington
1924–25	Otago
1925–26	Wellington
1926–27	Auckland
1927–28	Wellington
1928–29	Auckland
1929–30	Wellington
1930–31	Canterbury
1931–32	Wellington
1932–33	Otago
1933–34	Auckland
1934–35	Canterbury
1935–36	Wellington
1936–37	Auckland
1937–38	Auckland
1938–39	Auckland
1939–40	Auckland
1945–46	Canterbury
1946–47	Auckland
1947–48	Otago
1948–49	Canterbury

The Bombay Tournaments

QUADRANGULAR

1917–18	Drawn (Hindus v. Parsees)
1918–19	Europeans beat Parsees by 91 runs

1919–20	Hindus beat Muslims by an innings and 13 runs
1920–21	Drawn (Hindus v. Parsees)
1921–22	Europeans beat Parsees by an innings and 297 runs
1922–23	Parsees beat Hindus by 121 runs
1923–24	Hindus beat Europeans by 9 wickets
1924–25	Muslims beat Hindus by 5 wickets
1925–26	Hindus beat Europeans by 4 wickets
1926–27	Hindus beat Europeans by 11 runs
1927–28	Europeans beat Muslims by 4 wickets
1928–29	Parsees beat Europeans by 134 runs
1929–30	Hindus beat Parsees by 5 wickets
1930–34	*Not played*
1934–35	Muslims beat Hindus by 91 runs
1935–36	Muslims beat Hindus by 221 runs
1936–37	Hindus beat Europeans by 257 runs

PENTANGULAR

1937–38★	Muslims beat Europeans by an innings and 91 runs
1938–39	Muslims beat Hindus by 6 wickets
1939–40	Hindus beat Muslims by 5 wickets
1940–41★	Muslims beat Rest by 7 wickets
1941–42	Hindus beat Parsees by 10 wickets
1942–43	*Not played*
1943–44	Hindus beat Rest by an innings and 61 runs
1944–45	Muslims beat Hindus by 1 wicket
1945–46	Hindus beat Parsees by 310 runs

★ *Hindus did not compete*

C. SELECT BIBLIOGRAPHY

As E. W. Padwick has demonstrated in his *A Bibliography of Cricket* (2nd ed., 1984), there are over 8000 books and pamphlets written on the game. *Wisden*, since 1864, stands unchallenged as a primary source for the last century and a quarter. In the book-list given below, I list some sixty books which touch upon the period of *Cricket's Second Golden Age*. It should be possible to track any of them down – in bookshops, cricket libraries or the public library service. It has been said that few people read more than 2000 books in a lifetime: here the reader may make his or her inroads into the existing literature of cricket – enough for four lifetimes!

H. S. Altham and E. W. Swanton, *A History of Cricket* (1962)
John Arlott, *From Hambledon to Lord's* (1948)
Brian Bassano, *South Africa in International Cricket* (1979)
Rowland Bowen, *Cricket: A History of its Growth and Development throughout the World* (1970)
Sir Donald Bradman, *Farewell to cricket* (1950)
Sir Donald Bradman, *My cricketing life* (1938)
R. T. Brittenden, *Great days in New Zealand cricket* (1958)
Gerald Brodribb, *Maurice Tate* (1976)
Christopher Brookes, *English Cricket* (1978)
S. Canynge Caple, *The All-Blacks at cricket* (1958)
Neville Cardus, *Autobiography* (1947)
Neville Cardus, *Good Days* (1934)
Richard Cashman, *'Ave a Go, Yer Mug!* (1985)
Richard Cashman, *Patrons, Players and the Crowd* (1980)
Learie Constantine and Denzil Batchelor, *The changing face of cricket* (1966)
E. W. Docker, *History of Indian cricket* (1976)
Kenneth Farnes, *Tours and Tests* (1940)
Bill Frindall (ed.), *The Wisden Book of Cricket Records* (1979)
David Frith, *England versus Australia: A Pictorial History of the Test Matches since 1877* (1984)
David Frith, *Pageant of Cricket* (1987)

Chris Harte, *The History of the Sheffield Shield* (1987)

Alan Hill, *Hedley Verity* (1986)

Gerald Howat, *Cricketer Militant: The Life of Jack Parsons* (1980)

Gerald Howat, *Learie Constantine* (1975)

Gerald Howat, *Walter Hammond* (1984)

Sir Leonard Hutton, *Cricket is my Life* (1949)

Ray Illingworth and Kenneth Gregory, *The Ashes* (1982)

C. L. R. James, *Beyond a Boundary* (1963)

David Lemmon, *'Tich' Freeman and the decline of the leg-break bowler* (1982)

David Lemmon, *Percy Chapman: A biography* (1985)

Laurence Le Quesne, *The Bodyline Controversy* (1983)

Michael Manley, *A History of West Indies Cricket* (1988)

Ronald Mason, *Jack Hobbs* (1960)

Ronald Mason, *Walter Hammond* (1962)

Geoffrey Moorhouse, *Lord's* (1983)

A. G. Moyes, *Australian Cricket* (1959)

Patrick Murphy, *'Tiger' Smith* (1981)

M. A. Noble, *The Fight for the Ashes, 1928–29* (1929)

Bill O'Reilly, *The Bradman Era* (1984)

Gerald Pawle, *R. E. S. Wyatt: Fighting Cricketer* (1985)

I. A. R. Peebles, *Spinner's Yarn* (1977)

Jack Pollard, *Australian Cricket: The Game and the Players* (1982)

N. S. Ramaswami, *Indian Willow* (1971)

R. C. Robertson-Glasgow, *Cricket Prints* (1943)

R. C. Robertson-Glasgow, *46 Not Out* (1948)

Irving Rosenwater, *Sir Donald Bradman* (1978)

E. H. D. Sewell, *A searchlight on English cricket* (1926)

Ric Sissons and Brian Stoddart, *Cricket and Empire* (1984)

Ric Sissons, *The Players: A Social History of the Professional Cricketer* (1988)

Richard Streeton, *P. G. H. Fender* (1981)

E. W. Swanton and John Woodcock (eds.), *Barclays World of Cricket*, 3rd ed. (1986)

E. W. Swanton, *Gubby Allen: Man of Cricket* (1985)

E. W. Swanton, *Sort of a Cricket Person* (1972)

A. A. Thomson, *Cricket: the Golden Ages* (1961)

Sir Pelham Warner, *The Fight for the Ashes in 1926* (1926)

Sir Pelham Warner, *Cricket between two wars* (1942)

Sir Pelham Warner, *Long Innings* (1951)

Sir Pelham Warner, *Lord's, 1787–1945* (1946)

Marcus Williams, *The Way to Lord's: Cricketing Letters to The Times* (1983)

Peter Wynne-Thomas, *England on Tour* (1982)

D. SELECT INDEX

INDEX

Dacre, C. C., 212, 213
Dalton, E. L., 102, 104
Daniel, J., 48, 49
Deane, H. G., 93, 94, 95, 97
Dempster, C. S., 151, 213, 214,
    215, 216
Dennett, E. G., 42, 43
Deodhar, D. B., 241, 242, 244
De Selincourt, Hugh, 275
Dipper, A. E., 43, 68
Dooland, B., 147
D'Oliveira, B. L., 112, 268
Dollery, H. E., 149, 150
Donnelly, Sir Arthur, 223
Donnelly, M. P., 219, 221, 222, 223
Douglas, J. W. H. T., 57, 61, 62,
    66, 67, 68, 82, 203, 212
Ducat, A., 51, 68, 259
Duckworth, Sir George, 30
Duckworth, G., 30, 51, 98, 100
Duffus, Louis, 100, 102, 103, 108,
    111, 274
Deleepsinhji, K. S., 18, 19, 59,
    123, 166, 173, 174, 214, 217,
    268
Duminy, J. P., 96
Durston, F. J., 53

Eagar, E. D. R., 157
Eckersley, P. T., 44
Edrich, W. J., 54, 107, 108, 161,
    162, 163, 205, 207
Ellis, J. L., 252, 253
Evans, A. J., 68

Fagg, A. E., 164
Fairfax, A. G., 18, 261
Farnes, K., 58, 104, 131, 132, 133,
    169, 187, 189, 196, 199, 201,
    202, 208
Farrimond, W., 100
Faulkner, G. A., 71, 91, 92
Fender, P. G. H., 17, 50, 51, 52,
    53, 61, 62, 66, 67, 69, 82, 83,
    84, 85, 86, 173, 174, 175, 179,
    204, 272
Findlay Commission, The, 169,
    266

Findlay, W., 181, 266, 267
Fingleton, J. H., 103, 198, 202,
    205, 207, 256, 274
Fleetwood-Smith, L. O'B., 189,
    206, 253, 260, 261
Foot, David, 158
Fortune, Charles, 88
Foster, D. G., 149
Foster, F. R., 66
Foster, R. E., 207
Francis, G. N., 117, 119, 120, 122,
    128
Freeman, A. P., 55, 56, 93, 96,
    121, 164, 165
Fry, C. B., 15, 46, 67, 154, 196,
    221, 241, 272
Fuller, L. G., 110

Gandhi, M. K., 234, 236
Geary, G., 39, 40, 84, 93, 151
Gibb, P. A., 104, 107, 206,
    271
Gibson, C. H., 67, 71, 81
Giffen, G., 256, 257
Gilbert, H. R., 41
Gilligan, A. E. R., 56, 57, 74, 75,
    76, 82, 86, 90, 91, 167, 203,
    214, 218, 231, 232, 240, 270,
    272
Gilligan, A. H. H., 56
Gillingham, Canon F. H., 57,
    276
Gimblett, H., 50, 158, 159, 273
George V, King, 17, 21, 195
Goddard, T. W. J., 44, 98, 105,
    138, 154, 155
Gordon, Sir Home, 42, 56
Gordon, N., 103
Gover, A. R., 161
Grace, W. G., 15, 20, 25, 38, 41,
    42, 47, 48, 49, 51, 67, 95, 114,
    116, 160, 246
Grant, G. C., 116, 125, 126, 132,
    133, 134
Grant, R. S., 116, 134
Green, L., 30, 32
Gregory, J. M., 61, 63, 65, 66, 67,
    68, 77, 81, 84, 254, 264

295